Arnold Wesker

Plays: 1

Chicken Soup with Barley, Roots, I'm Talking About Jerusalem

Chicken Soup with Barley: 'Wesker is aware of history: he opens his characters' minds to world events. He confronts us, as sanely as the theatre has ever done, with a fundamental issue: is there a viable middle course between Welfare Socialism and Communism? He has written a fair, accurate and intensely exciting play . . . potentially a very important playwright.' Kenneth Tynan, *Observer*

'A sympathetic study of a group of people, who come alive under Mr Wesker's pen. The conflict of their beliefs is interesting because they are themselves interesting, not because Mr Wesker wants to argue that any particular belief is right or wrong.' *Daily Telegraph*

Roots: 'I have now seen this great, shining play three times, and it seems to have grown visibly in stature each time. It is the central pillar of Arnold Wesker's mighty Trilogy, and it is one on which the whole arch depends . . . The simple story still grips the audience . . . Beatie Bryant's betrayal by her Ronnie is still poignant beyond the reach of anything but the very greatest poetry, and her final triumphant budding is still the most heart-lifting single moment I have ever seen upon a stage.' Bernard Levin, *Daily Express*

I'm Talking About Jerusalem: 'A call for dignity in living, an individual shout of rejection in the face of scepticism and debased values . . . Wesker writes entirely from the heart. His craftsmanship is impeccable . . . It remains a great compassionate sigh of a play and our theatre is the richer for Wesker's endowment of talent . . . These three autobiographical dramas have taught us not only a great deal about Wesker, but also about ourselves, our time, and the loss of emotion which marks the epoch in which we live.' *Daily Mail*

Arnold Wesker was born in Stepney in 1932. His education came mainly from reading books and listening to BBC radio. He pursued many trades, from furniture maker to pastry cook, until 1958 when *Chicken Soup with Barley* was read by George Devine and produced at the Belgrade Theatre, Coventry. *Roots* followed in 1959, and together with *I'm Talking About Jerusalem* the three plays created an en   ^r* as the 'Wesker Trilogy' at the Royal Court in 1960. His other   '1961), *Chips with Everything* (1962, voted 'Play of   City* (1965; winner of the Italian Pre   *The Four Seasons* (1965), *The Frie   *Wedding Feast* (1974), *Shylock* (19   *Caritas* (1981), his six one-woman   *Merry-Go-Round* (1985), *Lady Othei...*   (1997), *Break, My Heart* (1997) and *Denial* (2000). ... written for film and television and published several collections of   , short stories, essays and lectures.

by the same author

plays

ARNOLD WESKER PLAYS: 2★
(Annie Wobbler, Four
Portraits – of Mothers,
Yardsale, Whatever
Happened to Betty
Lemon?, The Mistress,
Letter to a Daughter)

The Kitchen
The Four Seasons
Their Very Own and
Golden City
Chips with Everything
The Friends
The Old Ones
Love Letters on Blue
Paper
The Journalists
The Wedding Feast
Shylock
One More Ride on the
Merry-Go-Round
Caritas
When God Wanted a Son
Lady Othello
Bluey
Badenheim 1939

Shoeshine and Little Old
Lady (*plays for young
people*)
Boerhtel's Hill
Three Women Talking
Blood Libel
Wild Spring
Break, My Heart

short stories

Six Sundays in January
Love Letters on Blue Paper
Said the Old Man to the
Young Man
The King's Daughters

essays and non-fiction

Fears of Fragmentation
Distinctions
Say Goodbye, You May
Never See Them Again
Journey Into Journalism
As Much As I Dare
(*autobiography*)
The Birth of Shylock and
the Death of Zero Mostel

for children

Fatlips

★ *published by Methuen*

ARNOLD WESKER

Plays: 1
The Wesker Trilogy

Chicken Soup with Barley
Roots
I'm Talking About Jerusalem

introduced by the author

Methuen

METHUEN CONTEMPORARY DRAMATISTS

3 5 7 9 10 8 6 4 2

This edition first published in the United Kingdom in 2001 by
Methuen Publishing Limited
215 Vauxhall Bridge Road, London SW1V 1EJ

The Wesker Trilogy first published by Jonathan Cape 1960

Chicken Soup with Barley first published by Penguin Books 1959
Copyright © 1959, 1960 by Arnold Wesker

Roots first published by Penguin Books 1959
Copyright © 1959, 1960 by Arnold Wesker

I'm Talking About Jerusalem first published by Penguin Books 1960
Copyright © 1960, 1979 by Arnold Wesker

This collection and introduction copyright © 2001 by Arnold Wesker

The right of the author to be identified as the author of these works
has been asserted by him in accordance with the Copyright, Designs
and Patents Act, 1988

'April Showers' copyright © 1921 by Harms Inc. Used by permission.
Licence for performance in any production must be obtained from
Warner/Chappell Ltd, Griffin House, 161 Hammersmith Road,
London W6 8BS.

Methuen Publishing Limited Reg. No. 3543167

A CIP catalogue record for this book is available
from the British Library

ISBN 0 413 75830 3

Typeset by Deltatype Ltd, Birkenhead, Wirral
Printed and bound in Great Britain by
Cox & Wyman Ltd, Reading, Berks

Caution

Contents

Chronology of first performances

For more information about the author please visit website www.arnoldwesker.com

Introduction*

My memory of how and why I wrote *Chicken Soup with Barley* is clear. I had quarrelled with my mother over politics, raging at her continuing adherence to communism. We quarrelled constantly. I'm ashamed to recall how rarely I resisted a sarcastic observation about the misdemeanours of the Soviet Union or its satellites. 'There!' she'd say. 'He's attacking me again. Always criticising me.' 'No!' I'd say. 'I'm criticising the Soviet Union not you.' 'You're criticising the Soviet Union because you want to upset me, to get at me. Don't I know you by now?' Sometimes even she would see how absurd our exchanges were and we'd both end up laughing. It was not easy to handle a mother who never seriously believed the Americans had landed on the moon; the films and photos had been faked, she asserted, to divert the attention of the proletariat away from their exploitation. We quarrelled in varying degrees of absurdity and acrimony until she died.

On two memorable occasions, after bitter exchanges, I wrote down what she had said, feeling them to be remarkable and moving declarations of faith. Unfortunately they are not dated. Written on different types of paper in different inks they must have come at me on two different occasions. I fused them into one speech but it's the second part I recorded first, knowing with certainty when I heard it that it would become the speech to end this play turning over and over in my mind. I had screamed at her: how could she still remain a communist? The speech in the play is more or less what she replied in life.

*These notes are culled from my autobiography *As Much As I Dare* (Century, 1994).

All right, so I'm still a communist! Shoot me then! I'm a communist! I've always been one – since the time when all the world was a communist. You know that? When you were a baby and there was unemployment and anybody you talked to who was thinking – was a communist. But it's different now. Now the people have forgotten. I sometimes think they're not worth fighting for because they forget so easily. You give them a few shillings in the bank and they can buy a television so they think it's all over, there's nothing more, they don't have to think any more. Is that what you want? A world where people don't think any more? Is that what you want me to be satisfied with, a television set? Look at him. He wants to die. My son! You think it doesn't hurt me? The news about Hungary? You think I know what happened what didn't happen? Who do I know who to trust now? God! who is my friend now? All my life I fought. With your father and the rotten system that couldn't help him. All my life I worked with a party that meant glory and freedom and equality. You want me to give it up now? If the electrician who comes to mend my fuse he blows it instead so I should stop having electricity then? I should cut off my light? Socialism is my light, can you understand that? A way of life. A man *can* be beautiful. I hate ugly people, I can't bear meanness and fighting and jealousy – I've got to have light. I'm a simple person, Ronnie, and I've got to have light and love.

It's difficult, though, to be certain which are her lines and which are mine. I know she said things like: 'You give them a few shillings in the bank and they can buy a television set so they think it's all over, there's nothing more . . . I hate ugly people, I can't bear meanness and fighting and jealousy, I've got to have light.' But did she use the metaphor of the electrician?

If the disintegration of an ideology was the end of the play where was the beginning? I had learned from the huge sagas of Howard Spring and A.J. Cronin that for the impact of decline to be felt a story had to begin when the world was young and all things possible; the days of hope had to be chronicled first. Loss of faith could not be understood unless that faith was recreated in all its innocence. And when *were* those days of innocence? What crisis more than any other in recent history presented itself as black and white and could launch this family saga in which the central figure of the mother thought in black and white? The days of the Spanish Civil War and the anti-fascist demonstrations in the East End, of course, when Jews and gentiles for an incandescent moment respected one another, held hands, shared angers, threw barricades across the intersection of Whitechapel Road and Commercial Road and rolled thousands of marbles into the paths of mounted policemen with batons, toppling their ferocious steeds; that thrilling day when Sir Oswald Mosley's blackshirts were thrown off their provocative route through the Jewish streets of London and many were lured to believe the end of capitalism was imminent, the millennium just across the road at Aldgate Pump. The year was 1936. I was four, aware of nothing; but so electrifying had the riots been for my family, so full of anecdote, of little braveries and farce, of colourful personalities, that it was talked and talked about into my teens until I felt I had lived those days with them. I made notes. Scraps, typed and scribbled, accumulated. And I thought so long and intensely about the play that it came out in a rush, with ease, a swift if imperfect delivery. Pain, a little, but not for long. Only one other of my plays had such an effortless birth – *Caritas* – written in ten days, though I'd been preparing for it with months of research; ten days in a state of near delirium, intoxicated, like one drugged, driven. It shows in the work. The strangest of my plays, I feel.

The completion of *Chicken Soup with Barley* whirled me into a high like a dervish dancer and I came out of my room bursting to read the play to my mother. She was in the front room with her friend, Mrs Harris. I made them stop whatever it was they were doing to listen. These two women were my first audience for this family saga covering twenty years from 1936 to 1956, read to them by its author sitting at a heavy mahogany table (the kind into which could be slid an extra panel to make it longer for family feasts by winding it open with an iron handle), there in the little square room of an LCC flat off the Upper Clapton Road, E5, some time in mid November 1957.

When I had finished, my mother smiled her faintly sardonic smile and said something like: 'It's very good, no, really, I mean it, it's a big work, a lot of work, but who's going to be interested in any of it, silly boy? It's about us, it's between us. It won't mean anything to anyone else . . .' But I was elated and she could see I was elated, and though I can't remember her actually saying it – it was the 'silly boy, who's going to be interested in any of that' I remember more – yet I know she wished me well.

Whatever, I knew that at last I had written a work worthy of presenting to a public. It had substance, thrust, rich texture. There is no vanity in this. Artists know when the elements come together. Singers, actors, musicians – when every instrument in their body, every pulse, every nerve-end functions as it was ordained to and they and their audience know it – come off stage glowing, dazed sometimes. So it was with me having written the first play of *The Trilogy*. I wrote at

once to Lindsay Anderson* asking if he would read it.
Without hesitation he agreed, read it promptly, and on
18 December wrote a letter that changed my life.

Dear Arnold
    Thank you very much for letting me read the play,
which I enjoyed very much, and think is important
as well as very *good*. Obviously it needs reading
again; but at a first go, it held me, convinced me,
and presented its problems as well as its people in a
complete, *undeniable* way. Can I send it to George
Devine to read for the Court? It seems to me exactly
the sort of play they should be searching for – much
better, for instance, than one by Doris Lessing which
they planned to put on, and which I read and didn't
like. [But Doris, who subsequently became a good
friend, is a great novelist instead!] Of course I
haven't any idea what their reaction will be: they are
rather incalculable people ... and of course one
can't be sure that the play, being as real as it is,
would be a 'success' ... But surely they have had
enough of that recently to make them ready to put
on something as good as this. You really are a
playwright aren't you? I mean there it is, with
characters as solid as I can imagine, and a whole way
of life to them, and the necessary perspective, and a
much more mature grasp of the whole thing than
John Osborne (for instance) can provide. [Lindsay,
were he alive, might not think this now, and I
certainly view Osborne's work as inspirational.] I am
sure it would act, and stage, most excitingly. The
twenty years time-scheme presents its difficulties, of
course, but *they* aren't insoluble. Congratulations, as
I say, again, and thank you.

  * Lindsay Anderson, stage and film director, who had befriended me as a
student at the London School of Film Technique.

Oddly enough I have also been reading an interesting play from Poland, sent to the Court after it has been kept in the drawer for the last five years. Even more disillusioned than yours – I suppose you'll allow that yours *is* disillusioned? – and similarly obsessed with the Cause that failed. But of course they actually *lived* (and so to some extent no doubt still live) under the perversion of Socialism . . .

Let's meet some time anyway, if you have a moment. I am at home at least until 9.30 in the mornings – MAI 4719.

All best wishes –

Lindsay.

I rushed down to the red phone box on Upper Clapton Road to phone Lindsay my gratitude, and grant permission for him to offer the play to George Devine or whoever he liked. It was not an acceptance, I understood that. Lindsay was not the artistic director of the Court, not even – at that time – an assistant artistic director, but I had a champion! Not a father figure, more an elder-brother figure. Someone who was going to argue *for* me instead of me having to argue for myself. His letter lit candles and I glowed.

But neither George nor his young co-director, Tony Richardson, shared Lindsay's enthusiasm for *Chicken Soup with Barley*. They did however share an enthusiasm for Lindsay – all from the same college in Oxford, it must help. The personality of George Devine is central to an understanding of what gave the English Stage Company lift-off. As different as were writers like John Arden, John Osborne, Jellicoe and myself, so our experience with and perception of George were different. My mother was in awe of him. He was both the ruling class and a gentleman. He had warmth and grace, qualities my mother would forgive most things for, even being an intellectual and coming from an élite! She knew a 'mensch' when she saw one. George was a 'mensch'. Integrity saturated his being. His only blemish was – he didn't warm to my plays!

John Osborne, by supreme contrast, was both a personality George could relate to and a writer – whose marvellous old-fashioned English bile of moral outrage – George was more comfortable with. Quarrelling Jewish couples from East End ghettos, incontinent old men, earnest young idealists – these were hazy, unfamiliar, and perhaps implausible characters to him.

But his great virtue was his humility. He was prepared to risk being proven wrong about *Chicken Soup with Barley*. The English Stage Company had decided to celebrate fifty years of British repertory by inviting four regional theatres to present for a week one of the plays they were mounting in their season of fortnightly rep. Devine and Richardson, trusting the instinct of their trenchantly persuasive colleague, suggested to Brian Bailey, artistic director of the recently built theatre in Coventry, the Belgrade, that he should take on my play instead of the one he was proposing, of which they were not enamoured! Bailey read *Chicken Soup*, admired it and agreed Lindsay should direct it. Only one problem: Bailey could not afford to give Lindsay more than two weeks of rehearsal. Lindsay felt himself too inexperienced to tackle, in so short a rehearsal time, such a difficult play spanning twenty years of contemporary history. He needed three weeks. Rather than ask me to hang around until more propitious conditions obtained, until perhaps he could try again and persuade George to let him mount it at the Court – as a more opportunistic director might have done – he advised me to take the bird in hand and allow another director to direct it in Coventry. This other director – young, lean and hungry – was, in his opinion, more experienced, apparently talented and, to the point, had waxed lyrical about the play. Meet and talk with him, advised Lindsay, he appears to understand it and has ideas for mounting it. I was disappointed not to be working with Lindsay – by a quirk of fate I was never to work with him – but I too was lean and hungry and it was, after all, an alien world to me. If that was his advice I would take it and meet with this young man whose name was John Dexter.

Between 2 and 6 April 1958 Dusty, my wife-to-be, and I set off from London with a few hundred others on a four-day march to the nuclear weapons research station at Aldermaston. Our numbers grew to four thousand by arrival, an exhilarating experience. By 1961 the Aldermaston marchers grew to 50,000.

For the first three days it rained. Dexter, the same height as me, seven years older, animated from head to toe by a demonic, black-eyed, crackling enthusiasm that was as quirkily unpredictable as it could be thrillingly infectious – who hated rain and marches and any public spectacle other than theatrical – joined us on about the first or second day, suppressing his loathing of street politics in order to woo my confidence in him. If protesting against nuclear weaponry was what it took to land his first major production then he would rub shoulders with types he despised, and tolerate whatever drenching the indignity cost. He walked alongside me sharing our packed food of Jewish deli-filled sandwiches, cold chicken, cold fried fish (that was new for him), hating the political rowdies who chanted brave slogans at the handful of uninterested bystanders, getting soaked, talking talking talking non-stop to me about how marvellous he thought the play and what changes he felt would help it work even better. Those were the days when, to quote Lindsay Anderson: 'The text always came first, and writers were to be cherished

... There was never any suggestion that a director should *use* a text in order to show off his own prowess or personality . . .'*

In those first Aldermaston days, in the rain, collecting blisters, and singing Blake's 'Jerusalem', John was concerned only to help me make better that which I perceived to be the drama of my family and their times.

We lived in Fashion Street in the East End of London in an attic flat of two rooms where the kitchen was on the landing. Unsurprisingly, therefore, an early draft of *Chicken Soup with Barley* sets the first scene in the top rooms of a house in an East End street. John's first question was: does it have to be an attic room? Couldn't they live, he suggested, in the basement? I said they could because, it so happened, that row of tenement houses in Fashion Street was built with basements. (In our basement worked a furrier whose premises one evening caught fire.) So, yes, the Kahns *could* live in a basement. But why? Dexter explained. Living in a basement would permit two stage managers to run backwards and forwards again and again, only their legs showing, giving the impression that crowds were running to the barricades to join their comrades assembling against Mosley and his blackshirts. That was the kind of inspired idea John offered a writer.

I agreed to let him direct the play, and plans were set in motion to design and cast it. Rehearsals began on 23 June, it ran for a week in Coventry from 7 July, and a second week at the Royal Court from 14 July. After which I was awarded a £300 Arts Council grant which I spent on getting married. John went to prison for six months for seducing a minor. A full year was 1958.

* 'At the Royal Court', an essay for *Twenty-five Years of the English Stage Company* (Amber Lane Press, 1981).

Roots and rejection

Tony Richardson, assistant artistic director to George Devine, took me to lunch in the restaurant used by the Court's crowd – Au Père de Nico – the first time, possibly, I was taken to a 'posh' eating place of the 'artistic' kind. Tony enjoyed introducing me to this corner of Chelsea's sophisticated life. I think he thought he was corrupting me.

We talked about a future. Tony wanted to know if I was planning another play. I was, about a Norfolk farm-labourer's daughter who returns home after living in London with her Jewish boyfriend. Autobiography again. In a letter dated 30 May to Dusty, my Norfolk wife-to-be, on her twenty-second birthday, I had given more thought to it:

> In the Norfolk play . . . I'm spoken about all the time but I never appear. In the play I fail to turn up – ever, and after some terrible misery and 'there I told you so' from the family you turn round and say 'So what! I do not need him now! I'm better than I thought I was and I do not need him now!' And the triumph of the play is not my triumph but yours. The intellectual has betrayed but the ordinary girl has found her own voice, her own language. Funny that, the triumph of *Chicken Soup* is also not my triumph but my mother's. I wonder why . . .

On the 20 March 1958 Tony wrote offering a £25 option 'for your next play – the Norfolk one you outlined to me . . . a minimum amount but standard for all the plays we have commissioned . . .' Ten days later George Devine wrote to invite me to join the next Writers' Discussion Group. Giddy times.

Unlike many writers who complain they dread writing, that they must drag themselves to the desk, that it is all blood, sweat, tears and pain, it is not so for me. Or rather, yes, all those things, but as with the pleasures of sex they are part of the giddy times. I went to stay with my mother-in-law-to-be in Norfolk where I planned to begin writing. Letters from her tied cottage, called Beck Farm, to my wife-to-be describe the shaping of the play that was to become *Roots*.*

17 June
. . . It does not seem so strange me sitting here, in the front room, typing. Mother is laying the table for dinner in the kitchen and it is only twelve o'clock . . .

. . . I brought three of your paintings here for the family to see. The copy of the Van Gogh – which Joy and Ma like, the jazz band one in red, blue and white, and the two standing figures in green, red and blue. They didn't quite know what to say but I know they liked them – if only for the colours. I just asked Ma if she could live with a couple of them in the room and she say 'that would make no difference to me.' . . .

19 June
. . . Father Bicker was up most of the night helping two old sows give birth. He'll be tired today. He does work hard. The funny thing was how Mother was telling how some people don't think he works so hard and she was adding how he had offered to swop places with them. And then when I was discussing this with Joy she told me how Mother don't think he work hard! Your mother is a strange woman, she talks to you as though she were making a political speech. And when she tells a story she acts all the parts with such gusto that I feel sure she would have made a good dramatic actress. I find her stories

* I see the letters already contain attempts to capture Norfolk dialect and rhythms.

entertaining though, except when she repeats them. And how she hop from one anecdote to another . . .

20 June

The Norfolk play is beginning to take shape in my mind. I can see it a little more clearly now, I think I would like to start on the first act – perhaps I shall this afternoon when your mother goes into Harleston to post these letters. That would be wonderful if I managed to get the outline down of the first act . . .

. . . This morning she [Mother] asked Gully [Poppy Bicker] if he wanted a bath and he said yes, so she said to him he could have one after me. 'I don't mind that' he said to me 'as long as you don't shit in it so's it stick to me and I can't get it off.' That's a sign I am being treated as one of the family, isn't it? I couldn't quite make out whether Mother Bicker was embarrassed for me or not. He doesn't swear any more than Ann Jellicoe or Miriam or any of the other Court people do. That is something you shall have to get used to when we meet them – Lindsay too, they swear like troopers. I think it is slightly affectation with them though . . .

Roots was first entitled 'Not Only the Corn'. Thank God I renamed it. From the start it was to be about a girl whose boyfriend never turned up, for certain, that. And just as certain – the shock would lead to self-discovery. But what I was as excitedly eager to capture as much as anything was the slow pace of pause and silence in Norfolk rural life.

Many moments would have to be concocted – like the intimate conversations between Beatie and her sister Jenny, and Beatie's dance to Bizet's 'L'Arlesienne Suite' at the end of Act Two. But the stories told by Mrs Bryant would, I knew, be those I'd heard and noted down from Mother Bicker, while other moments would come from my relationship with Dusty. One of her dreams became the dream in Act Two when Beatie looks at herself in the mirror after her bath and observes:

> Isn't your nose a funny thing, and your ears. And your arms and your legs, aren't they funny things – sticking out of a lump –

But the denouement is concocted. The tea-party, the family's confusion, the mother's wrath and Beatie's last hosanna speech are pure invention, except for one element: I *did* write a letter to Dusty saying our relationship should end but she ignored it and replied asking me to pack and post a parcel of selected Jewish deli foods. I think that response of cheerful insouciance as much as any other aspect of her character suggested to me we could be lifelong partners.

I seem to remember *Roots* taking about three months to complete. By the end of August 1958 it must have been in the hands of Devine and Richardson. I was excited by its structure – a collection of moments juxtaposed in a way I thought added up to poetic impact. George and Tony turned it down.

I can't remember how I heard about it. I remember only the gist of what was explained: they were disappointed. Disappointed but – they had a suggestion. They felt, quite rightly, that nothing really happened in the first two acts and their suggestion was: combine the first and second acts into one act; make Act Three into Act Two; and write a new third act in which the London lover, Ronnie, appeared. After all, they reasoned most reasonably, everyone in the audience would by now be so keyed up and curious about this boy they would want to see him, witness his impact upon the family who had been driven mad with anticipation.

I said I would think about it, and did, though not for

long nor, I suspect, seriously. I knew the value of what I'd written. These brilliant men of the theatre had missed the point. Their suggestions had shocked me they were so banal. I rejected them and prepared to face the end of my career as a playwright.

Roots was turned down while still being read by council members one of whom was Dame Peggy Ashcroft. She not only admired the play but recognised it immediately as a role for Joan Plowright. Joan read it and announced she would play the role anywhere. Bryan Bailey of the Belgrade had by now read the play and was clamouring for the rights. What did John think? Poor John was languishing in Wormwood Scrubs (2952 Dexter) from where he wrote:

> Look here, I want to direct *Roots* – *Home is Where You Live*. [Did I ever call it that or is it John's humour? His humour, I hope!] I don't have to read it, I know you, I know the subject. If I had a cheque book I'd reach for it. Let's go to Coventry and use our kind of actors – (Alfie [Lynch] and Patsy Byrne for instance). I have more pleasure in remembering *Chicken Soup* than in anything I have ever done in my life . . . one of those absolutely enchanted times, when time and place perfectly cohered. If Bryan wants it, try to wait for me.

Of course I waited. Some time in the middle of March, it must have been, I met John out of prison with our first car, a secondhand Hillman Minx, convertible, and took him home to Clapton Common where he was fussed over and looked after for six weeks till his spirits recovered and he began sorting out his life. Dusty was working behind the counter at Sainsburys in Mare Street, Hackney, for £3 10s a week, and I was still having to help my brother-in-law, Ralph, in his basement joinery workshop to top up our weekly earnings.

John couldn't wait to read *Roots*. I have the sharpest memory of returning from work – it must have been the evening of the same day – to an excited ex-con who leapt into my arms declaring how wonderful the play was, that it didn't need changing as Tony and George had suggested, and that he knew exactly what to do with it.

He at once began assembling the elements to make *Roots* work. The Court didn't want it? Right, Bryan Bailey did – we'd go to Coventry, this time to enjoy the luxury of three weeks' rehearsal instead of two. Joan Plowright said she would do it anywhere? Splendid – we'll get her to Coventry. And there was this clever designer, a woman, tall, lean and beautiful – the daughter of the eminent writer and independent member of parliament, Sir Alan Herbert, 'Herbert' a name with ancient lineage – who had been a scene painter at the Court and had just been given her first chance by George to design Tony Richardson's production of Ionesco's *The Chairs*. Her second design project was John Dexter's production of the Yeats' play *Purgatory*. They had obviously worked well together and, like Joan Plowright, Jocelyn Herbert was a star in the making.

This is what I remember. We took Jocelyn to Norfolk. She wanted to see the settings on which I had based the play. John did *not*! Joan Plowright pointed to half a page in one act and suggested it really belonged to another. She was right. John decided that real liver and onions had to be fried on stage. 'It was,' he recorded, 'a practical problem of how long it needed to cook and serve and eat it . . .' The front rows gasped at the smell that wafted towards them as soon as the curtain went up. The major problem was pace. John's instructions to the cast were firm and clear: 'Don't be rushed. You'll hear shuffling, coughing – ignore it. *Dictate* the pace, they will accept it . . .' There may have been disagreements here and there between us, none stick in memory. We shared, and communicated it to the cast, a sense of being involved in something special. It was partly to do with the outrageousness of the play's rhythm, that long, delicate curve stretching from a very very slow beginning across three scenes to the end of Act Two and the exultant Bizet dance. We felt ourselves in possession of an experience in the theatre which, if we could pull it off, would be dynamic, unique.

What I see as plainly as yesterday is that first night – 25 May, the day after my twenty-seventh birthday, five days before Dusty's twenty-third – John on my left, Dusty on my right, sitting dead centre in the front row of the balcony at the Belgrade. The opening was breath-takingly slow. Patsy Byrne, solid, experienced, intelligent, trusting utterly in the play and John's direction, called to her child off stage, waited, went into her child's room, moved slowly back into the kitchen, returned to her frying pan, and cooked. Charlie Kay took his time coming in from work, placing his bike in the same room, arching his back with pain. Patsy looked at him for a long time, watching, before asking: 'Waas matter wi' you then?' Slowly they built up the exchange that was to become the running joke in the play about Mother Bryant saying the pain in his back was due to indigestion.

JIMMY. Don't be daft.
JENNY. That's what I say. Blast, Mother, I say, you don't git indigestion in the back. Don't you tell me, she say, I hed it!
JIMMY. What heven't she hed.

On which line the audience laughed, as we had hoped, planned, plotted, schemed, rehearsed day after intense day! The actors had captured and held them. John's hand reached to clutch mine. 'They've done it,' he whispered. When I turned to nod and share the moment, I saw – he had tears in his eyes.

The applause, after Beatie's dance – scattily and touchingly danced by Joan in a mixture of hornpipe and impromptu nothing-steps, sending shivers down our backs – was a great whoop of joy. By the end – after Gwen Nelson's poignant defence of Mother Bryant, and Joan's amazed, triumphant discovery that she was no longer quoting someone else but using her own words – we knew we had brought it off.

The next morning disparate groups of actors, friends, and theatre staff assembled in the Belgrade's restaurant upstairs to pour over enthusiastic local reviews. The buzz of excitement flew from table to table, and as I sat with my family I could see George Devine and Bryan Bailey, their heads down and huddled, negotiating a deal to transfer our production to the Royal Court. Bryan Bailey was killed not long afterwards in a motor accident on the first of the nation's motorways – the M1 from London to Coventry, a development rendering the city an industrial base of huge value. It just cost them one of their newest sons. Bryan fell asleep at the wheel. Overworked. Over-enthusiastic.

The London reviews were even more ecstatic. Milton Shulman in the *Evening Standard* 'begged' audiences to see the play. Ken Tynan, unprecedented for a critic, came out of the theatre in a state of such euphoria that he had to telephone and congratulate me. Giddy, giddy times until –

The play opened at the Royal Court on 30 June. A month later, 30 July, it transferred to the Duke of York's on St Martin's Lane during one of the hottest summers on record. Bernard Levin writing in the *Daily Express* claimed: 'I have now seen this great, shining play three times, and it seems to have grown visibly in stature each time . . .' It didn't help. Audiences stayed away. The play had to be taken off long before anticipated. It was the first of the gods' mean sporting with me.

When the play was first published at the end of 1959, a volume on its own, by Penguin Books, I signed and placed a copy in a plastic wrapping and gave it to Mother Bicker, who by then was my mother-in-law. It remained in its wrapping for years. She left it lying around on the window-ledge for neighbours to see. I don't think she ever read it.

I'm Talking About Jerusalem

There's little to say about the third play in *The Trilogy* except that while writing this story of my sister's and brother-in-law's rural experiment I was very conscious of wanting it to be different from the first two. It was, but no more than *Roots* was different from *Chicken Soup with Barley*. There is, I'd like to think, a progression from stark naturalism to a more lyrical naturalism. I think I was beginning to understand about the musicality of dramatic structure. There were hints of it in *Roots*. *Jerusalem* may be less successful but it aspired to take off from the ground in a way that happens only at the ends of Acts Two and Three of *Roots* – with the dance and the speech of self-discovery. By the time I came to write my fifth play, *Chips With Everything*, the ability to structure musically had matured. And with later plays like *The Friends*, *The Old Ones*, *Caritas*, and *Blood Libel* I was tackling musical structures of even greater complexity, reaching a zenith in the one-woman play that is my favourite – *Whatever Happened to Betty Lemon?* But it was with *I'm Talking About Jerusalem* that this passion for musical structures began.

Finally

Some twenty years later I was commissioned to write a film script of *The Trilogy*. John Dexter had once said he'd like to make the film using *Roots* as the spine. I took up his suggestion. The first shots are of Beatie returning home. From then on we flash back to the scenes of the other two plays. But I made changes. I threw out much and – notice my use of the word – 'remembered' new material. It's a fresh work. *The Trilogy* revisited. A fourth script rather than an adaptation of the three plays. A rethinking of my past. The film has not yet been made. Perhaps it's awaiting its time.

Arnold Wesker
Blaendigeddi
July 2000

AUTHOR'S NOTE

A play is ultimately a cooperative effort, and I would like to acknowledge my indebtedness to all the actors and actresses who eventually brought my plays alive on the stage. And in particular I cannot offer enough thanks for the understanding brought to the production by John Dexter, the director, many of whose ideas are contained in the versions as published.

NOTE TO ACTORS AND DIRECTORS OF THE *TRILOGY*

In twenty years of seeing the *Trilogy* performed I've observed one major weakness: an inability to make the characters physically – and thus intellectually – live on the stage. The emotion of a character often succeeds in coming through, but frequently there appears to be no comprehension of how the characters exchange ideas and thoughts, as though actors knew what made people weep but not what made them think; they have been made to stand still and utter 'significant' lines 'significantly', whereas debate in these plays, the cut and thrust of domestic polemic, should take place in the midst of physical action. Sarah should, for example, be cutting bread on a line like 'You can't have brotherhood without love'. The family inquest at the end of *Jerusalem* should be conducted while crates are being packed, floors swept, curtains pulled; thoughts should be thrown over shoulders, down the stairs, over the washing-line, from outside while emptying garbage. If the physical business of living does not continue then the dialogue will emerge pompously and fall with dull thuds from characters who will appear no more than cardboard cut-outs.

A.W.
July 1978

The complete *Wesker Trilogy* was first presented at the Royal Court Theatre, London, in 1960, with the following cast:

SARAH KAHN	Kathleen Michael
HARRY KAHN, *her husband*	Frank Finlay
MONTY BLATT	Alan Howard
DAVE SIMMONDS	Mark Eden
PRINCE SILVER	Charles Kay
HYMIE KOSSOF, *Sarah's brother*	John Colin
CISSIE, *Harry's sister, a trade-union organizer*	Cherry Morris
ADA KAHN, *daughter of Sarah and Harry*	Ruth Meyers
RONNIE KAHN, *son of Sarah and Harry*	David Saire
BESSIE BLATT, *wife of Monty*	Patsy Byrne
BEATIE BRYANT, *a friend of Ronnie*	Joan Plowright
JENNY BEALES, *her sister*	Patsy Byrne
JIMMY BEALES, *her brother-in-law*	Charles Kay
MRS BRYANT, *her mother*	Gwen Nelson
MR BRYANT, *her father*	John Colin
FRANK BRYANT, *her brother*	Alan Howard
PEARL BRYANT, *her sister-in-law*	Cherry Morrris
STAN MANN, *a neighbour of the Bealeses*	Frank Finlay
MR HEALEY, *a manager at the farm*	Anthony Hall
SAMMY, *Dave Simmonds's apprentice*	Terry Palmer
ESTHER, *Harry's sister*	Jessie Robins
IST REMOVAL MAN	Alan Howard
2ND REMOVAL MAN	Charles Kay
COLONEL DEWHURST	John Colin
DOBSON	Frank Finlay
DANIEL SIMMONDS	Michael Phillips

Directed by John Dexter
Designed by Jocelyn Herbert

Chicken Soup with Barley

For Leah and Joe

Chicken Soup with Barley was first presented at the Belgrade Theatre, Coventry, on 7 July 1958, and subsequently at the Royal Court Theatre, London, on 14 July 1958, with the following cast:

SARAH KAHN	Charmian Eyre
HARRY KAHN	Frank Finlay
MONTY BLATT	Alfred Lynch
DAVE SIMMONDS	Richard Martin
PRINCE SILVER	Patrick Carter
HYMIE KOSSOF	Henry Manning
CISSIE KAHN	Cherry Morris
ADA KAHN	Jacqueline Wilson
RONNIE KAHN	Anthony Valentine
BESSIE BLATT	Patsy Byrne

Directed by John Dexter

Act One, Scene One: 4 October 1936
        Scene Two: The same evening

Act Two, Scene One: April 1946
        Scene Two: October 1947

Act Three, Scene One: November 1955
        Scene Two: December 1956

THE SOLO GAME

	Clubs	*Hearts*	*Diamonds*	*Spades*
CISSIE:	K,4,3,2	3	K,2	A,K,J,6, 4,2
SARAH:	A,Q,6	10,5,4	A,6,5,4	9,8,3
PRINCE:	J,10,8	K,7,J	J,10,9,8,7	Q,5
HYMIE:	9,7,5	A,Q,9,8, 6,2	Q,3	10,7

1st Hand:

CISSIE:	3 Hearts – 10 – K – A
HYMIE:	3 Diamonds – 2 – 4 – J
PRINCE:	Q Spades – 10 – J – 9
PRINCE:	5 Spades – 7 – 6 – 8
SARAH:	5 Hearts – 7 – 6 – K Diamonds
PRINCE:	7 Diamonds – Q – K Clubs – A
SARAH:	3 Spades – J Clubs – 9 Clubs – 2 Spades

(CISSIE *shows Hand*)

ACT ONE

SCENE ONE

4 October 1936.

The basement of the KAHNS' *house in the East End of London. The room is warm and lived in. A fire is burning. One door, at the back and left of the room, leads to a bedroom. A window, left, looks up to the street. To the right is another door which leads to a kitchen, which is seen. At rear of stage are the stairs leading up into the street.*

SARAH KAHN *is in the kitchen washing up, humming to herself. She is a small, fiery woman, aged thirty-seven, Jewish, and of European origin. Her movements indicate great energy and vitality. She is a very warm person.* HARRY KAHN, *her husband, comes down the stairs, walks past her and into the front room. He is thirty-five and also a European Jew. He is dark, slight, rather pleasant looking, and the antithesis of* SARAH. *He is amiable but weak. From outside we hear a band playing a revolutionary song.*

SARAH (*from the kitchen*). You took the children to Lottie's?

HARRY (*taking up book to read*). I took them.

SARAH. They didn't mind?

HARRY. No, they didn't mind.

SARAH. Is Hymie coming?

HARRY. I don't know.

SARAH (*to herself*). Nothing he knows! You didn't ask him? He didn't say? He knows about the demonstration, doesn't he?

HARRY. I don't know whether he knows or he doesn't know. I didn't discuss it with him – I took the kids, that's all. Hey, Sarah – you should read Upton Sinclair's book about the meat-canning industry – it's an eye-opener . . .

SARAH. Books! Nothing else interests him, only books. Did you see anything outside? What's happening?

HARRY. The streets are packed with people, I never seen so many people. They've got barricades at Gardiner's Corner.

SARAH. There'll be such trouble.

HARRY. Sure there'll be trouble. You ever known a demonstration where there wasn't trouble?

SARAH. And the police?

HARRY. There'll be more police than blackshirts.

SARAH. What time they marching?

HARRY. I don't know.

SARAH. Harry, you know where your cigarettes are, don't you?

> *This is her well-meaning but maddening attempt to point out to a weak man his weakness.*

HARRY. I know where they are.

SARAH. And you know what's on at the cinema?

HARRY. So?

SARAH. And also you know what time it opens? (*He grins.*) So why don't you know what time they plan to march? (*Touché!*)

HARRY. Leave me alone, Sarah, will you? Two o'clock they plan to march – nah!

SARAH. So you do know. Why didn't you tell me straight away? Shouldn't you tell me something when I ask you?

HARRY. I didn't know what time they marched, so what do you want of me?

SARAH. But you did know when I nagged you.

HARRY. So I suddenly remembered. Is there anything terrible in that?

She shakes a disbelieving fist at him and goes out to see where the loudspeaker cries are coming from. The slogan 'Madrid today – London tomorrow' is being repeated. As she is out HARRY *looks for her handbag, and on finding it proceeds to take some money from it.*

SARAH (*she is hot*). Air! I must have air – this basement will kill me. God knows what I'll do without air when I'm dead. Who else was at Lottie's?

HARRY (*still preoccupied*). All of them.

SARAH. Who's all of them?

HARRY. All of them! You know. Lottie and Hymie and the boys, Solly and Martin.

He finds a ten-shilling note, pockets it and resumes his seat by the fire, taking up a book to read. SARAH *returns to front room with some cups and saucers.*

SARAH. Here, lay these out, the boys will be coming soon.

HARRY. Good woman! I could just do with a cup of tea.

SARAH. What's the matter, you didn't have any tea by Lottie's?

HARRY. No.

SARAH. Liar!

HARRY. I didn't have any tea by Lottie's, I tell you. (*Injured tone.*) Good God, woman, why don't you believe me when I tell you things?

SARAH. *You* tell *me* why. Why don't I believe him when he tells me things! As if he's such an angel and never tells lies. What's the matter, you never told lies before I don't think?

HARRY. All right, so I had tea at Lottie's. There, you satisfied now?

SARAH (*preparing things as she talks*). Well, of course you had tea at Lottie's. Don't I know you had tea at Lottie's. You think I'm going to think that Lottie wouldn't make you a cup of tea?

HARRY. Oh, leave off, Sarah.

SARAH. No! This time I won't leave off. (*Her logic again.*) I want to know why you told me you didn't have tea at Lottie's when you know perfectly well you did. I want to know.

> HARRY *raises his hands in despair.*

I know you had tea there and *you* know you had tea there – so what harm is it if you tell me? You think I care whether you had a cup of tea there or not? You can drink tea there till it comes out of your eyes and I wouldn't care only as long as you tell me.

HARRY. Sarah, will you please stop nagging me, will you? What difference if I had tea there or I didn't have tea there?

SARAH. That's just what I'm saying. All I want to know is whether you're all of a liar or half a liar!

HARRY (*together with her*). . . . all of a liar or half a liar!

> *A young man,* MONTY BLATT, *comes down the stairs. He is about nineteen, Jewish, working-class, and cockney. His voice is heard before he is seen, shouting:* 'Mrs Kahn! Sarah! Mrs Kahn!' *He has interrupted the row as he dashes into the room without knocking.*

MONTY. Ah, good! You're here! (*Moves to window and, looking out, shouts up.*) It's OK. They're here. Here! (*Offering parcel.*) Mother sent you over some of her strudel. C'mon down. (*To* HARRY.) Hello, Harry boy, how you going? All fighting fit for the demo?

HARRY. I'm fit, like a Trojan I'm fit!

SARAH. You won't see him at any demo. In the pictures you'll find him. (*Goes to landing to make tea.*)

MONTY. The pictures? Don't be bloody mad. You won't hear a thing! You seen the streets today? Sarah, you seen the streets yet? Mobbed Mo-obbed! The lads have been there since seven this morning.

Two other young men in their early twenties come down the stairs, DAVE SIMMONDS *and* PRINCE SILVER. *They are heatedly discussing something.*

PRINCE. But Dave, there's so much work here to do. Hello, Sarah!

DAVE. I know all about the work here, but there are plenty of party members to do it. Hello, Sarah. Spain is the battlefront. Spain is a real issue at last.

SARAH. Spain? Spain, Dave?

HARRY. Spain?

PRINCE. Dave is joining the International Brigade. He's leaving for Spain tomorrow morning. (*To* DAVE.) But Spain is only one issue brought to a head. You're too young to . . .

HARRY. Dave, don't go mad all of a sudden. It's not all glory, you know.

DAVE. Harry, you look as though you didn't sleep last night.

MONTY. He didn't – the old cossack. (*To the tune of 'All the nice girls love a sailor'.*) For you know what cossacks are . . . Am I right, Harry?

PRINCE. I saw your sister Cissie at Aldgate, Harry. She was waving your mother's walking-stick in the air.

HARRY. She's mad.

MONTY (*loudly calling*). Where's this cup of tea, Sarah?

SARAH (*bringing in tea*). Do your fly-buttons up, Monty, you tramp you. Now then, Dave, tell me what's happening and what the plans are.

Everyone draws up a chair by the table.

DAVE. It's like this. The Party loudspeaker vans have been out all morning – you heard them? The Fascists are gathering at Royal Mint Street near the bridge. They plan to march up to Aldgate, down Commercial Road to Salmon Lane in Limehouse – you know Salmon Lane? – where they think they're going to hold a meeting. Then they plan to go on to Victoria Park and hold another meeting.

SARAH. *Two* meetings? What do they want to hold two meetings for?

HARRY. Why shouldn't they hold two meetings?

SARAH. What, *you* think they should hold two meetings?

HARRY. It's not what I think – she's such a funny woman – it's not what I think, but they want to hold two meetings – so what's so strange about that?

SARAH. But it costs so much money.

HARRY. Perhaps you want we should have a collection for them?

DAVE. Now. They could go along the Highway by the docks and then up Cable Street, but Mosley won't take the Highway because that's the back way, though the police will suggest he does.

SARAH. I bet the police cause trouble.

PRINCE. They've had to call in forces from outside London.

SARAH. You won't make a real fight, boys, will you? I mean you won't get hurt?

MONTY. Sarah, you remember they threw a seven-year-old girl through a glass window? So don't fight the bastards?

PRINCE. Now Monty, there's to be discipline, remember. There's to be no attack or bottle-throwing. It's a test, you know that, don't you, it's a test for us. We're to stop them passing, that's all.

MONTY. Sure we'll stop them passing. If I see a blackshirt come by I'll tap his shoulder and I'll say: 'Excuse me, but you can't come this way today, we're digging up the road.' And he'll look at my hammer and sickle and he'll doff his cap and he'll say: 'I beg your pardon, comrade, I'll take the Underground.'

DAVE. Comrades! You want to know what the plans are

or you don't want to know? Again. As we don't know
what's going to happen we've done this: some of the
workers are rallying at Royal Mint Street – so if the
Fascists want to go through the Highway they'll have
to fight for it. But we guess they'll want to stick to the
main route so as not to lose face – you follow? We've
therefore called the main rally at Gardiner's Corner.
If, on the other hand, they do attempt to pass up
Cable Street –

SARAH. Everything happens in Cable Street.

HARRY. What else happened in Cable Street?

SARAH. Peter the Painter had a fight with Churchill
there, didn't he?

MONTY. You're thinking of Sidney Street, sweetheart.

HARRY. You know, she gets everything mixed up.

SARAH. You're very wonderful I suppose, yes? You're
the clever one!

HARRY. I don't get my facts mixed up, anyway!

SARAH. Per, per, per, per, per! Listen to him! My
politician!

MONTY. Sarah, do me a favour, leave the fists till later.

DAVE. If, on the other hand, they do try to come up
Cable Street then they'll meet some dockers and
more barricades. And if any get through that lot then
they still can't hold their meetings either in Salmon
Lane or Victoria Park Square.

SARAH. Why not?

PRINCE. Because since seven this morning there's been
some of our. comrades standing there with our
platforms.

MONTY. Bloody wonderful, isn't it? Makes you feel
proud, eh Sarah? Every section of this working-class
area that we've approached has responded. The
dockers at Limehouse have come out to the man.
The lot!

PRINCE. The unions, the Co–ops, Labour Party members and the Jewish People's Council –

SARAH. The Board of Deputies?

HARRY. There she goes again. Not the Jewish Board of Deputies – *they* asked the Jewish population to keep away. No, the Jewish People's Council – the one that organized that mass demo against Hitler some years back.

> SARAH *pulls face at him.*

MONTY. There's been nothing like it since the General Strike.

HARRY. Christ! The General Strike! That was a time, Sarah, eh?

SARAH. What you asking me for? You want I should remember that you were missing for six days when Ada was ill?

HARRY. Yes, I was missing, I'm sure.

SARAH. Well, sure you were missing?

HARRY. Where was I missing?

SARAH. How should I know where you were missing. If I'd have known where you were missing you wouldn't have been missing.

> *There is heard from outside a sound of running feet and voices shouting. Everyone except* HARRY *moves to the window.*

FIRST VOICE. They're assembling! They're assembling! Out to the barricades – the Fascists are assembling!

SECOND VOICE. Hey, Stan! Where's the best place?

FIRST VOICE. Take your boys to Cable Street. The Fascists are assembling! Come out of your houses! Come out of your houses!

MONTY. What about us, Dave?

SARAH. You haven't suggested to Harry and me where to go yet.

DAVE. There's plenty of time. They won't try to march till two, and it's only twelve thirty.

SARAH. You eaten? You boys had lunch?

PRINCE. We all had lunch at my place, Sarah; sit down, stop moving a few seconds.

DAVE. Take your pick, Sarah. If you fancy yourself as a nurse then go to Aldgate, we've got a first-aid post there, near Whitechapel Library.

SARAH. Such organization! And you lot?

DAVE. Monty is taking some of the lads to the left flank of Cable Street, Prince is organizing a team of cyclist messengers between the main posts and headquarters, I'm going round the streets at the last minute to call everyone out and – and that's the lot.

MONTY (*rubbing his hands*). All we have to do is wait.

DAVE. Where is Ada?

SARAH. Ada and Ronnie are at Hymie's place. I thought it best they get right out of the way.

DAVE (*guiltily*). You think she'll stay away? Your precocious daughter is a born fighter, Sarah.

MONTY. 'Course she is! She'll be round the streets organizing the pioneers – you see.

SARAH. Never! I told her to stay there and she'll stay there.

HARRY. I'm sure!

SARAH. God forbid she should be like you and run wild.

HARRY. All right, so she should be like you then!

SARAH. I'm jolly sure she should be like me! Ronnie isn't enough for him yet. A boy of five running about at nights and swearing at his aunts. (*Smiles at thought.*) Bless him! (*To the others.*) He didn't half upset them: they wouldn't let him mess around with the radio so he started effing and blinding and threw their books on the floor. (*Turning again to* HARRY.) Like you he throws things.

HARRY. Have you ever come across a woman like her before?

MONTY. I'd love another cup of tea.

HARRY (*jumps up and goes to kitchen*). I'll make it. I'll make it.

SARAH. He's so sweet when anybody else is around. I'll make some sandwiches.

PRINCE. But we've eaten, Sarah.

SARAH. Eat. Always eat. You don't know what time you'll be back.

> SARAH *goes to cupboard and cuts up bread ready for cheese sandwiches. A very distant sound of people chanting is heard:* 'They shall not pass, they shall not pass, they shall not pass.'

MONTY. The boys! Listen. Hear them? You know, Sarah, that's the same cry the people of Madrid were shouting.

PRINCE. And they didn't get past either. Imagine it! All those women and children coming out into the streets and making barricades with their beds and their chairs.

DAVE (*sadly*). It was a slaughter.

PRINCE. And then came the first International Brigade.

DAVE. The Edgar André from Germany, Commune de Paris from France, and the Dombrovsky from Poland.

MONTY. Wait till our Dave gets over there. You'll give 'em brass balls for breakfast, Dave, eh?

SARAH. You really going, Dave? Does Ada know?

DAVE. Don't tell her, Sarah. You know how dramatic calf-love is.

PRINCE. Calf-love? If you get back alive from Spain she'll marry you at the landing-stage – mark me.

SARAH. How are you going?

DAVE. They tell me it's a week-end trip to Paris and

then a midnight ramble over the Pyrenees. The back way!

SARAH. It's terrible out there, they say. They say we've lost a lot of good comrades already.

PRINCE. We've lost too many good comrades out there – you hear me, Dave?

MONTY. Sammy Avner and Lorimer Birch at Boadilla, Felicia Brown and Ernst Julius at Aragon.

SARAH. Julius? The tailor who used to work with us at Cantor's? But he was only a young boy.

PRINCE. And Felicia an artist and Lorimer an Oxford undergraduate.

MONTY. And Cornford was killed at Cordova.

PRINCE. And Ronnie Symes at Madrid.

MONTY. And Stevie Yates at Casa del Campo.

SARAH. Casa del Campo! Madrid! Such beautiful names and all that killing.

　　Pause.

MONTY. Hey! You know who organized the first British group? Nat Cohen! I used to go to school with him. Him and Sam Masters were on a cycling holiday in France. As soon as they heard of the revolt they cycled over to Barcelona and started the Tom Mann Centuria.

HARRY (*coming to the door*). He's a real madman, Nat Cohen. He chalks slogans right outside the police station. I used to work with him.

SARAH. God knows if they'll come back alive.

DAVE. When three Fascist deserters were asked how they reached our lines they said they came through the hills of the widows, orphans and sweethearts; they'd lost so many men attacking those hills.

MONTY. And may they lose many more!

DAVE (*angrily*). The war in Spain is not a game of cards, Monty. You don't pay in pennies when you lose.

May they lose many more! What kind of talk is that? Sometimes, Monty, I think you only enjoy the battle, and that one day you'll forget the ideal. You hate too much. You can't have brotherhood when you hate. There's only one difference between them and us – we know what we're fighting for. It's almost an unfair battle.

HARRY *now returns to kitchen to pour out tea.*

MONTY. Unfair, he says! When Germany and Italy are supplying them with guns and tanks and aeroplanes and our boys have only got rifles and mortars – is that unfair? You call that unfair, I don't think?

DAVE. When you fight men who are blind it's always unfair. You think I'm going to enjoy shooting a man because he calls himself a Fascist? I feel so sick at the thought of firing a rifle that I think I'll board that boat with a blindfold over my eyes. Sometimes I think that's the only way to do things. I'm not even sure that I want to go, only I know if I don't then – then – well, what sense can a man make of his life?

SARAH. You're really a pacifist, aren't you, Dave?

DAVE. I'm a terribly sad pacifist, Sarah.

HARRY. I understand you, Dave – I know what you mean, boy. What do you want we should say? You go – we're proud of you. You stay behind – we love you. Sometimes you live in a way you don't know why – you just do a thing. So you don't have to shout – you're shouting at yourself! But a pacifist, Dave? There's going to be a big war soon, a Fascist war: you think it's time for pacifism?

SARAH. He's right, Dave.

DAVE. I know it's not time yet. I know that. I know there is still some fighting to be done. But it'll come. It will come, you know – when there'll be a sort of long pause, and people will just be frightened of each other and still think they *have* to fight. That'll be the time – But now – well, I feel like an old gardener who knows he won't live through to the spring to plant his seeds.

> HARRY *comes in with the teas and at the same time a voice from the street is heard frantically shouting:* 'Man your posts! Men and women of the East End, come out of your houses! The blackshirts are marching! Come out! Come out!' *There is a hurried movement from the people in the room.* DAVE *and* MONTY *rush to the window.* PRINCE *rushes upstairs, knocking a cup of tea out of* HARRY*'s hand.*

MONTY. Christ! They've started before time.

DAVE. It might be a false alarm.

PRINCE (*from the stairs*). We can't take the risk. Let's get going.

> MONTY *moves off quickly, taking a poker from the fireplace on his way out and concealing it in his clothes.*

MONTY. I'll clean it and bring it back later.

HARRY. But I've made your tea.

DAVE. Stick it back in the pot. We'll drink it later. Now you two, you know where the posts are – Cable Street, Royal Mint Street and Gardiner's Corner.

HARRY (*at the window*). The street is mobbed. Jesus! Look at them, everybody is coming out, everybody.

SARAH (*putting on her coat in general rush*). Where's the first-aid post?

DAVE (*having helped* SARAH *with coat, moves off*). Whitechapel Library. Harry, you coming?

HARRY (*still at window*). I'm coming, I'm coming. You go on. Good God, there's Alf Bosky and his wife. She's got the baby with her. (*Shouts up.*) Hey Alf – good luck, comrade – we're coming. Sarah, there's Alf Bosky and his wife.

SARAH (*looking for something in kitchen*). I heard, I heard! (*She finds a rolling pin and, waving it in the air, dashes into the front room.*) Are you coming now, Harry? I'm going to Gardiner's Corner – come on, we'll be late.

HARRY (*backing away from rolling pin*). Don't hit anybody with that thing, Sarah, it hurts.

SARAH. Fool!

> SARAH *dashes to the stairs but stops and, remembering something, returns to front room. From a corner of the room she finds a red flag with a hammer and sickle on it and thrusts it in* HARRY's *hand.*

Here, wave this! Do something useful!

Exits upstairs.

HARRY (*grabbing his coat*). Hey, Sarah, wait for me – Sarah! Hey, wait for me!

> *He follows her, banner streaming. The voices outside grow to a crescendo:* 'They shall not pass, they shall not pass, THEY SHALL NOT PASS!'

Curtain.

SCENE TWO

Same room, later that evening. There is commotion and some singing from the streets outside. MONTY *and* PRINCE *are coming down the stairs leading* HYMIE KOSSOF. *He has blood all over his face. He is a short, rotund man with a homely appearance.*

MONTY (*leaving* PRINCE *and* HYMIE *to go into the room*). I'll get some water on the stove. Sit him in a chair. (*Shouts upstairs.*) Cissie! Don't come down yet, go and get some first-aid kit from somewhere. (*Fills kettle.*)

PRINCE. Now don't talk too much and don't move, Hymie. Jesus! What a state you're in. Sarah'll go mad.

HYMIE. Well, clean me up quickly then.

MONTY (*rushing from kitchen to window*). Cissie! *Cissie!* Try that sweet shop near Toynbee Hall. I saw a first-aid group there. They might still be there. (*Comes away, but, remembering something else, sticks his head out again.*) *Aspros!* Try and get hold of some Aspros.

SARAH (*from the top of stairs – off*). Monty! Is Hymie down there?

HYMIE. Oh, my goodness, she's here. If there is one thing Sarah loves it's someone who's ill to fuss over. Why didn't I go home?

MONTY. Because you know Lottie would say serves you right!

SARAH *appears;* MONTY *rushes to her.*

Now don't panic, Sarah, he's all right, he's all right.

SARAH (*entering*). Hymie!

HYMIE. Sarah Nightingale!

MONTY. Don't frighten him, I tell you.

SARAH (*taking over towel and wiping him*). Fool you! They told me you were hurt – I nearly died.

HYMIE. So did I!

SARAH. Fool! *You* had to go straight into it.

HYMIE. I was only hit by a truncheon. Now do me a favour, Sarah, and just make some tea, there's a good girl.

SARAH. Nobody else got hurt. Only him. The brave one!

MONTY (*significantly handling the poker*). Plenty got hurt! Oh, he's all right. Aren't you all right, Hymie?

HYMIE. I'm here, aren't I?

SARAH (*taking off her coat*). Well, why hasn't anybody done something?

PRINCE. Cissie has gone to get some first aid.

SARAH. Cissie? Harry's sister?

PRINCE. Yes. Where is Harry, by the way? Anybody seen him?

SARAH (*ominously*). Wait till I see him. I'll give him. You expected him to stay there?

MONTY. I saw him at Cable Street; he was waving the old red flag, but he didn't stay long. He took one look at the artillery and guns and said he was going to find us some sandwiches.

SARAH. They had guns at Cable Street? Did they use them?

MONTY. Nah! it was only brought out to frighten us. *Frighten* us, mark. If they'd have dropped a bomb today we wouldn't have been frightened. Christ! What a day!

HYMIE. I mean, did you ever see anything like it? We threw stones and bottles at them, Sarah. They were on horseback with batons and they kept charging us, so we threw stones. And you should have seen Monty when one policeman surrendered. Surrendered! A policeman! It's never happened before. He didn't know what to do, Monty didn't. None of us knew. I mean, who's ever heard of policemen surrendering? And after the first came others – half a dozen of them. My goodness, we made such a fuss of them. Gave them cigarettes and mugs of tea and called them comrade policemen.

PRINCE. There's no turning back now – nothing can stop the workers now.

MONTY. I bet we have a revolution soon. Hitler won't stop at Spain, you know. You watch him go and you watch the British Government lick his arse until he spits in their eye. Then *we'll* move in.

HYMIE. I'm not so sure, Monty. We won today but the same taste doesn't stay long. Mosley was turned back

at Aldgate pump and everyone shouted hurrah. But I
wonder how many of the people at Gardiner's
Corner were just sightseers. You know, in every
political movement there are just sightseers.

MONTY. Ten thousand bloody sightseers? Do me a
favour, it wasn't a bank holiday.

> SARAH *goes to kitchen to pour the water into the bowl.*
> CISSIE *appears.*

HYMIE. Any big excitement can be a bank holiday for a
worker, believe me.

> *Enter* CISSIE. *Woman of about thirty-three. She is a
> trade-union organizer – precise in her manner, dry
> sense of humour.*

CISSIE. Ointment, lint, bandage and plaster. Let's have
a look at him.

SARAH (*entering with bowl of water*). I'm coming, it's all
right, I can manage.

> CISSIE *makes way and* SARAH *begins to sponge her
> brother's face and then puts bandage round his head.*

PRINCE. Where were *you*, Cis?

CISSIE. Gardiner's Corner holding a banner. The union
banner. And you?

MONTY. Digging up the paving stones in Cable Street.

CISSIE. Paving stones? (*She hoists the back of her skirt to
warm her behind in front of the fire.*)

MONTY. We pulled out the railings from a near-by
church and the stones from the gutter. I'll get some
more coal for the fire. (*Goes to kitchen, pinching
CISSIE's behind on the way.*) We turned over a lorry.

SARAH. A lorry?

HYMIE. But it was the wrong one. The lorry we'd laid
on was in a near-by yard and when the call went up

to bring the lorry the boys, if you don't mind, grabbed one at the top of the street. I ask you!

SARAH. Keep still. There, you look more respectable now.

> MONTY *re-enters with coal and on his way to fire takes a feather from a hat near by and plants it among* HYMIE's *bandages.*

HYMIE. Anyone get hurt your way, Cissie?

CISSIE. Some of the boys from my union got arrested.

SARAH. I'll go and make some tea now.

CISSIE. Mick and Sammy and Dave Goldman – and that bloody fool, if you'll excuse the expression, Sonny Becks. Everybody is standing behind the barricades waiting for the blackshirts to appear. The place is swarming with policemen waiting, just waiting, for an opportunity to lay their hands on some of us. So look what he does: not content with just standing there – and Sonny knew perfectly well that the orders were for the strictest discipline – not content with just standing he chose that moment to get up on Mrs O'Laoghaire's vegetable barrow and make a political speech. 'Let us now remember the lessons of the Russian revolution', he starts like he was quoting Genesis, the nitwit. And then he finds that the barrow isn't safe so he steps over to an iron bedstead and put his foot through the springs just as he was quoting Lenin's letter to the toiling masses!

MONTY. You can never stop Sonny making a speech.

CISSIE. But not in bed! Anyway, you know Sonny – a mouth like a cesspool and no shame – so he lets out a torrent of abuse at the capitalist bed-makers and the police just make a dive at him. Mick and Sammy tried to argue with the police so they were hauled off and then Dave Goldman tried to explain – that was when he was hauled off, poor bastard, if you'll excuse the expression!

HYMIE. What'll happen?

CISSIE. The union'll have to find the laywers and probably pay their fine – what else? Which reminds me – Monty and Prince. Get all the boys and girls you can find and bring them to that social next Saturday, the one for Sally Oaks.

HYMIE. Wasn't it her husband caught his bicycle in a tram-line and was killed?

CISSIE. That's right. She's a Catholic. The local priest is trying to raise some money to keep her going for a bit and we promised we'd support it. Well, I'm going.

SARAH (*entering with tea*). Cissie, have you seen Harry?

CISSIE. Harry? No!

SARAH. He's not at your place, I suppose?

CISSIE. How should I know? I haven't been there all day.

SARAH. He always is at your place.

CISSIE. Sarah, I'm not responsible for my brother's actions. None of us have ever been able to control him, the eldest brother! We warned you what you were taking on – you wanted to change him! She wanted to change him.

SARAH. It's your mother who spoils him, you know that?

CISSIE. Spoils him! Do me a favour – the woman's been bed-ridden for the last ten years. Spoils him!

SARAH. He knows he can go to her – she'll feed him.

CISSIE. He's her son, for God's sake.

SARAH. Don't I know it. He's her son all right – and he wants to be looked after like everyone looks after her. Only it's such a pity – he can walk!

CISSIE. Yes, yes – so I know all this already. Good night, everyone.

CISSIE *exits amid varied good-byes and* 'I'll be seeing you'.

SARAH. I hate her!

HYMIE. Don't be a silly girl. Cissie is a good trade-union organizer.

SARAH. She's a cow! Not a bit of warmth, not a bit! What's the good of being a socialist if you're not warm.

HYMIE. But Cissie has *never* liked Harry.

SARAH. Not a bit of warmth. Everything cold and calculated. People like that can't teach love and brotherhood.

PRINCE. Love comes later, Sarah.

SARAH. Love comes now. You have to start with love. How can you talk about socialism otherwise?

MONTY. Hear, hear, Comrade Kahn. Come on now, what is this? We've just won one of the biggest fights in working-class history and all we do is quarrel.

MONTY *settles down and all is quiet. Suddenly, softly, he starts to sing.*

England arise, the long long night is over.

Others join in.

Faint in the East behold the dawn appears.
Out of your evil sleep of toil and sorrow,
England arise, the long long day is here.
England arise . . .

SARAH (*suddenly*). Hymie! The children! God in heaven, I've forgotten the children.

HYMIE. They're at my place. What's the matter with you?

SARAH (*putting on her coat*). But I can't leave them there. How could I forget them like that; what am I thinking of? Won't be long.

Exits.

HYMIE (*calling up to her*). But Ronnie'll be asleep. Don't tell Lottie I got hit. Tell her I'm coming home soon. (*Returning to front room.*) Impetuous woman!

They all settle themselves comfortably around the fire. SARAH *is heard calling from the street.*

SARAH (*off*). Make yourself some food! And there's tea in the pot.

HYMIE (*coming away from window*). Make yourself some food! With her it's food all the time. Food and tea. No sooner you finished one cup than you got another.

MONTY. She's a sweetheart.

HYMIE. God forbid you should ever say you're not hungry. She starts singing that song: As man is only human he must eat before he can think.

MONTY (*picking up the song and singing it*).
    As man is only human
    He must eat before he can think,
    Fine words are only empty air
    But not his meat or his drink.

Others join in chorus.

    Then left right left, then left right left,
    There's a place, comrade, for you.
    March with us in the ranks of the working class
    For you are a worker too.

HARRY *enters. As they finish the song he stands in the doorway and, waving the banner, cries:*

HARRY. We won! Boys, we won the day!

MONTY. Harry! Welcome home the hero! Where are those bloody sandwiches?

HYMIE. Your wife's looking for you.

HARRY. What, she's gone *out* for me? (*Places banner in corner and looks concerned.*)

MONTY. Yes! Just this minute.

HARRY. Did she have a rolling pin in her hand?

HYMIE. No, no. She's gone to my place to collect the children.

HARRY. Blimey, Hymie! What happened to you? You all right?

HYMIE. Now don't you fuss, Harry; drink your tea.

MONTY. That's it, Harry, swill up, mate.

HARRY. Sure, sure. (*Goes to kitchen.*) The children, you say? But I saw Ada in the streets.

PRINCE (*looking to* MONTY). She was helping me, Harry, but don't tell Sarah. She was taking messages from Cable Street to headquarters. I knew she wouldn't stay in on such a day. Marched with us on the victory march, then went to look for Dave.

MONTY. She'll break her little heart when she hears he's going to Spain.

> ADA *comes tearing down the stairs at this point – she is the* KAHNS' *daughter, aged fourteen.*

ADA. Mother! Mother! Hello everyone – Dad, where's Mother?

> *She snatches a slice of bread and butter from table.*

HARRY. Hello, Ada – you haven't seen her yet? You'll cop it. She's gone to look for Ronnie.

ADA (*going off again*). Be back in quarter of an hour – excuse me.

HARRY. Where are you going now?

ADA. Must check up on the last few posts, see that all the other pioneers are safe. (*She calls back through the window.*) Christ, what a day, comrades! (*Exits.*)

HARRY. Comrades! And *we* didn't force her to be in the pioneers. Wasn't necessary. I tell you, show young people what socialism means and they recognize life! A future! But it won't be pure in our lifetime, you know that, don't you, boys? Not even in hers, maybe – but in her children's lifetime – *then* they'll begin to feel it, all the benefits, despite our mistakes – you'll see, despite our mistakes. Now boys, tell me everything that happened.

PRINCE. Don't you know? Sir Philip Game, the police commissioner, got the wind up and banned the march. He told Mosley to fight it out with the Home Secretary. He wasn't going to have any trouble. And what happened to you?

HARRY (*proudly*). I was nearly arrested.

MONTY. You?

HARRY. I was running through the streets waving a red banner Sarah gave me and a policeman told me to drop it.

PRINCE. So?

HARRY. I dropped it! And when I turned into Flower and Dean Street I raised it again. He must have guessed what I was going to do. Christ! I never saw so many policemen appear so quickly. They seemed to pour out of all the windows when they heard that penny-farthing whistle. I only just had time to hop into my mother's place.

MONTY. And you stayed there?

HARRY. I had a cup of tea and at about four o'clock I came out. I got to Gardiner's Corner and police were charging the barricades. I didn't see no Fascists. Any get there?

PRINCE. They stayed in the back streets. The police did all the attacking. So?

HARRY. So I saw the police were picking our boys off like flies and then I saw my policeman – his hat was missing by this time. Oooh! There was a vicious look came into his eye when he saw me. I didn't stop to ask him where he'd lost it. I just ran back to my mother's and read a book.

HYMIE (*ominously*). So you *were* at your mother's (*To the others.*) I think we'd better go before Sarah comes back. Harry, we're going.

HARRY. You're not staying for something to eat?

HYMIE. Lottie's waiting for me, Harry. Come on, you two.

HARRY. Hey, Hymie. You won't tell her I was at my mother's all the time, will you? No?

> *The boys assure him with pats and shakes of the head.*
> HARRY *pours himself out a cup of tea and, taking it into the front room, he settles down to a book by the fire. After some seconds* SARAH *comes down the stairs with* RONNIE, *a boy of about five. He is asleep in her arms. She takes him straight into the bedroom.* HARRY *tries to appear very absorbed.* SARAH *comes out of the room, takes off her coat and hangs it up. She is eyeing* HARRY *most of the time with a gaze to kill while he does his best to avoid it. She clears a few things from the table, then goes out to get herself a cup of tea. As she watches* HARRY *she seats herself at the table and slowly stirs her drink. He shrinks under her gaze as her head begins to nod. It is an 'I-know-you-don't-I' nod.*

SARAH. You think I'm a fool, don't you?

> HARRY *shifts uncomfortably, doesn't answer.* SARAH *watches him.*

Think I can't see, that I don't know what's going on. (*Pause.*) Look at him! The man of the house! Nothing matters to him! (*Pause.*) Well, Harry, why don't you look at me? Why don't you talk to me? I'm your wife, aren't I? A man is supposed to discuss things with his wife.

HARRY (*at last*). What do you want me to say?

SARAH. Must I tell you what to say? Don't you know?

Don't you *just* know! (*Pause.*) Artful! Oh, you're so
artful!

HARRY. Yes, yes, I'm artful.

SARAH. Aren't you artful, then? You think because you
sit there pretending to read that I won't say anything?
That's what you'd like – that I should just come in
and carry on and not say anything. You'd like that,
wouldn't you? That you should carry on your life just
the same as always and no one should say anything.

HARRY. Oh, leave me alone, Sarah.

SARAH. Oh, leave me alone, Sarah! I'll leave you alone
all right. There'll be blue murder, Harry, you hear
me? There'll be blue murder if it carries on like this.
All our life is it going to be like this? I can't leave a
handbag in the room. You remember what happened
last time? You left me! Remember?

> HARRY *tries to turn away out of it all and* SARAH
> *shakes him back again.*

Remember? And you wanted to come back? And you
came back – full of promises. What's happened to
them now?

HARRY. Nothing's happened! Now stop nagging! Good
God, you don't let a man live in peace.

SARAH. You can still pretend? After you took ten
shillings from my bag and you know that I know you
took it and you can still be righteous? Say you don't
know anything about it, go on. Say you don't know
what I'm talking about.

HARRY. No. I *don't* know what you're talking about.

SARAH (*finally unable to control herself, cursing him*). Fire
on your head! May you live so sure if you don't know
what I'm talking about. The money fell out of my
purse, I suppose. I dropped it in the street. (*Screaming at him.*) Fire on your head!

HARRY (*rising and facing her in a rage*). I'll throw this book at you – so help me I'll throw this book at you.

At this point ADA *rushes in.*

ADA. Harry, stop it. (*She cries.*) Oh, stop it!

HARRY (*shouting*).Tell your mother to stop it, she's the cause, it's her row. Don't you know your mother by now? (*He has moved away to the door.*)

SARAH. I'm the cause? Me? You hear him, Ada, you hear him? I'm the cause! (*Throws a saucer at him.*) Swine, you!

HARRY (*in speechless rage, throws his book to the ground*). She's mad, your mother, she's stark raving mad!

> HARRY *rushes out of the room up the stairs.* SARAH *follows him to bottom of stairs and, picking up a basin in her hands, brandishes it.* ADA *goes to look out of the window.*

SARAH. That's it, run away. Go to your mother! She'll give you peace! She'll do everything for you! Weakling, you! *Weakling!*

ADA (*crying*). Everybody's outside, Mummy. Everybody is looking down at us.

SARAH (*turning to comfort her*). There, there, Boobola. There, there, meine kindt. Shuh! Shuh! I'm sorry. (*Bends over her and strokes her.*) Shuh! Shuh! It's finished, I'm sorry, it's over.

HARRY (*from the street*). She's mad, she's gone mad, she has.

SARAH. Shuh! shuh! Ada, don't listen. It'll pass. Shuh – shuh! (*Cooing.*) Loolinka, Ada, Ada, Ada.

> *As she comforts* ADA, RONNIE *comes out and stands watching them – listening and bewildered . . .*
>
> *Curtain.*

ACT TWO

SCENE ONE

Late April 1946 – the war has come and gone.

The scene is now changed. The KAHNS have moved to an LCC block of flats in Hackney – the 1930 kind, with railings. The working class is a little more respectable now, they have not long since voted in a Labour Government. The part of the flat we can see is: the front room, from which lead off three rooms; the passage to the front door – and a door leading from the passage to the kitchen (off); and part of the balcony with its iron railings.

It is late on Friday afternoon. HARRY is lying down on the sofa. SARAH walks along the balcony, puts her hand through the letter box, withdraws the key, and enters the front room – energetic as ever.

SARAH. What! You here already? (*Accepting the fact.*) You haven't been working!

HARRY. The place closed down.

SARAH (*takes off coat and unpacks shopping bag*). The place closed down! But you only started there on Monday.

HARRY. Well! So the place closed down! Is it my fault?

SARAH. It always happens where *he* works. You can't bring luck anywhere, can you! When it's a slump you always manage to be the first one sacked and when the season starts again you're the last one to find work. Ah, Harry, you couldn't even make money during the war. The war! When *everybody* made money.

HARRY (*laying pay packet on table*). Nah!

SARAH (*reading it*). What's this? Seven pounds thirteen? Why only seven pounds thirteen?

HARRY. Four days' work.

SARAH. You haven't worked *all* day today? So what you been doing?

HARRY. I felt tired.

SARAH. Sleep! That's all he can do. You didn't peel potatoes or anything? (*No answer.*) Oh, what am I standing here talking to you for? Don't I know you by now?

HARRY. I got a headache.

SARAH (*going to kitchen and talking from there*). Yes, yes – headache! Ronnie not home yet?

HARRY. He's distributing leaflets.

SARAH. What leaflets?

HARRY. I don't know what leaflets. What leaflets! Leaflets!

SARAH. Come and make some tea. Ada will be here soon.

HARRY. Leave me alone, Sarah.

SARAH (*from the kitchen*). Make some tea when I ask you!

> HARRY *rises, and* ADA *is seen coming along the balcony. She enters through the front door in the same manner as* SARAH. *She is twenty-five years of age, well-spoken, a beautiful Jewess and weary of spirit.*

HARRY (*kissing her*). Hello, Ada.

SARAH. Ada? Ada? You here? Go inside, Daddy'll make some tea. Supper will soon be ready. (*Appears cheerfully from kitchen with all the signs of a cook about her. Kisses* ADA.) Got a nice supper.

ADA. What nice supper?

SARAH. Barley soup. I left it on a small light all day while I was at work. (*Returns to kitchen.*)

ADA. Do you know if Ronnie has gone to my place to see if there is mail from Dave?

SARAH. Suppose so. He usually does when he knows you're coming here straight from work.

> RONNIE *appears on the balcony and lets himself in. Aged fifteen, enthusiastic, lively, well-spoken like his sister.*

(*Hearing the noise at the door.*) Ronnie?

RONNIE. I'm here.

SARAH. He's here.

RONNIE (*to* ADA *as he enters*). Two hundred and fifty leaflets in an hour and a half!

ADA. Very good. What for?

RONNIE. The May Day demo. Are you coming?

ADA. I doubt it.

RONNIE (*mocking her*). I doubt it! Don't you find the march exciting any longer?

ADA. I do *not* find the march exciting any longer.

RONNIE. Can't understand it. You and Dave were such pioneers in the early days. I got all my ideas from you two – and now –

ADA. And now the letters, please.

RONNIE. Letters? Letters? What letters?

ADA. Oh, come on, Ronnie – Dave's letters.

RONNIE (*innocently*). But I've been distributing leaflets!

ADA. You didn't go to my home to find . . . ?

RONNIE. Miles away – other direction.

ADA (*sourly*). Thank you.

> *While* ADA *sits down to read a newspaper* RONNIE *withdraws three letters from his pocket and reads some initials on the back.*

RONNIE. I.L.T. Now what could that mean – I love thee?

ADA. Give me those letters, please.

RONNIE (*teasing*). Oh, I love thee, sister.

ADA. You've been reading them.

RONNIE (*reading front of envelope*). Letter number 218 – Christ! he's prolific. And here's number 215 – lousy service, isn't it? And number 219. This one says I.L.T.T., I love thee terribly, I suppose. And if I loved you I'd also love you terribly. (*Bends over and kisses her.*)

ADA. Idiot! (*Reads.*)

RONNIE. Isn't it time that husband of yours was demobbed? The war's been over a year already. Imagine! I was only nine when he left. I've still kept all his letters, Ada, all of them. (*Ambles round the room to wall and tears off a little piece of wallpaper which he hurriedly crumples and stuffs into his pocket, making sure no one has seen him.*) We've been living here for five years – he hasn't even seen this place, God help him! (*Shouting to kitchen.*) Harry! Harry! Where's Harry?

> HARRY *comes in with some tea and* RONNIE *goes to take a cup.*

Good old Pops. Dad, I saw Monty Blatt. He says you must attend the meeting tonight.

HARRY. Ach! Do me a favour!

RONNIE. Listen to him! Party member! Won't attend branch meetings! How can you know what's going *on* in the world? That's where Ada gets her apathy from. She's you! And you're a lazy old sod – whoopee!

> RONNIE *hoists* HARRY *over his shoulder, fireman fashion, and dances round the room.*

Are you going to the meeting?

HARRY. Let me down, you fool! Let me down!

RONNIE. The meeting?

HARRY. Stop it, you idiot – I've got a headache.

ADA. Do be quiet, you two.

RONNIE (*lowering his father*). I'll fight you. Come on, fists up, show your mettle; I just feel in the mood. (*Assumes quixotic boxing stance.*)

HARRY (*grinning*). Bloody fool! Leave off!

RONNIE. Windy! (*Playfully jabs* HARRY.)

HARRY (*raising his fists*). I'll knock your block off.

> *They follow each other round – fists raised. First* RONNIE *moves forward, then he backs away and* HARRY *moves forward. Thus they move – to and fro, without touching each other, until* SARAH *comes in with some soup in plates.*

SARAH. The table! the table! Lay the table someone.

RONNIE. The table, the table – oh, oh, the table!

> *Everyone moves to lay the table;* RONNIE *in haste,* ADA *while reading, and* HARRY *clumsily. Then they all sit down.*

ADA. Lovely soup, Mummy.

RONNIE. Magnificent!

SARAH. You like it?

HARRY. They just said they did.

SARAH. I wasn't talking to you.

RONNIE. She wasn't talking to you.

HARRY. Your mother never talks *to* me.

RONNIE. You're so ugly, that's why. I wouldn't talk to you either only you wouldn't give me any spending money.

SARAH. He won't give you any spending money this week anyway.

RONNIE. Don't tell me. He's out of work.

HARRY (*pathetically*). The shop closed down.

ADA. Oh, Daddy, why does it always happen to you?

HARRY. It doesn't always happen to me.

ADA. Always! All my life that's all I can remember, just one succession of jobs which have fallen through.

HARRY. Is it my fault if the garment industry is so unstable?

ADA. It's not the industry – it's you.

HARRY. Yes, me.

ADA. Well, isn't it you?

HARRY. Oh, Ada, leave off. I have enough with your mother. I've got a headache.

ADA. I don't wonder you have a headache, you spend most of your time sleeping.

HARRY. Yes, sleeping.

ADA. What are you going to do now?

HARRY. I'll look for another job on Monday.

ADA. What's wrong with Sunday – on the Whitechapel Road? There's always governors looking for machinists.

HARRY. Those people aren't there for work. They go to gossip. Gossip, that's all! Monday I'll find a job and start straight away. It's busy now, you know.

SARAH (*collecting the soup dishes and taking them out*). Morgen morgen nor nischt heite, sagen alle faule leite.

ADA. Daddy – you are the world's biggest procrastinator.

RONNIE. Give the boy a break, Addy, that's a big word.

ADA. He ought to be ashamed of himself. The industry's booming with work, and he's out of a job. You probably got the sack, didn't you?

HARRY (*offended*). I did not get the sack.

ADA. All her life Mummy's had to put up with this. I shall be glad to get away.

> SARAH, *entering with the next course, hears this remark and glares bitterly at* HARRY.

RONNIE. Get away where?

ADA. Anywhere. When Dave comes back we shall leave London and live in the country. That'll be our socialism. Remember this, Ronnie: the family should be a unit, and your work and your life should be part of one existence, not something hacked about by a bus queue and office hours. A man should see, know, and love his job. Don't you want to feel your life? Savour it gently? In the country we shall be somewhere where the air doesn't smell of bricks and the kids can grow up without seeing grandparents who are continually shouting at each other.

SARAH. Ada, Ada.

RONNIE. And no more political activity?

ADA. No more political activity.

RONNIE. I bet Dave won't agree to that. Dave fought in Spain. He won't desert humanity like that.

ADA. Humanity! Ach!

RONNIE. Listen to her! With a Labour majority in the House? And two of our own Party members? It's only just beginning.

ADA. It's always only just beginning for the Party. Every defeat is victory and every victory is the beginning.

RONNIE. But it is, it is the beginning. Plans for town and country planning. New cities and schools and hospitals. (*Jumping up on chair to* HARRY's *facetious applause.*) Nationalization! National health! Think of it, the whole country is going to be organized to cooperate instead of tear at each other's throat. That's what I said to them in a public speech at school and all the boys cheered and whistled and stamped their feet – and blew raspberries.

ADA. I do not believe in the right to organize people. And anyway I'm not so sure that I love them enough to *want* to organize them.

SARAH (*sadly*). This – from *you*, Ada? You used to be such an organizer.

ADA. I'm tired, Mother. I spent eighteen months waiting for Dave to return from Spain and now I've waited six years for him to come home from a war against Fascism and I'm tired. Six years in and out of offices, auditing books and working with young girls who are morons – lipsticked, giggling morons. And Dave's experience is the same – fighting with men who he says did not know what the war was about. Away from their wives they behaved like animals. In fact they wanted to get away from their wives in order to behave like animals. Give them another war and they'd run back again. Oh yes! the service killed any illusions Dave may have once had about the splendid and heroic working class.

HARRY (*pedantically*). This is the talk of an intellectual, Ada.

ADA. God in heaven save me from the claptrap of a threepenny pamphlet. How many friends has the Party lost because of lousy, meaningless titles they gave to people. *He* was a bourgeois intellectual, *he* was a Trotskyist, *he* was a reactionary Social Democrat. Whisht! Gone!

HARRY. But wasn't it true? Didn't these people help to bolster a rotten society?

ADA. The only rotten society is an industrial society. It makes a man stand on his head and then convinces him he is good-looking. I'll tell you something. It wasn't the Trotskyist or the Social Democrat who did the damage. It was progress! There! Progress! And nobody dared fight progress.

SARAH. But that's no reason to run away. Life still carries on. A man gets married, doesn't he? He still has children, he laughs, he finds things to make him laugh. A man can always laugh, can't he?

ADA. As if that meant he lived? Even a flower can grow in the jungle, can't it? Because there is always some earth and water and sun. But there's still the jungle,

struggling for its own existence, and the sick screech-
ing of animals terrified of each other. As if laughter
were proof!

HARRY. And we and the Party don't want to do away
with the jungle, I suppose?

ADA. No, you do not want to do away with the jungle, I
suppose. You have *never* cried against the jungle of
an industrial society. You've never wanted to destroy
its *values* – simply to own them yourselves. It only
seemed a crime to you that a man spent all his
working hours in front of a machine because he did
not own that machine. Heavens! the glory of owning
a machine!

SARAH. So what, we shouldn't care any more? We must
all run away?

ADA. Care! Care! What right have we to care? How can
we care for a world outside ourselves when the world
inside is in disorder? Care! Haven't you ever stopped,
Mother – I mean stopped – and seen yourself
standing with your arms open, and suddenly paused?
Come to my bosom. Everyone come to my bosom.
How can you possibly imagine that your arms are
long enough, for God's sake? What audacity tells you
you can harbour a billion people in a theory? What
great, big, stupendous, egotistical audacity, tell me?

RONNIE. Whoa, whoa!

HARRY. But it *is* an industrial age, you silly girl. Let's
face facts –

ADA (*mocking*). Don't let us kid ourselves.

HARRY (*with her*). Don't let us kid ourselves – it's a
challenge of our time.

ADA. Balls!

HARRY. You can't run away from it.

ADA. Stop me!

HARRY. Then you're a coward – that's all I can say –
you're a coward.

SARAH (*sadly*). She had a fine example from her father, didn't she?

HARRY (*to this stab in the back*). What do you mean – a fine example from her father?

SARAH. You don't understand what I'm saying, I suppose?

HARRY (*he is hurt and throws a hand at her in disgust*). Ach! you make me sick.

SARAH (*mocking*). Ach, you make me sick. *I* make *him* sick. Him, my fine man! You're the reason why she thinks like this, you know that?

HARRY. Yes, me.

SARAH. Well, of course you. Who else?

RONNIE (*collecting dishes and escaping to the kitchen*). I'll wash up.

HARRY. I didn't bring her up – she's all your work.

SARAH. That's just it! You didn't bring her up. You weren't concerned, were you? You left it all to me while you went to your mother's or to the pictures or out with your friends.

HARRY. Yes. I went out with my friends. Sure!

SARAH. Well, didn't you? May I have so many pennies for the times you went up West to pictures.

HARRY. Oh, leave off, Sarah.

SARAH. Leave off! That's all you can say – leave off, leave me alone. That was it. I did leave you alone. That's why I had all the trouble.

ADA. I'm going home, Mummy.

SARAH (*caressingly and apologetically*). Oh no, Ada, stay, it's early yet. Stay. We'll play solo.

ADA. I'm feeling tired and I must write to Dave.

SARAH. Well, stay here and write to Dave. We'll all be quiet. Ronnie's going out. Daddy'll go to bed and I've got some washing to do. Stay, Ada, stay. What do you want to rush home for? A cold, miserable, two-roomed flat, all on your own. Stay. We're a family, aren't we?

ADA (*putting on her coat*). I've also got washing to do, I must go –

SARAH. I'll do it for you. What's a mother for? Straight from work I'll go to your place and bring it back with me. Stay. You've got company here – perhaps Uncle Hymie and Auntie Lottie'll come up. What do you want to be on your own for, tell me?

ADA. I'm not *afraid* of being on my own – I must go.

SARAH (*wearily*). Go then! Will we see you tomorrow?

ADA. Yes, I'll come for supper tomorrow night. Good night. (*Calling.*) Good night, Ronnie.

RONNIE (*appearing from kitchen*). 'Night, Addy.

SARAH. You washing up, Ronnie?

RONNIE. I'm washing up.

SARAH. You I don't have to worry about – but your sister runs away. At the first sight of a little bother she runs away. Why does she run away, Ronnie? Before she used to sit and discuss things, now she runs to her home – such a home to run to – two rooms and a shadow!

RONNIE. But, Ma, she's a married woman herself. You think she hasn't her own worries wondering what it'll be like to see Dave after all these years?

SARAH. But you never run away from a discussion. At least I've got you around to help me solve problems.

RONNIE. Mother, my one virtue – if I got any at all – is that I always imagine you can solve things by talking about them – ask my form master! (*Returns to kitchen.*)

SARAH (*wearily to* HARRY). You see what you do? That's your daughter. Not a word from her father to ask her to stay. The family doesn't matter to you. All your life you've let the family fall around you, but it doesn't matter to you.

HARRY. I didn't drive her away.

SARAH (*bitterly*). No – you didn't drive her away. How could you? You were the good, considerate father.

HARRY *turns away and hunches himself up miserably.*

Look at you! Did you shave this morning? Look at the cigarette ash on the floor. Your shirt! When did you last change your shirt? He sits. Nothing moves him, nothing worries him. He sits! A father! A husband!

HARRY (*taking out a cigarette to light*). Leave me alone, please leave me alone, Sarah. You started the row, not me, you!

SARAH (*taking cigarette from his hand*). Why must you always smoke? – talk with me. Talk, talk, Harry.

HARRY. Sarah! (*He stops, chokes, and then stares wildly around him.*) Mamma. Mamma. (*He is having his first stroke.*)

SARAH (*frightened but not hysterical*). Harry! Harry! What is it?

HARRY (*in Yiddish, gently*). Vie iss sie – der mamma?

SARAH. Stop it, Harry.

HARRY. Sie iss dorten – der mamma?

SARAH. Ronnie! Ronnie!

RONNIE *comes in from the kitchen.*

Doctor Woolfson – quick, quick, get him.

RONNIE. What's happening?

SARAH. I don't know.

RONNIE *runs out.*

Harry, it was only a quarrel, you silly man. None of your tricks now, Harry – Harry, you hear me?

HARRY. Vie iss sie? Mamma, mamma.

Curtain.

SCENE TWO

October 1947.

We are in the same room. RONNIE *is making a fire in the grate. When this is done he puts on the radio and goes into the kitchen. The 'Egmont' overture comes over the radio.* RONNIE *comes out of the kitchen with a cup of tea. On hearing the music he lays down the cup and picks up a pencil and proceeds to conduct an imaginary orchestra, until* CISSIE *is seen moving along the balcony. She lets herself in and surprises* RONNIE. *She is carrying a brief-case.*

RONNIE. Aunt!

CISSIE. Hello, Junior. I've come to see your father.

RONNIE. Not back from work yet. Just in time for a cuppa.

Goes off to make one.

CISSIE. He still has that job, then?

RONNIE (*from kitchen*). Can't hear you.

CISSIE. Turn this bloody wireless down. (*Does so.*)

RONNIE. Aunty! Please! Beethoven!

CISSIE. I know, I know. Some other time. I'm not feeling so good. (*Takes cigarette from handbag.*)

RONNIE (*entering with tea*). What price partition in Palestine, Aunt?

CISSIE. Russia's backing the plan.

RONNIE. Yes – and haven't the Arabs got upset over that. They're taking it to the high courts. They expected Russia to attack the United Nations plan if only to upset the West. Power politics!

CISSIE. Has your father still got that job?

RONNIE. No, he's a store-keeper in a sweet factory now. Look. (*Shows her a biscuit tin full of sweets.*) Jelly babies. Can't help himself. Doesn't do it on a large scale, mind, just a handful each night. Everyone does it.

CISSIE. How long has he been there?

RONNIE. Three weeks. You know he can't stay long at a job – and now he has got what he has always wanted – a legitimate excuse.

CISSIE. He can *walk*, can't he?

RONNIE. He walks – slowly and stooped – with his head sunk into his shoulders, hands in his pockets. (*Imitates his father.*) His step isn't sure – frightened to exert himself in case he should suddenly drop dead. You ought to see him in a strong wind – (*Moves drunkenly round the room.*) like an autumn leaf. He seems to have given up the fight, as though *thank God* he was no longer responsible for himself. You know, Aunt, I don't suppose there is anything more terrifying to a man than his own sense of failure, and your brother Harry is really a very sensitive man. No one knows more than he does how he's failed. Now that's tragedy for you: having the ability to see what is happening to yourself and yet not being able to do anything about it. Like a long nightmare. God! fancy being born just to live a long nightmare. He gets around. But who knows how sick he is? Now we can't tell his lethargy from his illness.

CISSIE. It sounds just like Mother. Mother was bed-ridden for years. He seems to be moving that way –

RONNIE. Almost deliberately. Here! (*Goes to a drawer and takes out a notebook.*) Did you know he once started to write his autobiography? Listen. (*Reads.*) 'Of me, the dummy and my family.' How's that for a poetic title! 'Sitting at my work in the shop one day my attention was drawn to the dummy that we all try the work on. The rhythm of the machines and my constant looking at the dummy rocked me off in a kind of sleepy daze. And to my surprise the dummy began to take the shape of a human, it began to speak. Softly at first, so softly I could hardly hear it. And then louder and still louder, and it seemed to raise its eyebrows and with a challenge asked: Your life, what of your life? My life? I had never thought, and I began to take my mind back, way back to the time when I was a little boy.' There, a whole notebook full, and then one day he stopped! Just like that! God knows why a man stops doing the one thing that can keep him together.

CISSIE. How's Ada and Dave?

RONNIE. Struggling in a tied cottage in the country. Ada suckles a beautiful baby, Dave lays concrete floors in the daytime and makes furniture by hand in the evening.

CISSIE. Lunatics!

RONNIE. They're happy. Two Jews in the Fens. They had to get a Rabbi from King's Lynn to circumcise the baby. A Rabbi from King's Lynn! Who'd ever think there were Rabbis in King's Lynn?

CISSIE. And you?

RONNIE. A bookshop.

CISSIE. Same one?

RONNIE. Same one.

CISSIE. You're also crazy and mixed up, I suppose?

RONNIE (*highly indignant*). Don't call me that! God in heaven, don't call me that! I'm a poet.

CISSIE. Another one!

RONNIE. A socialist poet.

CISSIE. A socialist poet!

RONNIE. I have all the world at my fingertips. Nothing is mixed up. I have so much life that I don't know who to give it to first. I see beyond the coloured curtains of *my* eyes to a world – say, how do you like that line? Beyond the coloured curtains of *my* eyes, waiting for time and timing nothing but the slow hours, lay the thoughts in the mind. Past the pool of *my* smile . . .

CISSIE. What does that mean?

RONNIE. What, the pool of my smile? It's a metaphor – the pool of my smile – a very lovely metaphor. How's trade-union activity?

CISSIE. We've got a strike on. Dillingers are probably going to lock out its workers.

RONNIE. Ah, Dillingers! 'Dillinger styles get all the men's smiles, this is the wear for everywhere!' No wonder the workers don't like poetry.

CISSIE. The old boy wants to reduce their wages because they're doing sale work.

RONNIE. What's that?

CISSIE. You know – sale work – specially made-up clothes for the big West End sales.

RONNIE. You mean a sale is not what is left over from the season before?

CISSIE. Oh, grow up, Ronnie. You should know that by now. It's cheaper stuff, inferior quality.

RONNIE. And the union doesn't protest? (*Jumping on a chair and waving his arms in the air.*) Capitalist exploiters! The bastards – if you'll excuse the expression. I'll write a book about them! I'll expose them in their true light. What a novel, Aunt – set in a clothing factory, the sweat shops, the –

CISSIE. Look, you want to hear about this strike or you don't want to hear about this strike?

RONNIE *sits down.*

So because it's sale work Dillinger wants to cut the women's wages by ten per cent and the men's by twelve and a half per cent. So what does he plan to do? I'll tell you what he plans to do – he plans to pay all thirty of them for one full week, sack them, and then re-employ them, which would mean they were new employees and only entitled to Board of Trade rate, which is considerably less.

RONNIE. But can he do that?

CISSIE. He did it! He did it! The girls told me. But this year the shop stewards got together and asked me to go down and negotiate. They didn't all want it, mind you. One wagged his finger at me and cried: 'We're not taking your advice, we're not taking your advice!' I gave them – you know me. First I read the Riot Act to them and then I lashed out. You ought to be ashamed of yourselves, I told them, after the union struggled hard, tooth and nail, for every penny you get and at the first sign of intimidation you want to give in. For shame! I yelled at them – for shame! I tell you, Ronnie – a boss you can always handle because he always wants to bribe you, and that gives you the upper hand – but the worker . . .

> HARRY *has by this time entered through the front door, and he shuffles down the passage into the front room. He is slightly paralysed down one side but is still very able to move around. The first stroke has just made him age prematurely.*

HARRY. Hello, Cissie, what are you doing here?

CISSIE. I've come to see you. Well, how are you?

HARRY. I'm all right, Cissie, I'm fine.

CISSIE. Can you work all right?

HARRY. I can't move my left hand very well. Lost its grip or something. (*Clutches and unclutches fist to prove the point.*)

RONNIE (*gripping* HARRY'*s hand in a shake*). Strong as an ox. You're a sham, Harry boy. Want some tea?

HARRY. Yes please, son.

CISSIE. What do the doctors say is wrong with you?

HARRY. I had a stroke – that's all they know. They don't tell you anything in the hospitals these days. Sarah's gone to the doctor's now to find out if I can go back again for observation.

CISSIE. More observation?

HARRY. Ach! Don't talk to me about them, they make me sick.

CISSIE. All those blood tests they took and they still don't know – after a year. I'm surprised you had that much blood. Well, I'm going. Here, smoke yourself to death. (*Hands him forty cigarettes.*)

RONNIE (*bringing in the tea*). Going?

CISSIE. I've got a strike meeting.

RONNIE. In the evening?

CISSIE. Any time. So long, Junior.

> *She kisses* HARRY *and* RONNIE *and goes out. On the landing she meets* SARAH.

Hello, Sarah. I just come to see Harry. Sorry I must go. How are you?

SARAH. I'm all right. Why don't you stay for supper?

CISSIE (*out of sight by now*). I've got a strike meeting. I'll be seeing you.

HARRY (*to* SARAH *as she comes in*). Did you go to the doctor's?

SARAH (*wearily*). I've been, I've been. Oh, those stairs will kill me.

HARRY. What does he say?

SARAH (*taking out a letter from her bag and placing it on the mantelpiece*). He gave me a letter: you should take it to the hospital.

HARRY. What does it say; show me.

SARAH. It's sealed; you mustn't open it.

HARRY. Show me it.

SARAH. What can you see? It's sealed.

HARRY (*irritably*). Oh, I want to see who it's addressed to.

Too tired to cope with him she hands him the letter and then goes to the kitchen.

SARAH (*from the kitchen*). Did anybody make supper?

RONNIE. We've not long come in. (*To* HARRY, *taking away the envelope he is trying to open.*) Uh-uh. Mustn't open. It's for the hospital.

SARAH (*entering with a cup of tea and sitting down*). I've got a branch meeting tonight. Ronnie, you can take your own supper. It's fried fish from yesterday. You want to come with me, Harry?

HARRY. I don't feel like going to any branch meeting.

SARAH. You want to get well, don't you? You don't want to become an invalid, do you? So come to a meeting tonight. Mix with people. They're your comrades, aren't they?

HARRY. Yes, my comrades.

SARAH. Nothing is sacred for him. Ach! Why should I worry whether you come or not. What are you doing, Ronnie?

RONNIE. An evening in. I want to write a novel tonight.

SARAH. What, all in one night? Ronnie, do you think you'll ever publish anything? I mean, don't you have to be famous or be able to write or something? There must be such a lot of people writing novels.

RONNIE. Not socialist novels. Faith, Mother, faith! I am one of the sons of the working class, one of its own artists.

HARRY. You mean a political writer like Winston Churchill?

SARAH. What, does he write novels as well? I thought he was only a politician.

RONNIE. Well, he's both – *and* he paints pictures.

SARAH. A painter? He paints pictures? Landscapes and things?

RONNIE. Of course! And in his spare time he –

SARAH. What, he has spare time also?

RONNIE. In his spare time he builds walls at the bottom of his garden.

SARAH (*in admiration*). A bricklayer! Ronnie, I told you you should take up a trade! Why don't you? Go to evening classes. Why should you waste your time in a bookshop? If I were young, oh, what wouldn't I study! All the world I would study. How properly to talk and to write and make sentences. You'll be sorry – don't be like your father, don't be unsettled. Learn a good trade and then you have something to fall back on. You can always write – and when you work then you'll have something to write about.

RONNIE. Give me a chance, Ma. I only left school a year ago.

SARAH. That's what he kept on saying. Give me a chance! Everybody had to give him a chance: now look at him. Harry – you're not working in the sweet factory any more, are you?

HARRY. Who said I'm not?

RONNIE. Well, isn't he?

SARAH. Well, ask him, he knows.

RONNIE *inclines his head enquiringly.*

HARRY. Of course I'm still working there.

SARAH (*wearily, the time has gone for violent rows*). Harry, answer me. What do you gain by telling me this lie? Tell me, I want to know. All my life I've wanted to know what you've gained by a lie. *I* know you're not working because I saw the foreman. You're not even a good liar. I've always known when you've lied. For twenty-five years it's been the same and all the time I've not known what it's about. But *you* know – no one else knows, but you do. I'm asking you, Harry – let me be your doctor, let me try and help you. What is it that makes you what you are? Tell me – only tell me. Don't sit there and say nothing. I'm entitled to

know – after all this time, I'm entitled to know. Well,
aren't I, Ronnie?

> *Nobody answers her.* HARRY *avoids her gaze,*
> RONNIE *waits till it's all over.*

So look at him. He sits and he sits and he sits and all
his life goes away from him. (*To* RONNIE.) You won't
be like that, will you?

RONNIE. I shall never take up a trade I hate as he did –
if that's what you mean; and I shall never marry – at
least not until I'm real and healthy. (*Cheerfully.*) But
what's there to grumble about, little Sarah? You have
two splendid children, a fine son-in-law and a
grandson.

SARAH. I haven't seen my grandson yet. My daughter
lives two hundred miles away from me and my
husband is a sick man. That's my family. Well, it's a
family, I suppose. (*She rises to go.*)

RONNIE. What about me? (*He regards himself in a
mirror.*) Young, good-looking, hopeful, talented . . .
hopeful, anyway.

SARAH (*sadly*). You? I'll wait and see what happens to
you. Please God you don't make a mess of your life,
please God. Did you ask for that rise?

RONNIE. I did ask for that rise. 'Mr Randolph,' I said –
he's the manager of that branch – 'Mr Randolph, I
know that the less wages you pay us bookshop
assistants the more you get in your salary. But don't
you think I've sold enough books for long enough
time to warrant you foregoing some of your commission?'

SARAH. So what did he say, you liar?

RONNIE. 'You're our best salesman,' he said, 'but I've
got to keep head office happy.'

SARAH. So what did you say, you liar?

RONNIE. So I said, 'It's not head office, it's your wife.'

SARAH. So what did he say, you liar?

RONNIE. He said, 'Kahn,' he said, 'as you're so frank and you know too much I'll give you a two-pound rise.'

SARAH. Ronnie, did you get a rise, I asked you?

RONNIE (*kissing her*). No, I did not get a rise.

SARAH. Mad boy, you! I'm going to the meeting.

RONNIE. That's it, Mother. You go to the meeting. At least if you keep on fighting them there's hope for me. (*He helps her on with a coat as he speaks, then she goes. Returning to room.*) You want supper, Dad? It's the old dead fish again. I'll lay it for you. (*Moves to kitchen.*)

HARRY. Aren't you going to eat?

RONNIE (*from kitchen*). I'm not hungry. I'll eat later. I must work now. You want me to read the first chapter to you, Dad?

HARRY. Oh, leave me alone, Ronnie – I'm tired.

RONNIE. Tired! You're not tired, Harry – you're just drowning with heritage, mate! (*Re-enters with an assortment of plates, which he lays on the table.*) There, you can wash up after you. I'm going to my room now.

> RONNIE *goes to his room.* HARRY *moves to the table and begins to eat. He eats in silence for a few seconds, then stretches out for a newspaper. After glancing through this he turns to the mantelpiece and sees the letter. He looks to* RONNIE*'s room to make sure he is not coming and then moves slowly across to get the letter. First of all he tries to prise it open without tearing anything. Then not succeeding in this he moves to the table to get a knife. As he picks up the knife* RONNIE *enters again.*

RONNIE. Christ! It's bloody cold in that room: I – now, then, Harry – (*As though playfully scolding a child.*)

you know you must not read the letter, remember what Mummykins said.

He moves to take it.

HARRY (*retaining it*). Let me read the letter, I want to know what's in it.

RONNIE (*making another bid for it*). Use some will-power, Dad; you know the letter is not for you. Now leave it be, there's a good boy.

HARRY (*still retaining it*). I want to see it; it's about me, isn't it? Now leave off, Ronnie.

RONNIE (*snatching it from his father's hand*). No!

HARRY (*banging his hand on the table in rapid succession with the words, like a child in anger, hating to be like a child, and shrieking*). GIVE ME THAT LETTER. GIMME. S'mine. S'mine. I WAN' THAT ENVELOPE. Now. This instant. I – wan' – that – envelope!

> RONNIE *stands there trembling. He had not meant to provoke such anger, and now, having done so, is upset. He is not quite sure what to do. Almost involuntarily he hands over the envelope, and when he has done so he goes to a wall and cries. He is still a boy – he has been frightened.* HARRY *picks up envelope, himself distraught. He does not bother to open it now. Seeing that* RONNIE *is crying he goes over to him and clasps him.*

HARRY. You shouldn't do these things. I'm a sick man. If I want to open the envelope you shouldn't stop me. You've got no right to stop me. Now you've upset me and yourself – you silly boy.

RONNIE. Can't you see that I can't bear what you are. I don't want to hear your lies all my life. Your weakness frightens me, Harry – did you ever think about that? I watch you and I see myself and I'm terrified.

HARRY (*wandering away from him; he does not know what to say*). What I am – I am. I will never alter. Neither you nor your mother will change me. It's too late now; I'm an old man and if I've been the same all my life so I will always be. You can't alter people, Ronnie. You can only give them some love and hope they'll take it. I'm sorry. It's too late now. I can't help you. (*He shuffles miserably to his room, perceptibly older.*) Don't forget to have supper. Good night.

Curtain.

ACT THREE

SCENE ONE

November 1955.

HARRY *has had his second stroke, and now paralysis has made him completely unfit for work. He can only just move around, has difficulty in talking, and is sometimes senile.* SARAH *retains much of her energy but shows signs of age and her troubles – her tone of speaking is compassionate now.*

Evening, in the same LCC flat. HARRY *sits in a chair – huddled by the fireplace, listening to Ravel's* La Valse *on the radio. He smokes more than ever, it is his one comfort.* SARAH *is sitting by the table struggling to fill out an official Government form – she talks a lot to herself.*

SARAH (*reading form*). Have you an insurance policy for life or death? Name of company. Amount insured for. Annual payments. How should I know the annual payments? I pay one and a penny a week – that's fifty-two shillings and fifty-two pennies. (*Makes mental reckoning.*)

> *The music on the radio has by this time reached a climax and is too loud.* SARAH *goes to turn it off.*

Oh, shut that off! Classical music! All of a sudden it starts shouting at you.

HARRY. No, no, no, no, I was – I was listening.

SARAH. You *liked* it?

HARRY. I liked it. It reminds me of – of – of – of – it reminds me of Blackfriars Bridge in a fog.

SARAH. Blackfriars Bridge in a fog it reminds you of?

Why a fog?

HARRY. Oh, I don't know why a fog. Why a fog?

SARAH. And why Blackfriars Bridge?

HARRY. Because I said so! Och, you're such a silly woman sometimes, Sarah.

SARAH (*playing with him*). But if it's in a fog so what difference whether it's Blackfriars Bridge or London Bridge? Ach, I must get these forms done before Bessie and Monty arrive. You remember Bessie and Monty are coming tonight? (SARAH *continues to complete forms.*) If Ronnie were here I'd get him to fill it in for me . . . as if they don't know how many times I was at work this year. Forms! You tell the National Insurance office that you started work on such and such a day so they tell the National Assistance and the National Assistance tells the Income Tax and then there's forms, forms, forms, forms. Oi – such forms. They can't get enough of them into one envelope. (*Writing.*) No, I haven't got any property, I haven't got any lodgers, I haven't got a housekeeper. A housekeeper! A housekeeper wouldn't do what I do for you, Harry – washing all those sheets.

> MONTY BLATT *and his wife* BESSIE *appear on the balcony. They knock.* SARAH *jumps up.*

They're here already. Now Harry, sit up. Do your flies up and brush that cigarette ash off you. And remember – don't let me down – you promised. You want to go now?

> *She takes* HARRY's *arm but he pushes her away; he doesn't want to go.* SARAH *opens the door to her visitors. Both are richly dressed – over-dressed – and full of bounce and property.*

MONTY. Sarah – little Sarah. How are you, sweetheart? You remember Bessie?

They all shake hands and enter the front room.

Harry boy! How's Harry? You're looking well. You feeling well? They haven't changed a bit. Neither of them.

SARAH. Sit down, both of you; I'll get the kettle on. (*Goes off to kitchen.*)

MONTY (*to* BESSIE). Always put the kettle on – that was the first thing Sarah always did. Am I right, Harry? I'm right, aren't I? (*Shouting to* SARAH.) Remember, Sarah? It was always a cup of tea first.

SARAH (*coming in*). I remember, I remember.

MONTY (*to* BESSIE). We used to *live* in their old place in the East End, all the boys. Remember Prince and your brother Hymie? How is Hymie? Since we moved to Manchester I've lost contact with everybody, everyeeebody!

SARAH. Hymie's all right. He's got a business. His children are married and he stays at home all the time. Prince works in a second-hand shop.

MONTY. A second-hand shop? But I thought – and Cissie?

SARAH. The union members retired her. She lives on a pension, visits the relatives – you know . . .

MONTY. It's all broken up, then?

SARAH. What's broken up about it? They couldn't keep up with the Party – so? The *fight* still goes on.

MONTY (*hastily changing the subject*). And Ada and Dave and Ronnie? Where are they all? Tell me everything. Tell me all the news. I haven't seen you for so long, Sarah – it's so good to see you – isn't it good to see them, Bessie?

SARAH. Ada and Dave are still in the country. They've got two children. Dave is still making furniture by hand –

MONTY. He makes a living?

SARAH. They live! They're not prosperous, but they live.

MONTY. And Ronnie? Ronnie has such ambitions; what's he doing?

SARAH. My Ronnie? He's in Paris.

MONTY. There, I told you he'd go far.

SARAH. As a cook.

MONTY (*not so enthusiastically*). A cook? Ronnie?

BESSIE (*helping them out*). A cook makes good money.

MONTY (*reviving*). Sure a cook makes good money. Ronnie is a smart boy, isn't he, Sarah? Didn't I always say Ronnie was a smart boy? Nobody could understand how an East End boy could speak with such a posh accent. But cooking! He likes it? I mean he's happy?

SARAH. I tell you something, Monty. People ask me what is Ronnie doing and, believe me, I don't know what to answer. He used to throw his arms up in the air and say 'I want to do something worthwhile, I want to create.' Create! So, he's a cook in Paris.

MONTY. Please God he'll be a hotel manager one day.

SARAH. Please God.

MONTY. And Harry? (*He indicates with his head that* HARRY *has dozed off.*)

SARAH. Poor Harry. He's had two strokes. He won't get any better. Paralysed down one side. He can't control his bowels, you know.

BESSIE. Poor man.

SARAH. You think *he* likes it? It's ach-a-nebish Harry now. It's not easy for him. But he won't do anything to help himself. I don't know, other men get ill but they fight. Harry's never fought. Funny thing. There were three men like this in the flats, all had strokes. And all three of them seemed to look the same. They walked the same, stooped the same, and all needing a shave. They used to sit outside together and talk for hours on end and smoke. Sit and talk and smoke. That was their life. Then one day one of them decided he wanted to live so he gets up and finds himself a job – running a small shoe-mender's – and he's earning money now. A miracle! Just like that. But the other one – he wanted to die. I used to see him standing outside in the rain, the pouring rain, getting all wet so that he could catch a cold and die. Well, it happened: last week he died. Influenza! He just didn't want to live. But Harry was not like either of them. He didn't want to die but he doesn't seem to care about living. So! What can you do to help a man like that? I make his food and I buy him cigarettes and he's happy. My only dread is that he will mess himself. When that happens I go mad – I just don't know what I'm doing.

MONTY. It's like that, is it?

SARAH. It's like that. That's life. But how about you, Monty? You still in the Party?

MONTY. No, Sarah – I'm not still in the Party, and I'll tell you why if you want to know –

BESSIE. Now, Monty, don't get on to politics. Sarah, do me a favour and don't get him on to politics.

MONTY. Don't worry, I won't say much –

SARAH. Politics is living, Bessie. I mean everything that happens in the world has got to do with politics.

BESSIE. Listen, Sarah. Monty's got a nice little green-grocer's business in Manchester, no one knows he was ever a member of the Party and we're all happy. It's better he forgets it.

MONTY. No, no – I'll tell her, let me tell her.

BESSIE. I'm warning you, Monty, if you get involved in a political argument I shan't stay. No political argument, you hear me?

MONTY. Listen, Sarah. Remember Spain? Remember how we were proud of Dave and the other boys who answered the call? But did Dave ever tell you the way some of the Party members refused to fight alongside the Trotskyists? And one or two of the Trotskyists didn't come back and they weren't killed in the fighting either? And remember Itzack Pheffer – the Soviet Yiddish writer? We used to laugh because Itzack Pheffer was a funny name – ha, ha. Where's Itzack Pheffer? everyone used to say. Well, we know now, don't we. The great 'leader' is dead now, and we know. The whole committee of the Jewish Anti-Fascist League were shot! Shot, Sarah! In our land of socialism. That was *our* land – what a land that was for us! We didn't believe the stories then; it wasn't possible that it could happen in our one-sixth of the world.

SARAH. And you believe the stories now, Monty?

MONTY (*incredulously*). You don't –

BESSIE. Now, Monty –

MONTY. You don't believe it, Sarah? You won't believe it!

SARAH. And supposing it's true, Monty? So? What should we do, bring back the old days? Is that what you want?

MONTY. I don't know, sweetheart. I haven't got any solutions any more. I've got a little shop up north – I'm not a capitalist by any means – I just make a comfortable living and I'm happy. Bessie – bless her – is having a baby. (*Taps* BESSIE*'s belly.*) I'm going to give him all that I can, pay for his education, university if he likes, and then I shall be satisfied. A man can't do any more, Sarah, believe me. There's nothing more to life than a house, some friends, and a family – take my word.

SARAH. And when someone drops an atom bomb on your family?

MONTY (*pleading*). So what can I do – tell me? There's

nothing I can do any more. I'm too small; who can I trust? It's a big, lousy world of mad politicians – I can't trust them, Sarah.

SARAH. The kettle's boiling – I'll make some tea. (*Goes to kitchen.*)

BESSIE. Enough now, Monty, enough.

MONTY (*he has upset himself*). All right, all right. I didn't tell her anything she doesn't know. She's a fine woman is Sarah. She's a fighter. All that worry and she's still going strong. But she has one fault. For her the world is black and white. If you're not white so you must be black. She can't see shades in character – know what I mean? She can't see people in the round. 'They' are all the same bunch. The authorities, the governments, the police, the Post Office – even the shopkeepers. She's never trusted any of them, always fighting them. It was all so simple. The only thing that mattered was to be happy and eat. Anything that made you unhappy or stopped you from eating was the fault of capitalism. Do you think she ever read a book on political economy in her life? Bless her! Someone told her socialism was happiness so she joined the Party. You don't find many left like Sarah Kahn. I wish you'd have known us in the old days. Harry there used to have a lovely tenor voice. All the songs we sang together, and the strikes and the rallies. I used to carry Ronnie shoulder high to the May Day demonstrations. Everyone in the East End was going somewhere. It was a slum, there was misery, but we were going somewhere. The East End was a big mother.

SARAH *comes in with the tea.*

We'll talk about the good times now, shall we, Sarah? Blimey, sweetheart, it's not often that I come to London for a weekend. Here, remember the stall I used to have in Petticoat Lane? I'll take you there tomorrow, Bessie. And Manny the Corn King? Him and his wife used to go to Norwich, to sell phoney corn cures. His wife used to dress up as a nurse and they'd hang letters round the stall from people who were supposed to have been cured.

SARAH. And what about Barney?

MONTY. And Barney, that's it! He used to sell all the old farmers a lucky charm to bring them fortune. Sixpence each he'd sell them for and you know what they were? Haricot beans! Haricot beans dropped in dye to colour them. You could get them for three-pence a pound in a grocer's shop and Barney sold them for sixpence each! Sixpence! A pound of beans used to last him for months.

SARAH. Ach! Horrible times! Horrible times – dirty, unclean, cheating!

MONTY. But friendly.

SARAH. Friendly, you call it? You think it was friendly to swindle people?

MONTY. Sweetheart, you take life too seriously. Believe me, those farmers knew very well what they were buying. Nobody swindled anybody because everyone knew.

SARAH. You think so, Monty?

> HARRY *wakes up with a jerk. Something has happened. He tries hurriedly to rise.*

HARRY. Sarah, quick, help me.

SARAH. What! It's happened? (*She moves quickly to him.*)

MONTY. What is it, Harry boy?

SARAH. It's happened, Harry? Well, quickly then, quickly.

> HARRY, *crippled by paralysis and this attack of incontinence, shuffles, painfully, towards the toilet,*

with SARAH *almost dragging him along. He whines and groans pathetically.*

In front of Monty and Bessie. I'm so ashamed.

MONTY *attempts to help* HARRY *move.*

(*Abruptly.*) No, leave him. It's all right. I'll manage. Leave him, Monty.

They struggle out and into the passage. When they have left the front room, BESSIE *turns her head away and shudders.*

BESSIE. Oh, good God!
MONTY. Poor Sarah and Harry. Jesus! It's all come to this?

Curtain.

SCENE TWO

December 1956.

The KAHNS' *room, late one evening.* SARAH, PRINCE, HYMIE *and* CISSIE *are sitting round the table playing solo.* HARRY *is by the fire, gazing into it, quite oblivious of what is going on. The cards have just been dealt for a round. Everyone is evaluating his cards in silence. After some seconds:*

PRINCE (*studying his cards*). What time you expecting Ronnie, Sarah?
SARAH (*studying her cards*). He's supposed to arrive at nine thirty tonight.

Again silence.

HYMIE (*to* CISSIE). Nu? Call!
CISSIE. Misère.

SARAH. How can you call a misère when I want to call a misère?

CISSIE. Please, Sarah – don't give the game away.

PRINCE. Wait a minute, not everybody has passed.

CISSIE. All right then, call!

SARAH. Pass.

PRINCE. Pass.

HYMIE. Pass.

CISSIE. Thank you. Can I start now?

SARAH. Is it your lead? I thought Prince dealt the cards.

CISSIE. What's the matter with you, Sarah? – Hymie dealt them.

PRINCE. I could have sworn Sarah dealt them.

CISSIE. Hymie, who dealt the cards?

HYMIE. We've been so long deciding what to call that I don't know any more. Did I deal them? I don't remember.

There is a general discussion as to who dealt them.

CISSIE. Now quiet, everybody. Quiet! Every time I come to this house to play solo there's the same confusion. Why don't you pay attention to the game? Now then, what was laid on the table for trumps?

SARAH. The two of spades.

HYMIE. That was the last round. It was the six of diamonds.

SARAH. But I saw it with my own eyes, it was the –

HYMIE. You aren't wearing your glasses, Sarah.

PRINCE. It was the six of hearts, I remember now.

CISSIE. Ah, thank God! We've got two people to agree. I also saw the six of hearts on the table. Who's got the six of hearts?

HYMIE. I have.

CISSIE. Which means that you dealt and if you dealt that means that I lead. Everybody happy now? There!

CISSIE throws down a card. The others follow. It's HYMIE's trick. He lays down a card and the others follow, but SARAH realizes she has made a mistake.

SARAH. Wait a minute, wait a minute. I didn't mean to play that card.

CISSIE. Too late; you should watch the game.

SARAH. Ach! fool that I am. But you can see I shouldn't have played that card.

CISSIE. Of course I can see, but I'm glad that you did!

SARAH. Now, Hymie, would I normally play that card?

HYMIE. You aren't wearing your glasses, Sarah: I told you. We can still catch her. Now play.

SARAH. A second, a second. Let me get my glasses. (*Finds her bag, takes out her glasses and proceeds to puff on them and clean them.*) I don't know what's happened to my eyes lately. I went to have my glasses changed the other day – the rims were too big for me, kept slipping into my mouth – so I went to have them changed. The man said he couldn't change them because they were National Health glasses. So you know me, I tell him what for and he says, 'Madam,' he says, 'you want your money back?' So I say, 'Sure I want my money back.' And then I go up to the National Health offices – now listen to this – I go up to the National Health offices and I complain about the small allowance they made me for Harry. So the chap behind the desk – may he wake up dead – he says, 'What do you want, madam, ten pounds a week?' Did you ever hear? So I said, 'Son,' I said, 'when you were still peeing all over the floor I was on strike for better conditions, and don't you be cheeky.' 'Oh dear, you mustn't talk to me like that per, per, per, per!'

PRINCE. Come on, Sarah, the game.

It is PRINCE's lead. The others follow; it is his trick

68   CHICKEN SOUP WITH BARLEY

*again. Again he leads and the others follow. Now it is
for* SARAH *to lead, and she does so.*

What did you play hearts for? Couldn't you see what
suits I was showing you?

SARAH. Prince, let me play my own game. Don't I know
what I'm doing?

PRINCE. Well, it doesn't look like it, Sarah, so help me
it doesn't. You can't be watching the game. Couldn't
you guess she was going to throw off on hearts?

CISSIE. What is this! In the middle of the game!

SARAH. Of course I could see, but how do you know
that I can't play anything else?

CISSIE. Are you going to play solo or aren't you going to
play solo? No inquests, please.

HYMIE. Prince, play your game.

CISSIE. It's always the same. You can't even get a good
game of solo these days!

PRINCE *plays his card and they all follow.*

SARAH. Look at him! Now he comes out diamonds and
he wants to teach me how to play solo.

SARAH *leads next time, and after that* CISSIE *lays
down her cards and shows that she can't be caught.*

CISSIE. There! Three-halfpence from everybody,
please.

*Now everybody looks at everybody else's hand to see
where everybody else went wrong.*

SARAH. Well, of course I couldn't catch her, not with
my hand.

PRINCE. Why did you come out with hearts when you
knew she might be throwing off on them?

SARAH. Because I wanted to give the lead away – *I*
couldn't do anything.

HYMIE. But why give the lead away with hearts when you knew she might not have any?

SARAH. How was I to know? It was my smallest card.

CISSIE. You never could play a good game of solo, Sarah.

SARAH. But do me a favour –

CISSIE. Spades! That was the suit to play.

SARAH. Spades? Never!

> *Again everybody starts to speak at once until a loud scream brings them to silence. It comes from the playground below and is followed by a young girl's voice crying.*

GIRL'S VOICE. Philip! Philip! I want my Philip. Leave me alone – go away.

MAN'S VOICE. Go 'ome, I tell you, 'ome, you silly cow. 'Ome!

GIRL'S VOICE. I won't go till· I see Philip. I love him! I love him!

CISSIE. They making a film out there or something?

> *They all go out to the balcony and look down.* SARAH *walks along it off-stage to see what the commotion is all about.*

Can't see a thing. There's always something happening in these flats. Last week a woman tried to gas herself. Come on, let's go in.

> *They return to room.*

HARRY. What happened?

PRINCE. Your neighbours are having a party. Sarah's gone to see who's dead.

HYMIE. Why did the woman want to commit suicide?

CISSIE (*raising her skirt to warm her behind*). Who knows why a woman of thirty-two wants to commit suicide? These flats are a world on their own. You live a whole lifetime here and not know your next-door neighbour.

HARRY. I don' – I don' – I don' –

CISSIE. Do you want to write it down?

HARRY. I don' know the woman downstairs yet.

Everyone smiles for him, and having said his piece he returns to gazing at the fire. SARAH *re-enters.*

SARAH. Children! They don't know what to do with themselves. Seems she'd just spent the evening watching television with Philip and it was a horror film or something and he kept frightening her. Frightening her! That's all they can do to each other! She got home late and her father started on her so she ran back and started screaming for Philip. The great lover! He came out in his pyjamas to soothe her.

CISSIE (*going to get her coat*). Well, Sarah, I had a nice supper, a nice game of solo, and I'm going before the washing up. It doesn't look as though Ronnie caught that train anyway.

SARAH. I can't understand it. He wrote he was leaving Paris at eight this morning.

HYMIE. Well, it's nearly ten thirty and I must be going as well.

PRINCE. Me too, Sarah.

SARAH. Won't you stay for a cup of tea at least? It's so long since we've played a game of solo. Harry and I don't see many people these days.

HYMIE. It's been a nice evening, Sarah. Why don't you come up to *us* sometimes? I'm always at home.

SARAH. What chance do I get to leave Harry now?

CISSIE. Good night, Sarah.

HYMIE *kisses* SARAH *and* CISSIE *kisses* HARRY, *and all leave.* SARAH *waves to them from the balcony and returns to the room. She collects the cards and tidies up.*

SARAH. Harry, you want a cup of tea?

HARRY (*slowing rising*). I'm going to bed.

SARAH. You won't wait up for Ronnie?

HARRY. I'll – I'll – I'll –

SARAH. You'll what?

HARRY. See him in the morning.

> SARAH *helps* HARRY *shuffle away to bed, and then settles down in the armchair to read. But she is tired now and lets the paper fall, and dozes.* RONNIE *appears on the balcony with his cases. He gently opens the door and lets himself in. He tiptoes over to* SARAH *and stands looking at her. It is no longer an enthusiastic* RONNIE. *She opens her eyes and after a second of looking at him she jumps up into his arms.*

SARAH. I fell asleep.

RONNIE. So I saw.

SARAH. I thought you were a dream.

RONNIE. Perhaps I am.

SARAH (*pushing him away to look at him*). I hope not, Ronnie. Oh God, I hope not. Don't go away again. It's been so lonely without you and your friends. I don't mind not having any money, we can always eat, you know that, but I can't bear being on my own. (*Begins to cry.*)

RONNIE. I've only once ever seen you cry.

SARAH. What's the good of crying?

RONNIE. I wish I could cry sometimes. Perhaps if you'd have cried more often it would have been easier.

SARAH. It's just that I can't cope any longer, that's all. Three times a week Daddy has that accident and it gets too much. I'm an old woman now.

RONNIE. What makes you think I shall be able to cope?

SARAH. You? What are you talking about? Of course

you'll be able to cope. You're young, aren't you?
You're going to settle down.

RONNIE. I – I'm sick, Sarah.

SARAH. Sick?

RONNIE. Oh, not physically. That's why I came home.

SARAH. Didn't you like the place where you worked?
You always wrote how happy you were – what an
experience it was.

RONNIE. I hated the kitchen.

SARAH. But –

RONNIE. I – hated – the – kitchen! People coming and
going and not staying long enough to understand
each other. Do you know what I finally discovered –
it's all my eye! This notion of earning an honest
penny is all my eye. A man can work a whole lifetime
and when he is sixty-five he considers himself rich if
he has saved a thousand pounds. Rich! A whole
lifetime of working in a good, steady, settled, enter-
prising, fascinating job! For every manager in a
restaurant there must be twenty chefs terrified of old
age. That's all we are – people terrified of old age,
hoping for the football pools to come home. It's all
my eye, Sarah.

SARAH. I'll make you some tea. Are you hungry?

RONNIE. No, I don't want anything to eat, thank you – I
want to talk to you about something.

SARAH. But you must have to eat, you've been travelling
all day.

RONNIE (*categorically*). I do not want to eat – I want to
talk.

SARAH. I'll just make some tea, then; the water's boiled.
You sit and relax and then you'll go straight to sleep.
You'll see, by the morning you'll feel much better.
(*Goes to kitchen.*)

RONNIE. Still optimistic, Mother. Food and sleep and

you can see no reason why a person should be
unhappy.

SARAH (*from the kitchen*). I'd have looked blue all these
years if I hadn't've been optimistic.

RONNIE. How's Harry?

SARAH (*entering with two cups of tea*). You'll see him
tomorrow; he was too tired to wait up. Want some
biscuits? Have a piece of cake. Look, cake I made
specially for you – your favourite.

RONNIE (*loudly*). Mother, don't fuss, I'm sorry.

SARAH. Is this how you've come home? You start by
shouting? Is this a nice homecoming?

RONNIE (*something is obviously boiling in him*). Are you
still in the Party?

SARAH (*quizzically*). Yes.

RONNIE. Active?

SARAH. So?

RONNIE (*suddenly*). I don't suppose you've bothered to
read what happened in Hungary.

SARAH. Hungary?

RONNIE. Look at me, Mother. Talk to me. Take me by
the hand and show me who was right and who was
wrong. Point them out. Do it *for* me. I stand here and
a thousand different voices are murdering my mind.
Do you know, I couldn't wait to come home and
accuse you.

SARAH. Accuse me?

RONNIE. You didn't tell me there were any doubts.

SARAH. What doubts? What are you talking about?

RONNIE. Everything has broken up around you and you
can't see it.

SARAH (*shouting*). What, what, what, you mad boy?
Explain what you mean.

RONNIE. What has happened to all the comrades,
Sarah? I even blush when I use that word. Comrade!
Why do I blush? Why do I feel ashamed to use words

like democracy and freedom and brotherhood? They don't have meaning any more. I have nothing to write about any more. Remember all that writing I did? I was going to be a great socialist writer. I can't make sense of a word, a simple word. You look at me as if I'm talking in a foreign language. Didn't it hurt *you* to read about the murder of the Jewish Anti-Fascist Committee in the Soviet Union?

SARAH. You as well. Monty Blatt came up some months ago and said the same thing. He's also left the Party. He runs a greengrocer shop in Manchester.

RONNIE. And Dave and Ada in the Fens, and Prince working in a second-hand shop, and Uncle Hymie stuck smugly at home and Auntie Cissie once devoted – once involved – wandering from relative to relative. What's happened to us? Were we cheated or did we cheat ourselves? I just don't know, God in heaven, I just do not know! Can you understand what it is suddenly not to know? (*Collapses into armchair.*) And the terrifying thing is – I don't care either.

They sit in silence for some seconds.

SARAH. Drink your tea, darling.

RONNIE *closes his eyes and talks.*

RONNIE. Do you know what the trouble is, Mother? Can't you guess?

SARAH. You're tired, Ronnie.

RONNIE. You *do* know what the trouble is. You just won't admit it.

SARAH. In the morning you'll feel better.

RONNIE. Think hard. Look at my face. Look at my nose and my deep-set eyes; even my forehead is receding.

SARAH. Why don't you listen to me? Go to bed and –

RONNIE. Political institutions, society – they don't really affect people that much.

SARAH. Ronnie!

RONNIE. Who else was it who hated the jobs he had, who couldn't bear the discipline imposed by a daily routine, couldn't make sense of himself and gave up?

SARAH (*frightened*). Are you mad?

RONNIE. I've lost my faith and I've lost my ambition. Now I understand him perfectly. I wish I hadn't shouted at him as I used to.

SARAH. Mad boy!

RONNIE (*rising, opens his eyes and shouts*). You know that I'm right. *You've* never been right about anything. You wanted everybody to be happy but you wanted them to be happy your way. It was strawberries and cream for everyone – whether they liked it or not. And now look what's happened. The family you always wanted has disintegrated, and the great ideal you always cherished has exploded in front of your eyes. But you won't face it. You just refuse to face it. I don't know how you do it but you do – you just do. (*Louder.*) You're a pathological case, Mother – do you know that? You're still a *communist!*

He wants to take back his words but he has lost the power to express anything any more.

SARAH. All right! So I'm still a communist! Shoot me then! I'm a communist! I've always been one – since the time when all the world was a communist. You know that? When you were a baby and there was unemployment and everybody was thinking so – all the world was a communist. But it's different now. Now the people have forgotten. I sometimes think they're not worth fighting for because they forget so easily. You give them a few shillings in the bank and they can buy a television so they think it's all over, there's nothing more to be got, they don't have to think any more! Is that what you want? A world where people don't think any more? Is that what you want me to be satisfied with – a television set? Look at him! My son! He wants to die!

RONNIE. Don't laugh at me, Sarah.

SARAH. You want me to cry again? We should all sit down and cry?

RONNIE. I don't see things in black and white any more. My thoughts keep going pop, like bubbles. That's my life now – you know? – a lot of little bubbles going pop.

SARAH. And he calls me a pathological case! Pop! Pop, pop, pop, pop – shmop! You think it doesn't hurt me – the news about Hungary? You think I know what happened and what didn't happen? Do any of us know? Who do I know who to trust now – God, who are our friends now? But all my life I've fought. With your father and the rotten system that couldn't help him. All my life I worked with a party that meant glory and freedom and brotherhood. You want me to give it up now? You want me to move to Hendon and forget who I am? If the electrician who comes to mend my fuse blows it instead, so I should stop having electricity? I should cut off my light? Socialism is my light, can you understand that? A way of life. A man *can* be beautiful. I hate ugly people – I can't bear meanness and fighting and jealousy – I've got to have light. I'm a simple person, Ronnie, and I've got to have light and love.

RONNIE *looks up at her meaningfully.*

You think I didn't love your father enough, don't you? I'll tell you something. When Ada had diphtheria and I was pregnant I asked Daddy to carry her to the hospital. He wouldn't. We didn't have money because he didn't care to work and I didn't know what to do. He disappeared. It was Mrs Bernstein who saved her – you remember Mrs Bernstein? No, of course not, she died before you were born. It was Mrs Bernstein's soup. Ada still has that taste in her mouth – chicken soup with barley. She says it is a friendly taste – ask her. That saved her. Not even my brothers had money in those days, and a bit of dry crust with a cup of tea – ah! it was wonderful. But Daddy had the relief money. Someone told me they saw him eating salt-beef sandwiches in Bloom's. He didn't care. Maybe it was his illness *then* – who knows! He was never really a bad man. He never beat us or got drunk or gambled – he wasn't vulgar or coarse and he always had friends. So what was wrong? *I* could never understand him. All I did was fight him because he didn't care. Look at him now. He doesn't care to live. He's never cared to fully undress himself and put on pyjamas; never cared to keep shaved or washed; or to be on time or even turn up! And now he walks around with his fly-buttons and his shoelaces undone because he still doesn't care to fight his illness – and the dirt gathers around him. He doesn't care! And so I fought him because he didn't care. I fought everybody who didn't care. All the authorities, the shopkeepers, even today – those stinking assistance officers – I could buy them with my little finger – even now I'm still fighting them. And you want to be like them, like your father? I'll fight you then.

RONNIE. And lose again.

SARAH. But your father was a weak man. Could you do any of the things he did?

RONNIE. I would not be surprised.

SARAH. Ronnie, your father would never have left his mother to go abroad as you did. I don't tell you all this now to pull you down but on the contrary – so you should know, so you should care. Learn from us, for God's sake learn from us. What does it matter if your father was a weakling, or the man you worked with was an imbecile. They're human beings.

RONNIE. That doesn't mean a thing.

SARAH. There will always be human beings and as long as there are there will always be the idea of brotherhood.

RONNIE. Doesn't mean a thing.

SARAH. Despite the human beings.

RONNIE. Not a thing.

SARAH. Despite them!

RONNIE. It doesn't mean . . .

SARAH (*exasperated*). All right then! Nothing, then! It all comes down to nothing! People come and people go, wars destroy, accidents kill and plagues starve – it's all nothing, then! Philosophy? You want philosophy? Nothing means anything! There! Philosophy! I know! So? Nothing! Despair – die then! Will that be achievement? To die? (*Softly.*) You don't want to do that, Ronnie. So what if it all means nothing? When you know *that* you can start again. Please, Ronnie, don't let me finish this life thinking I lived for nothing. We got through, didn't we? We got scars but we got through. You hear me, Ronnie? (*She clasps him and moans.*) You've got to care, you've got to care or you'll die.

> RONNIE *unclasps her and moves away. He tries to say something – to explain. He raises his arms and some jumbled words come from his lips.*

RONNIE. I – I can't, not now, it's too big, not yet – it's too big to care for it, I – I . . .

> RONNIE *picks up his case and brokenly moves to his*

room mumbling: 'Too big, Sarah – too big, too big.'

SARAH (*shouting after him*). You'll die, you'll die – if you don't care you'll die. (*He pauses at door.*) Ronnie, if you don't care you'll die. (*He turns slowly to face her.*)

Curtain.

ENGLAND ARISE

AS MAN IS ONLY HUMAN

Roots

For Dusty

NOTE TO ACTORS AND PRODUCERS

My people are not caricatures. They are real (though fiction), and if they are portrayed as caricatures the point of all these plays will be lost. The picture I have drawn is a harsh one, yet my tone is not one of disgust – nor should it be in the presentation of the plays. I am at one with these people: it is only that I am annoyed, with them and myself.

NOTE ON PRONUNCIATION

This is a play about Norfolk people; it could be a play about any country people and the moral could certainly extend to the metropolis. But as it is about Norfolk people it is important that some attempt is made to find out how they talk. A very definite accent and intonation exists and personal experience suggests that this is not difficult to know. The following may be of great help:

When the word 'won't' is used, the 'w' is left out. It sounds the same but the 'w' is lost.

Double 'ee' is pronounced 'i' as in 'it' – so that 'been' becomes 'bin', 'seen' becomes 'sin', etc.

'Have' and 'had' become 'hev' and 'hed' as in 'head'.

'Ing' loses the 'g' so that it becomes 'in'.

'Bor' is a common handle and is a contraction of neighbour.

Instead of the word 'of' they say 'on', e.g. 'I've hed enough on it' or 'What do you think on it?'

Their 'yes' is used all the time and sounds like 'year' with a 'p' – 'yearp'.

'Blast' is also common usage and is pronounced 'blust', a short sharp sound as in 'gust'.

The cockney 'ain't' becomes 'ent' – also short and sharp.

The 't' in 'that' and 'what' is left out to give 'thaas' and 'whaas', e.g. 'Whaas matter then?'

Other idiosyncrasies are indicated in the play itself.

Roots was first presented at the Belgrade Theatre, Coventry, on 25 May 1959, with the following cast:

JENNY BEALES	Patsy Byrne
JIMMY BEALES	Charles Kay
BEATIE BRYANT	Joan Plowright
STAN MANN	Patrick O'Connell
MRS BRYANT	Gwen Nelson
MR BRYANT	Jack Rodney
MR HEALEY	Richard Martin
FRANKIE BRYANT	Alan Howard
PEARL BRYANT	Brenda Peters

Directed by John Dexter
Designed by Jocelyn Herbert

The play transferred to the Royal Court Theatre, London, on 30 June 1959, and subsequently to the Duke of York's on 30 July 1959. At the Duke of York's the part of Mr Healey was played by Barry Wilsher.

Act One: An isolated cottage in Norfolk, the house of the Bealeses

Act Two, Scene One: Two days later at the cottage of Mr and Mrs Bryant, in the kitchen
Scene Two: The same a couple of hours later

Act Three: Two weeks later in the front room of the Bryants'

Time: 1959

ACT ONE

A rather ramshackle house in Norfolk where there is no water laid on, nor electricity, nor gas. Everything rambles and the furniture is cheap and old. If it is untidy it is because there is a child in the house and there are few amenities, so that the mother is too overworked to take much care.

An assortment of clobber lies around: papers and washing, coats and basins, a tin wash-tub with shirts and underwear to be cleaned, Tilley lamps and Primus stoves. Washing hangs on a line in the room. It is September.

JENNY BEALES *is by the sink washing up. She is singing a recent pop song. She is short, fat and friendly, and wears glasses. A child's voice is heard from the bedroom crying* 'Sweet, Mamma, sweet.'

JENNY (*good-naturedly*). Shut you up Daphne and get you to sleep now. (*Moves to get a dishcloth.*)

CHILD'S VOICE. Daphy wan' sweet, sweet, sweet.

JENNY (*going to cupboard to get sweet*). My word child, Father come home and find you awake he'll be after you. (*Disappears to bedroom with sweet.*) There – now sleep, gal, don't wan' you grumpy wi' me in the mornin'.

> *Enter* JIMMY BEALES. *Also short, chubby, blond though hardly any hair left, ruddy complexion. He is a garage mechanic. Wears blue dungarees and an army pack slung over his shoulder. He wheels his bike in and lays it by the wall. Seems to be in some sort of pain – around his back.* JENNY *returns.*

Waas matter wi' you then?

JIMMY. I don' know gal. There's a pain in my guts and

one a'tween my shoulder blades I can hardly stand
up.

JENNY. Sit you down then an' I'll git you your supper
on the table.

JIMMY. Blust gal! I can't eat yit.

> JIMMY *picks up a pillow from somewhere and lies
> down on the sofa holding pillow to stomach.* JENNY
> *watches him a while.*

JENNY. Don't you know what 'tis yit?

JIMMY. Well, how should *I* know that 'tis.

JENNY. I told Mother about the pain and she says it's
indigestion.

JIMMY. What the hell's indigestion doin' a'tween my
shoulder blades then?

JENNY. She say some people get indigestion so bad it go
right through their stomach to the back.

JIMMY. Don't be daft.

JENNY. That's what I say. Blust Mother, I say, you
don't git indigestion in the back. Don't you tell me,
she say, I hed it!

JIMMY. What hevn't she hed.

> JENNY *returns to washing up while* JIMMY *struggles a
> while on the sofa.* JENNY *hums. No word. Then –*

JENNY. Who d'you see today?

JIMMY. Only Doctor Gallagher.

JENNY (*wheeling round*). You see who?

JIMMY. Gallagher. His wife driv him up in the ole
Armstrong.

JENNY. Well I go t'hell if that ent a rum thing.

JIMMY (*rising and going to table; pain has eased*). What's
that then?

JENNY (*moving to get him supper from oven*). We was
down at the whist drive in the village and that Judy
Maitland say he were dead. 'Cos you know he've hed

a cancer this last year and they don't give him no longer'n three weeks don't you?

JIMMY. Ole crows. They don' wan' nothin' less than a death to wake them up.

JENNY. No. No longer'n three weeks.

GIRL'S VOICE (*off*). Yoo-hoo! Yoo-hoo!

JIMMY. There's your sister.

JENNY. That's her.

GIRL'S VOICE (*off*). Yoo-hoo! Anyone home?

JENNY (*calling*). Come you on in gal, don't you worry about yoo-hoo.

> *Enter* BEATIE BRYANT, *an ample, blonde, healthy-faced young woman of twenty-two years. She is carrying a case.*

JIMMY. Here she is.

JENNY (*with reserve, but pleased*). Hello, Beatrice – how are you?

BEATIE (*with reserve, but pleased*). Hello, Jenny – how are you? What's that lovely smell I smell?

JENNY. Onions for supper and bread for the harvest festival.

BEATIE. Watcha Jimmy Beales, how you doin' bor?

JIMMY. Not so bad gal, how's yourself?

BEATIE. All right you know. When you comin' to London again for a football match?

JIMMY. O blust gal, I don' wanna go to any more o' those things. Ole father Bryant was there in the middle of that crowd and he turn around an' he say (*Imitating.*), Stop you a-pushin' there, he say, stop you a-pushin'.

JENNY. Where's Ronnie?

BEATIE. He's comin' down at the end of two weeks.

JIMMY. Ent you married yit?

BEATIE. No.

JIMMY. You wanna hurry then gal, a long engagement don't do the ole legs any good.

JENNY. Now shut you up Jimmy Beales and get that food down you. Every time you talk, look, you miss a mouthful! That's why you complain of pain in your shoulder blades.

BEATIE. You bin hevin' pains then Jimmy?

JIMMY. Blust yes! Right a'tween my shoulder blades.

JENNY. Mother says it's indigestion.

BEATIE. What the hell's indigestion doin' a'tween his shoulder blades?

JENNY. Mother reckon some people get indigestion so bad it go right through their stomach to the back.

BEATIE. Don't talk daft!

JENNY. That's what I say. Blust Mother, I say, you don't git indigestion in the back. Don't you tell me, she say, I hed it!

BEATIE. What hevn't she hed. How is she?

JENNY. Still the same you know. How long you staying this time?

BEATIE. Two days here – two weeks at home.

JENNY. Hungry gal?

BEATIE. Watcha got?

JENNY. Watcha see.

BEATIE. Liver? I'll hev it!

> BEATIE *makes herself at home. Near by is a pile of comics. She picks one up and reads.*

JENNY. We got some ice-cream after.

BEATIE (*absorbed*). Yearp.

JENNY. Look at her. No sooner she's in than she's at them ole comics. You still read them ole things?

JIMMY. She don't change much do she?

BEATIE. Funny that! Soon ever I'm home again I'm like I always was – it don' even seem I bin away. I do the same lazy things an' I talk the same. Funny that!

JENNY. What do Ronnie say to it?

BEATIE. He ent never bin here, not in the three years I know him so he don't even know. But I'll tell you (*She jumps up and moves around as she talks.*) I used to read the comics he bought for his nephews and he used to get riled –

> *Now* BEATIE *begins to quote Ronnie, and when she does she imitates him so well in both manner and intonation that in fact as the play progresses we see a picture of him through her.*

'Christ, woman, what can they give you that you can *be* so absorbed?' So you know what I used to do? I used to get a copy of the *Manchester Guardian* and sit with that wide open – and a comic behind!

JIMMY. *Manchester Guardian?* Blimey Joe – he don' believe in hevin' much fun then?

BEATIE. That's what I used to tell him. 'Fun?' he say, 'fun? Playing an instrument is fun, painting is fun, reading a book is fun, talking with friends is fun – but a comic? A comic? for a young woman of twenty-two?'

JENNY (*handing out meal and sitting down herself*). He sound a queer bor to me. Sit you down and eat gal.

BEATIE (*enthusiastically*). He's alive though.

JIMMY. Alive? Alive you say? What's alive about someone who can't read a comic? What's alive about a person that reads books and looks at paintings and listens to classical music?

> *There is a silence at this, as though the question answers itself – reluctantly.*

Well, it's all right for some I suppose.

BEATIE. And then he'd sneak the comic away from me and read it his-self!

JENNY. Oh, he didn't really mind then?

BEATIE. No – 'cos sometimes I read books as well.
'There's nothing wrong with comics,' he'd cry – he
stand up on a chair when he want to preach but don't
wanna sound too dramatic.

JIMMY. Eh?

BEATIE. Like this, look. (*Stands on a chair.*) 'There's
nothing wrong with comics only there's something
wrong with comics all the time. There's nothing
wrong with football, only there's something wrong
with *only* football. There's nothing wrong with rock
'n' rolling, only God preserve me from the girl that
can do nothing else!' (*She sits down and then stands up
again, remembering something else.*) Oh yes, 'and
there's nothing wrong with talking about the
weather, only don't talk to me about it!' (*Sits down.*)

> JIMMY *and* JENNY *look at each other as though she,
> and no doubt Ronnie, is a little barmy.* JIMMY *rises
> and begins to strap on boots and gaiters ready for
> going out to an allotment.*

JENNY. He never really row with you then?

BEATIE. We used to. There was a time when he handled
all official things for me you know. Once I was in
between jobs and I didn't think to ask for my
unemployment benefit. *He* told me to. But when I
asked they told me I was short on stamps and so I
wasn't entitled to benefit. *I* didn't know what to say
but he did. He went up and argued for me – he's just
like his mother, she argues with everyone – and I got
it. I didn't know how to talk see, it was all foreign to
me. Think of it! An English girl born and bred and I
couldn't talk the language – except for to buy food
and clothes. And so sometimes when he were in a
black mood he'd start on me. 'What can you talk of?'
he'd ask. 'Go on, pick a subject. Talk. Use the
language. Do you know what language is?' Well, I'd

never thought before – hev you? – it's automatic to you isn't it, like walking? 'Well, language is words,' he'd say, as though he were telling me a secret. 'It's bridges, so that you can get safely from one place to another. And the more bridges you know about the more places you can see!' (*To* JIMMY.) And do *you* know what happens when you can see a place but you don't know where the bridge is?

JIMMY (*angrily*). Blust gal, what the hell are you on about.

BEATIE. Exactly! You see, you hev a row! Still, rows is all right. I like a row. So then he'd say: 'Bridges! bridges! bridges! Use your bridges woman. It took thousands of years to build them, use them!' And that riled me. 'Blust your bridges,' I'd say. 'Blust you and your bridges – I want a row.' Then he'd grin at me. 'You want a row?' he'd ask. 'No bridges this time?' 'No bridges,' I'd say – and we'd row. Sometimes he hurt me but then, slowly, he'd build the bridge up *for* me – and then we'd make love! (*Innocently continues her meal.*)

JENNY. You'd what, did you say?

BEATIE. Make love. Love in the afternoon gal. Ever had it? It's the only time *for* it. Go out or entertain in the evenings; sleep at night, study, work and chores in the mornings; but love – alert and fresh, when you got most energy – love in the afternoon.

JIMMY. I suppose you take time off from work every afternoon to do it?

BEATIE. I'm talking about weekends and holidays – daft.

JENNY. Oh, Beatie, go on wi' you!

BEATIE. Well, go t'hell Jenny Beales, you're blushin'. Ent you never had love in the afternoon? Ask Jimmy then.

JENNY (*rising to get sweet*). Shut you up gal and get on

wi' your ice-cream. It's strawberry flavour. Want some more James?

JIMMY (*taking it in the middle of lacing up boots*). Yes please, vanilla please. (*Eating.*) Good cream ent it? Made from the white milk of a Jersey cow.

BEATIE. This is good too – made from pink milk ent it?

Pause.

JIMMY. Yearp! (*Pause.*) Come from a pink cow!

Pause. They are all enjoying the cream.

JENNY (*eating*). You remember Dickie Smart, Beatie?

BEATIE (*eating*). Who?

JENNY (*eating*). We had a drink wi' him in the Storks when you was down last.

BEATIE (*eating*). Yearp.

JENNY (*eating*). Well, he got gored by a bull last Thursday. His left ear was nearly off, his knee were gored, his ribs bruised, and the ligaments of his legs torn.

Pause as they finish eating.

BEATIE (*euphemistically*). He had a rough time then!

JENNY. Yearp. (*To* JIMMY.) You off now?

JIMMY. Mm.

JENNY *collects dishes.*

BEATIE. Still got your allotment Jimmy?

JIMMY. Yearp.

BEATIE. Bit heavy-going this weather.

JIMMY. That ent too bad just yit – few more weeks an' the old mowld'll cling.

BEATIE. Watcha got this year?

JIMMY. Had spuds, carrots, cabbages, you know. Beetroot, lettuces, onions, and peas. But me runners let me down this year though.

JENNY. I don't go much on them old things.
BEATIE. You got a fair owle turn then?
JIMMY. Yearp.

    JIMMY *starts to sharpen a reap hook.*

BEATIE (*jumping up*). I'll help you wash.
JENNY. That's all right gal.
BEATIE. Where's the cloth?
JENNY. Here 'tis.

> BEATIE *helps collect dishes from table and proceeds to help wash up. This is a silence that needs organizing. Throughout the play there is no sign of intense living from any of the characters –* BEATIE'*s bursts are the exception. They continue in a routine rural manner. The day comes, one sleeps at night, there is always the winter, the spring, the autumn, and the summer – little amazes them. They talk in fits and starts mainly as a sort of gossip, and they talk quickly too, enacting as though for an audience what they say. Their sense of humour is keen and dry. They show no affection for each other – though this does not mean they would not be upset were one of them to die. The silences are important – as important as the way they speak, if we are to know them.*

JENNY. What about that strike in London? Waas London like wi'out the buses?
BEATIE. Lovely! No noise – and the streets, you should see the streets, flowing with people – the city looks human.
JIMMY. They wanna call us Territorials out – we'd soon break the strike.
BEATIE. That's a soft thing for a worker to say for his mates.
JIMMY. Soft be buggered, soft you say? What they

earnin' those busmen, what they earnin'? And what's
the farm worker's wage? Do you know it gal?

BEATIE. Well, let the farm workers go on strike too
then! It don't help a farm labourer if a busman don't
go on strike do it now?

JENNY. You know they've got a rise though. Father
Bryant's go up by six and six a week as a pigman, and
Frank goes up seven 'n' six a week for driving a
tractor.

JIMMY. But you watch the Hall sack some on 'em.

JENNY. Thaas true Beatie. They're such sods, honest to
God they are. Every time there's bin a rise someone
gets sacked. Without fail. You watch it – you ask
father Bryant when you get home, ask him who's bin
sacked since the rise.

BEATIE. One person they 'ont sack is him though. They
'ont find many men'd tend to pigs seven days a week
and stay up the hours he do.

JENNY. Bloody fool! (*Pause.*) Did Jimmy tell you he've
bin chosen for the Territorials' Jubilee in London this
year?

BEATIE. What's this then? What'll you do there?

JIMMY. Demonstrate and parade wi' arms and such
like.

BEATIE. Won't do you any good.

JIMMY. Don't you reckon? Gotta show we can defend
the country you know. Demonstrate arms and you
prevent war.

BEATIE (*she has finished wiping up*). Won't demonstrate
anything bor. (*Goes to undo her case.*) Present for the
house! Have a hydrogen bomb fall on you and you'll
find them things silly in your hands. (*Searches for
other parcels.*)

JIMMY. So you say gal? So you say? That'll frighten
them other buggers though.

BEATIE. Frighten yourself y'mean. (*Finds parcels.*) Presents for the kid.

JIMMY. And what do you know about this all of a sudden?

JENNY (*revealing a tablecloth*). Thank you very much Beatie. Just what I need.

BEATIE. You're not interested in defending your country Jimmy, you just enjoy playing soldiers.

JIMMY. What did I do in the last war then – *sing* in the trenches?

BEATIE (*explaining – not trying to get one over on him*). Ever heard of Chaucer, Jimmy?

JIMMY. No.

BEATIE. Do you know the MP for this constituency?

JIMMY. What you drivin' at gal – don't give me no riddles.

BEATIE. Do you know how the British Trade Union Movement started? And do you believe in strike action?

JIMMY. No to both those.

BEATIE. What you goin' to war to defend then?

JIMMY (*he is annoyed now*). Beatie – you bin away from us a long time now – you got a boy who's educated an' that and he's taught you a lot maybe. But don't you come pushin' ideas across at us – we're all right as we are. You can come when you like an' welcome but don't bring no discussion of politics in the house wi' you 'cos that'll only cause trouble. I'm telling you. (*He goes off.*)

JENNY. Blust gal, if you hevn't touched him on a sore spot. He live for them Territorials he do – that's half his life.

BEATIE (*she is upset now*). What's he afraid of talking for?

JENNY. He ent afraid of talking Beatie – blust he can do that, gal.

BEATIE. But not talk, not really talk, not use bridges. I

sit with Ronnie and his friends sometimes and I listen
to them talk about things and you know I've never
heard half of the words before.

JENNY. Don't he tell you what they mean?

BEATIE. I get annoyed when he keep tellin' me – and he
want me to ask. (*Imitates him half-heartedly now.*)
'Always ask, people love to tell you what they know,
always ask and people will respect you.'

JENNY. And do you?

BEATIE. No! I don't! An' you know why? Because I'm
stubborn, I'm like Mother, I'm stubborn. Somehow I
just can't bring myself to ask, and you know what? I
go mad when I listen to them. As soon as they start to
talk about things I don't know about or I can't
understand I get mad. They sit there, casually
talking, and suddenly they turn on you, abrupt.
'Don't you think?' they say. Like at school, pick on
you and ask a question you ent ready for. Sometimes
I don't say anything, sometimes I go to bed or leave
the room. Like Jimmy – just like Jimmy.

JENNY. And what do Ronnie say to that then?

BEATIE. He get mad too. 'Why don't you ask me
woman, for God's sake why don't you ask me? Aren't
I dying to tell you about things? Only ask!'

JENNY. And he's goin' to marry you?

BEATIE. Why not?

JENNY. Well I'm sorry gal, you mustn't mind me saying
this, but it don't seem to me like you two got much in
common.

BEATIE (*loudly*). It's not true! We're in love!

JENNY. Well, you know.

BEATIE (*softly*). No, I don't know. I won't know till he
come here. From the first day I went to work as
waitress in the Dell Hotel and saw him working in
the kitchen I fell in love – and I thought it was easy. I
thought everything was easy. I chased him for three

months with compliments and presents until I finally give myself to him. He never said he love me nor I didn't care but once he'd taken me he seemed to think he was responsible for me and I told him no different. I'd *make* him love me I thought. I didn't know much about him except he was different and used to write most of the time. And then he went back to London and I followed him there. I've never moved far from home but I did for him and he felt all the time he couldn't leave me and I didn't tell him no different. And then I got to know more about him. He was interested in all the things I never even thought about. About politics and art and all that, and he tried to teach me. He's a socialist and he used to say you couldn't bring socialism to a country by making speeches, but perhaps you could pass it on to someone who was near you. So I pretended I was interested – but I didn't understand much. All the time he's trying to teach me but I can't take it Jenny. And yet, at the same time, I want to show I'm willing. I'm not used to learning. Learning was at school and that's finished with.

JENNY. Blust gal, you don't seem like you're going to be happy then. Like I said.

BEATIE. But I love him.

JENNY. Then you're not right in the head then.

BEATIE. I couldn't have any other life now.

JENNY. Well, I don't know and that's a fact.

BEATIE (*playfully mocking her*). Well I don't know and that's a fact! (*Suddenly.*) Come on gal, I'll teach you how to bake some pastries.

JENNY. Pastries?

BEATIE. Ronnie taught me.

JENNY. Oh, you learnt that much then?

BEATIE. But he don't know. I always got annoyed when

he tried to teach me to cook as well – Christ! I had to know something – but it sank in all the same.

By this time it has become quite dark and JENNY *proceeds to light a Tilley lamp.*

JENNY. You didn't make it easy then?

BEATIE. Oh don't you worry, gal, it'll be all right once we're married. Once we're married and I got babies I won't need to be interested in half the things I got to be interested in now.

JENNY. No you won't will you! Don't need no education for babies.

BEATIE. Nope. Babies is babies – you just have 'em.

JENNY. Little sods!

BEATIE. You gonna hev another Jenny?

JENNY. Well, course I am. What you on about? Think Jimmy don't want none of his own?

BEATIE. He's a good man Jenny.

JENNY. Yearp.

BEATIE. Not many men'd marry you after you had a baby.

JENNY. No.

BEATIE. He didn't ask you any questions? Who was the father? Nor nothing?

JENNY. No.

BEATIE. You hevn't told no one hev you Jenny?

JENNY. No, that I hevn't.

BEATIE. Well, that's it gal, don't you tell me then!

By this time the methylated spirit torch has burned out and JENNY *has finished pumping the Tilley lamp and we are in brightness.*

JENNY (*severely*). Now Beatie, stop it. Every time you come home you ask me that question and I hed enough. It's finished with and over. No one don't say nothing and no one know. You hear me?

BEATIE. Are you in love with Jimmy?

JENNY. Love? I don't believe in any of that squit – we just got married, an' that's that.

BEATIE (*suddenly looking around the room at the general chaos*). Jenny Beales, just look at this house. Look at it!

JENNY. I'm looking. What's wrong?

BEATIE. Let's clean it up.

JENNY. Clean what up?

BEATIE. Are you going to live in this house all your life?

JENNY. You gonna buy us another?

BEATIE. Stuck out here in the wilds with only ole Stan Mann and his missus as a neighbour and sand pits all around. Every time it rain look you're stranded.

JENNY. Jimmy don't earn enough for much more 'n we got.

BEATIE. But it's so untidy.

JENNY. You don' wan' me bein' like sister Susan do you? 'Cos you know how clean she is don' you – she's so bloody fussy she's gotten to polishing the brass overflow pipe what leads out from the lavatory.

BEATIE. Come on gal, let's make some order anyway – I love tidying up.

JENNY. What about the pastries? Pastries? Oh my sainted aunt, the bread! (*Dashes to the oven and brings out a most beautiful-looking plaited loaf of bread. Admiring it.*) Well, no one wanna complain after that. Isn't that beautiful Beatie?

BEATIE. I could eat it now.

JENNY. You hungry again?

BEATIE (*making an attack upon the clothes that are lying around*). I'm always hungry again. Ronnie say I eat more'n I need. 'If you get fat woman I'll leave you – without even a discussion!'

JENNY (*placing bread on large oval plate to put away*). Well, there ent nothin' wrong in bein' fat.

BEATIE. You ent got no choice gal. (*Seeing bike.*) A bike! What's a bike doin' in a livin' room – I'm putting it outside.

JENNY. Jimmy 'ont know where it is.

BEATIE. Don't be daft, you can't miss a bike. (*Wheels it outside and calls from there.*) Jenny! Start puttin' the clothes away.

JENNY. Blust gal, I ent got nowhere to put them.

BEATIE (*from outside*). You got drawers – you got cupboards.

JENNY. They're full already.

BEATIE (*entering – energy sparks from her*). Come here – let's look. (*Looks.*) Oh, go away – you got enough room for ten families. You just bung it all in with no order, that's why. Here – help me.

> They drag out all manner of clothes from the cupboard and begin to fold them up.

How's my Frankie and Pearl?

JENNY. They're all right. You know she and Mother don't talk to each other?

BEATIE. What, again? Who's fault is it this time?

JENNY. Well, Mother she say it's Pearl's fault and Pearl she say it's Mother.

BEATIE. Well, they wanna get together quick and find whose fault 'tis 'cos I'm going to call the whole family together for tea to meet Ronnie.

JENNY. Well, Susan and Mother don't talk neither so you got a lot of peace-making to do.

BEATIE. Well go t'hell, what's broken them two up?

JENNY. Susan hev never bin stuck on her mother, you know that don't you – well, it seems that Susan bought something off the club from Pearl and Pearl give it to Mother and Mother sent it to Susan through the fishmonger what live next door her in the council houses. And of course Susan were riled 'cos she didn't want her neighbours to know that she bought anything off the club. So they don't speak.

BEATIE. Kids! It makes me mad.

JENNY. And you know what 'tis with Pearl don't you – it's 'cos Mother hev never thought she was good enough for her son Frankie.

BEATIE. No more she wasn't neither!

JENNY. What's wrong wi' her then? I get on all right.

BEATIE. Nothing's wrong wi' her, she just wasn't good enough for our Frankie, that's all.

JENNY. Who's being small-minded now?

BEATIE. Always wantin' more'n he can give her.

JENNY. An' I know someone else who always wanted more'n she got.

BEATIE (*sulkily*). It's not the same thing.

JENNY. Oh yes 'tis.

BEATIE. 'Tent.

JENNY. 'Tis my gal. (*Mimicking the child* BEATIE.) I wan' a 'nana, a 'nana, a 'nana. Frankie's got my 'nana, 'nana, 'nana.

BEATIE. Well, I liked bananas.

JENNY. You liked anything you could get your hands on and Mother used to give in to you 'cos you were the youngest. Me and Susan and Frankie never got nothing 'cos o' you – 'cept a clout round the ear.

BEATIE. 'Tent so likely. You got everything and I got nothing.

JENNY. All we got was what we pinched out the larder and then you used to go and tell tales to Mother.

BEATIE. I never did.

JENNY. Oh, didn't you my gal? Many's the time I'd've willingly strangled you – with no prayers – there you are, no prayers whatsoever. Strangled you till you was dead.

BEATIE. Oh go on wi' you Jenny Beales.

By now they have finished folding the clothes and

have put away most of the laundry and garments that have till this moment cluttered up the room. BEATIE *says 'There', stands up and looks around, finds some coats sprawled helter-skelter, and hangs them up behind the door.*

I'll buy you some coat-hangers.

JENNY. You get me a couple o' coats to hang on 'em first please.

BEATIE (*looking around*). What next. Bottles, jars, nicknacks, saucepans, cups, papers – everything anywhere. Look at it! Come on!

BEATIE *attempts to get these things either into their proper places or out of sight.*

JENNY. You hit this place like a bloody whirlwind you do, like a bloody whirlwind. Jimmy'll think he've come into the wrong house and I shan't be able to find a thing.

BEATIE. Here, grab a broom. (*She is now gurgling with sort of animal noises signifying excitement. Her joy is childlike.*) How's Poppy?

JENNY. Tight as ever.

BEATIE. What won't he give you now?

JENNY. 'Tent nothing wi' me gal. Nothing he do don't affect me. It's Mother I'm referring to.

BEATIE. Don't he still give her much money?

JENNY. Money? She hev to struggle and skint all the time – *all* the time. Well it ent never bin no different from when we was kids hev it?

BEATIE. No.

JENNY. I tell you what. It wouldn't surprise me if Mother were in debt all the time, that it wouldn't. No. It wouldn't surprise me at all.

BEATIE. Oh, never.

JENNY. Well, what do you say that for Beatie – do you know how much he allow her a week look?

BEATIE. Six pounds?

JENNY. Six pound be buggered. Four pounds ten! An' she hev to keep house *an'* buy her own clothes out of that.

BEATIE. Still, there's only two on 'em.

JENNY. You try keepin' two people in food for four pound ten. She pay seven an' six a week into Pearl's club for clothes, two and six she hev on the pools, and a shilling a week on the Labour Tote. (*Suddenly.*) Blust! I forgot to say. Pearl won the Tote last week.

BEATIE. A hundred pounds?

JENNY. A hundred pounds!

BEATIE. Well no one wrote me about it.

JENNY. 'Cos you never wrote no one else.

BEATIE. What she gonna do wi' it – buy a TV?

JENNY. TV? Blust no. You know she hevn't got electricity in that house. No, she say she's gonna get some clothes for the kids.

> *There is a sound now of a drunk old man approaching, and alongside of it the voice of* JIMMY. *The drunk is singing:* 'I come from Bungay Town, I calls I Bungay Johnnie.'

Well I go t'hell if that ent Stan Mann drunk again. And is that Jimmy wi' him? (*Listens.*)

BEATIE. But I thought Stan Mann was paralysed.

JENNY. That don't stop him getting paralytic drunk. (*Listens again.*) That's Jimmy taking him into the house I bet. A fortune that man hev drunk away – a whole bleedin' fortune. Remember the fleet of cars he used to run and all that land he owned, and all them cattle he had and them fowl? Well, he've only got a few acres left and a few ole chickens. He drink it all away. Two strokes he've had from drinking and now he's paralysed down one side. But that don't stop him getting drunk – no it don't.

JIMMY enters and throws his jacket on the couch, takes off his boots and gaiters, and smiles meanwhile.

JIMMY. Silly ole bugger.

JENNY. I was just telling Beatie how he've drunk a fortune away hevn't he?

JIMMY. He wanna drink a little more often and he'll be finished for good.

JENNY. Didn't he hev all them cows and cars and land Jimmy? And didn't he drink it all away bit by bit?

JIMMY. Silly ole sod don't know when to stop.

JENNY. I wished I had half the money he drink.

JIMMY. He messed his pants.

JENNY. He what? Well where was this then?

JIMMY. By the allotment.

JENNY. Well, what did *you* do then?

JIMMY. He come up to me – 'course I knowed he were drunk the way he walk – he come up to me an' he say, "Evenin' Jimmy Beales, thaas a fine turnover you got there.' An' I say, 'Yearp 'tis.' An' then he bend down to pick a carrot from the ground an' then he cry, 'Oops, I done it again!' An' 'course, soon ever he say 'done it again' I knowed what'd happened. So I took his trousers down an' ran the ole hose over him.

BEATIE. Oh, Jimmy, you never did.

JIMMY. I did gal. I put the ole hose over him an' brought him home along the fields with an ole sack around his waist.

BEATIE. He'll catch his death.

JIMMY. Never – he's strong as an ox.

JENNY. What'd you do with his trousers and things?

JIMMY. Put it on the compost heap – good for the land!

Now STAN MANN enters. He's not all that drunk. The cold water has sobered him a little. He is old – about seventy-five – and despite his slight stoop one can see he was a very strong upright man. He probably looks like everyman's idea of a farmer – except that he wears no socks or boots at this moment and he hobbles on a stick.

STAN. Sorry about that ole son.

JIMMY. Don't you go worrying about that my manny – get you along to bed.

JENNY. Get some shoes on you too Stan, or you'll die of cold *and* booze.

STAN (*screwing up his eyes across the room*). Is that you Jenny? Hello ole gal. How are you?

JENNY. It's you you wanna worry about now ole matey. I'm well enough.

STAN (*screwing his eyes still more*). Who's that next to you?

JENNY. Don't you recognize her? It's our Beatie, Stan.

STAN. Is that you Beatie? Well blust gal, you gotten fatter since I seen you last. You gonna be fat as Jenny here? Come on over an' let's look at you.

BEATIE (*approaching*). Hello Stan Mann, how are you?

STAN (*looking her up and down*). Well enough gal, well enough. You married yit?

BEATIE. No.

STAN. You bin courtin' three years. Why ent you married yit?

BEATIE (*slightly embarrassed*). We ent sure yit.

STAN. You ent sure you say? What ent you sure of? You know how to do it don't you?

JENNY. Go on wi' you to bed Stan Mann.

STAN. Tell your boy he don't wanna waste too much time or I'll be hevin' yer myself for breakfast – on a plate.

JENNY. Stan Mann, I'm sendin' you to your bed – go on now, off wi' you, you can see Beatie in the mornin'.

STAN (*as he is ushered out – to* BEATIE). She's fat ent she? I'm not sayin' she won't do mind, but she's fat. (*As he goes out.*) All right ole sweetheart, I'm goin'. I'm just right for bed. Did you see the new bridge they're building? It's a rum ole thing isn't it . . . (*Out of sound.*)

JENNY *makes up bed on couch for* BEATIE.

JIMMY. Well, I'm ready for bed.

BEATIE. I can't bear sick men. They smell.

JIMMY. Ole Stan's all right – do anythin' for you.

BEATIE. I couldn't look after one you know.

JIMMY. Case of hevin' to sometimes.

BEATIE. Ronnie's father's paralysed like that. I can't touch him.

JIMMY. Who see to him then?

BEATIE. His mother. She wash him, change him, feed him. Ronnie help sometimes. I couldn't though. Ronnie say, 'Christ, woman, I hope you aren't around when I'm ill.' (*Shudders.*) Ole age terrify me.

JIMMY. You sleepin' on that ole couch tonight?

BEATIE. Suppose so.

JIMMY. You comfortable sleepin' on that ole thing? You wanna sleep with Jenny while you're here?

BEATIE. No thanks, Jimmy. (*She is quite subdued now.*) I'm all right on there.

JIMMY. Right, then I'm off. (*Looking around.*) Where's the *Evening News* I brought in?

JENNY (*entering*). You off to bed?

JIMMY. Yearp. Reckon I've had 'nough of this ole day. Where's my *News*?

JENNY. Where d'you put it Beatie?

JIMMY (*suddenly seeing the room*). Blust, you movin' out?

BEATIE. Here you are Jimmy Beales. (*Hands him paper.*) It's all tidy now.

JIMMY. So I see. Won't last long though will it? 'Night. (*Goes to bed.*)

JENNY. Well I'm ready for my bed too – how about you Beatie?

BEATIE. Yearp.

JENNY (*taking a candle in a stick and lighting it*). Here, keep this with you. Your bed's made. Want a drink before you turn in?

BEATIE. No thanks gal.

JENNY (*picking up Tilley lamp. Leaving*). Right then. Sleep well gal.

BEATIE. Good night Jenny. (*Pause. Loud whispers from now on.*) Hey Jenny.

JENNY. What is it?

BEATIE. I'll bake you some pastries when I get to Mother's.

JENNY. Father won't let you use his electricity for me, don't talk daft.

BEATIE. I'll get Mother on him. It'll be all right. Your ole ovens weren't big 'nough anyways. Good night.

Moves to door.

JENNY. Good night.

BEATIE (*an afterthought*). Hey Jenny.

JENNY (*returning*). What now?

BEATIE. Did I tell you I took up painting?

JENNY. Painting?

BEATIE. Yes – on cardboard and canvases with brushes.

JENNY. What kind of painting?

BEATIE. Abstract painting – designs and patterns and such like. I can't do nothing else. I sent two on 'em home. Show you when you come round – if Mother hevn't thrown them out.

JENNY. You're an artist then?

Pause. Such a thought had not occurred to her before. It pleases, even thrills, her.

BEATIE. Yes. Good night.

JENNY. Good night.

> BEATIE *is left alone. Looks out of window. Blows out candle. We see only the faint glow of moonlight from outside and then –*

> *The curtain falls.*

ACT TWO

SCENE ONE

Two days have passed. BEATIE *will arrive at her own home, the home of her parents. This is a tied cottage on a main road between two large villages. It is neat and ordinary inside. We can see a large kitchen – where most of the living is done – and attached to it is a large larder; also part of the front room and a piece of the garden where some washing is hanging.*

MRS BRYANT *is a short, stout woman of fifty. She spends most of the day on her own, and consequently when she has a chance to speak to anybody she says as much as she can as fast as she can. The only people she sees are the tradesmen, her husband, the family when they pop in occasionally. She speaks very loudly all the time so that her friendliest tone sounds aggressive, and she manages to dramatize the smallest piece of gossip into something significant. Each piece of gossip is a little act done with little looking at the person to whom it is addressed. At the moment she is at the door leading to the garden, looking for the cat.*

MRS BRYANT. Cossie, Cossie, Cossie, Cossie, Cossie, Cossie! Here Cossie! Food Cossie! Cossie, Cossie, Cossie! Blust you cat, where the hell are you. Oh hell on you then, I ent wastin' my time wi' you now.

> *She returns to the kitchen and thence the larder, from which she emerges with some potatoes. These she starts peeling.* STAN MANN *appears round the back door. He has a handkerchief to his nose and is blowing vigorously, as vigorously as his paralysis will allow.* MRS BRYANT *looks up, but continues her peeling.*

STAN. Rum thing to git a cold in summer, what you say Daphne?

MRS BRYANT. What'd you have me say my manny. Sit you down bor and rest a bit. Shouldn't wear such daf' clothes.

STAN. Daf' clothes? Blust woman! I got on half a cow's hide, what you sayin'! Where's the gal?

MRS BRYANT. Beatie? She 'ent come yit. Didn't *you* see her?

STAN. Hell, I was up too early for her. She always stay the weekend wi' Jenny 'fore comin' home?

MRS BRYANT. Most times.

STAN *sneezes.*

What you doin' up this way wi' a cold like that then? Get you home to bed.

STAN. Just come this way to look at the vicarage. Stuff's comin' up for sale soon.

MRS BRYANT. You still visit them things then?

STAN. Yearp. Pass the ole time away. Pass the ole time.

MRS BRYANT. Time drag heavy then?

STAN. Yearp. Time drag heavy. She do that. Time drag so slow, I get to thinkin' it's Monday when it's still Sunday. Still, I had my day gal I say. Yearp. I had that all right.

MRS BRYANT. Yearp. You had that an' a bit more ole son. I shant grumble if I last as long as you.

STAN. Yearp. I hed my day. An' I'd do it all the same again, you know that? Do it all the same I would.

MRS BRYANT. Blust! All your drinkin' an' that?

STAN. Hell! Thaas what kep' me goin' look. Almost anyways. None o' them young 'uns'll do it, hell if they will. There ent much life in the young 'uns. Bunch o' weak-kneed ruffians. None on 'em like livin' look, none on 'em! You read in them ole papers what go on look, an' you wonder if they can see. You do! Wonder if they got eyes to look around them. Think they know where they live? 'Course they don't, they don't you know, not one. Blust! the winter go an' the spring come on after an' they don't see buds an' they don't smell no breeze an' they don't see gals, an' when they see gals they don't know whatta do wi' 'em. They don't!

MRS BRYANT. Oh hell, they know *that* all right.

STAN. Gimme my young days an' I'd show 'em. Public demonstrations I'd give!

MRS BRYANT. Oh shut you up Stan Mann.

STAN. Just gimme young days again Daphne Bryant an' I'd mount you. (*Pause.*) But they 'ont come again will they gal?

MRS BRYANT. That they 'ont. My ole days working in the fields with them other gals, thems 'ont come again, either.

STAN. No, they 'ont that! Rum ole things the years ent they? (*Pause.*) Them young 'uns is all right though. Long as they don't let no one fool them, long as they think it out theirselves. (*Sneezes and coughs.*)

MRS BRYANT (*moving to help him up*). Now get you back home Stan Mann. (*Good-naturedly.*) Blust, I aren't hevin' no dead 'uns on me look. Take a rum bor, take a rum an' a drop o' hot milk and get to bed. What's Mrs Mann thinking of lettin' you out like this.

> She pulls the coat round the old man and pushes him off. He goes off mumbling and she returns, also mumbling, to her peeling.

STAN. She's a good gal, she's right 'nough, she don't think I got it this bad. I'll pull this ole scarf round me. Hed this scarf a long time, hed it since I started wi' me cars. *She* bought it me. Lasted a long time. Shouldn't need it this weather though ... (*Exits.*)

MRS BRYANT (*mumbling same time as* STAN). Go on, off
you go. Silly ole bugger, runnin' round with a cold
like that. Don't know what 'e's doin' half the time.
Poor ole man. Cossie? Cossie? That you Cossie?
(*Looks through door into front room and out of window
at* STAN.) Poor ole man.

> *After peeling for some seconds she turns the radio on,
> turning the dial knob through all manner of stations
> and back again until she finds some very loud dance
> music which she leaves blaring on. Audible to us, but
> not to* MRS BRYANT, *is the call of* 'Yoo-hoo Mother,
> yoo-hoo'. BEATIE *appears round the garden and
> peers into the kitchen.* MRS BRYANT *jumps.*

MRS BRYANT. Blust, you made me jump.
BEATIE (*toning radio down*). Can't you hear it? Hello,
Mother. (*Kisses her.*)
MRS BRYANT. Well, you've arrived then.
BEATIE. Didn't you get my card?
MRS BRYANT. Came this morning.
BEATIE. Then you knew I'd arrive.
MRS BRYANT. 'Course I did.
BEATIE. My things come?
MRS BRYANT. One suitcase, one parcel in brown
paper –
BEATIE. My paintings.
MRS BRYANT. And one other case.
BEATIE. My pick-up. D'you see it?
MRS BRYANT. I hevn't touched a thing.
BEATIE. Bought myself a pick-up on the HP.
MRS BRYANT. Don't you go telling that to Pearl.
BEATIE. Why not?
MRS BRYANT. She'll wanna know why you didn't buy
off her on the club.
BEATIE. Well, hell, Mother, I weren't gonna hev an ole

pick-up sent me from up north somewhere when we lived next door to a gramophone shop.

MRS BRYANT. No. Well, what bus you come on – the half-past-ten one?

BEATIE. Yearp. Picked it up on the ole bridge near Jenny's.

MRS BRYANT. Well I looked for you on the half-past-nine bus and you weren't on that so I thought to myself I bet she come on the half-past-ten and you did. You see ole Stan Mann?

BEATIE. Was that him just going up the road?

MRS BRYANT. Wearin' an ole brown scarf, that was him.

BEATIE. I see him! Just as I were comin' off the bus. Blust! Jimmy Beales give him a real dowsin' down on his allotment 'cos he had an accident.

MRS BRYANT. What, another?

BEATIE. Yearp.

MRS BRYANT. Poor ole man. Thaas what give him that cold then. He come in here sneezin' fit to knock hisself down.

BEATIE. Poor ole bugger. Got any tea Ma? I'm gonna unpack.

> BEATIE *goes into front room with case. We see her take out frocks, which she puts on hangers, and underwear and blouses, which she puts on couch.*

MRS BRYANT. Did you see my flowers as you come in? Got some of my hollyhocks still flowering. Creeping up the wall they are – did you catch a glimpse on 'em? And my asters and geraniums? Poor ole Joe Simonds gimme those afore he died. Lovely geraniums they are.

BEATIE. Yearp.

MRS BRYANT. When's Ronnie coming?

BEATIE. Saturday week – an' Mother, I'm heving all the

family along to meet him when he arrive so you patch your rows wi' them.

MRS BRYANT. What you on about gal? What rows wi' them?

BEATIE. You know full well what rows I mean – them ones you hev wi' Pearl and Susan.

MRS BRYANT. 'Tent so likely. They hev a row wi' me gal but I give 'em no heed, that I don't. (*Hears van pass on road.*) There go Sam Martin's fish van. He'll be calling along here in an hour.

BEATIE (*entering with very smart dress*). Like it Mother?

MRS BRYANT. Blust gal, that's a good 'un ent it! Where d'you buy that then?

BEATIE. Swan and Edgar's.

MRS BRYANT. Did Ronnie choose it?

BEATIE. Yearp.

MRS BRYANT. He've got good taste then.

BEATIE. Yearp. Now listen Mother, I don't want any on you to let me down. When Ronnie come I want him to see we're proper. I'll buy you another bowl so's you don't wash up in the same one as you wash your hands in and I'll get some more tea cloths so's you 'ont use the towels. And no swearin'.

MRS BRYANT. Don't he swear then?

BEATIE. He swear all right, only I don't want him to hear *you* swear.

MRS BRYANT. Hev you given it up then?

BEATIE. Mother, I've never swore.

MRS BRYANT. Go to hell, listen to her!

BEATIE. I never did, now! Mother, I'm *telling* you, listen to me. Ronnie's the best thing I've ever had and I've tried hard for three years to keep hold of him. I don't care what you do when he's gone but don't show me up when he's here.

MRS BRYANT. Speak to your father gal.

BEATIE. Father too. I don't want Ronnie to think I

come from a small-minded family. 'I can't bear mean people,' he say. 'I don't care about their education, I don't care about their past as long as their minds are large and inquisitive, as long as they're generous.'

MRS BRYANT. Who say that?

BEATIE. Ronnie.

MRS BRYANT. He *talk* like that?

BEATIE. Yearp.

MRS BRYANT. Sounds like a preacher.

BEATIE (*standing on a chair*). 'I don't care if you call me a preacher, I've got something to say and I'm going to say it. I don't care if you don't like being told things – we've come to a time when you've got to say this is right and this is wrong. God in heaven, have we got to be wet all the time? Well, have we?' Christ, Mother, you've got them ole wasps still flying around. (*She waves her arms in the air flaying the wasps.*) September and you've still got wasps. Owee! shoo-shoo! (*In the voice of her childhood.*) Mammy, Mammy, take them ole things away. I doesn't like them – ohh! Nasty things.

> BEATIE *jumps off chair and picks up a coat-hanger. Now both she and her mother move stealthily around the room 'hunting' wasps. Occasionally* MRS BRYANT *strikes one dead or* BEATIE *spears one against the wall.* MRS BRYANT *conducts herself matter-of-fact-like but* BEATIE *makes a fiendish game of it.*

MRS BRYANT. They're after them apples on that tree outside. Go on! Off wi' you! Outside now! There – that's got 'em out, but I bet the buggers'll be back in a jiffy look.

BEATIE. Oh yes, an' I want to have a bath.

MRS BRYANT. When d'you want that then?

BEATIE. This morning.

MRS BRYANT. You can't hev no bath this morning, that copper won't heat up till after lunch.

BEATIE. Then I'll bake the pastries for Jenny this morning and you can put me water on now. (*She returns to sort her clothes.*)

MRS BRYANT. I'll do that now then. I'll get you the soft water from the tank.

> MRS BRYANT *now proceeds to collect bucket and move back and forth between the garden out of view and the copper in the kitchen. She fills the copper with about three buckets of water and then lights the fire underneath. In between buckets she chats.*

(*Off – as she hears lorry go by.*) There go Danny Oakley to market. (*She returns with first bucket.*)

BEATIE. Mother! I dreamt I died last night and heaven were at the bottom of a pond. You had to jump in and sink and you know how afeared I am of water. It was full of film stars and soldiers and there were two rooms. In one room they was playing skiffle and – and – I can't remember what were goin' on in the other. Now who was God? I can't remember. It was someone we knew, a she. (*Returns to unpacking.*)

MRS BRYANT (*entering with second bucket; automatically*). Yearp. (*Pause.*) You hear what happened to the headache doctor's patient? You know what they say about him – if you've got a headache you're all right but if you've got something more you've had it! Well he told a woman not to worry about a lump she complained of under her breast and you know what that were? That turned out to be thrombosis! There! Thrombosis! She had that breast off. Yes, she did. Had to hev it cut off. (*Goes for next bucket.*)

BEATIE (*automatically*). Yearp. (*She appears from front room with two framed paintings. She sets them up and admires them. They are primitive designs in bold masses,*

*rather well-balanced shapes and bright poster colours –
red, black, and yellow – see Dusty Wesker's work.*)
Mother! Did I write and tell you I've took up
painting? I started five months ago. Working in
gouache. Ronnie says I'm good. Says I should carry
on and maybe I can sell them for curtain designs.
'Paint girl,' he say. 'Paint! The world is full of people
who don't do the things they want so you paint and
give us all hope!'

MRS BRYANT *enters.*

BEATIE. Like 'em?

MRS BRYANT (*looks at them a second*). Good colours ent
they. (*She is unmoved and continues to empty a third
bucket while* BEATIE *returns paintings to other room.*)
Yes gal, I ent got no row wi' Pearl but I ask her to
change my Labour Tote man 'cos I wanted to give
the commission to Charlie Gorleston and she didn't
do it. Well, if she can be like that I can be like that
too. You gonna do some baking you say?

BEATIE (*enters from front room putting on a pinafore and
carrying a parcel*). Right now. Here y'are Daphne
Bryant, present for you. I want eggs, flour, sugar, and
marg. I'm gonna bake a sponge and give it frilling.
(*Goes to larder to collect things.*)

MRS BRYANT (*unpacking parcel; it is a pinafore*). We both
got one now.

> MRS BRYANT *continues to peel potatoes as* BEATIE
> *proceeds to separate four eggs, the yolks of which she
> starts whipping with sugar. She sings meanwhile a
> ringing folk song.*

BEATIE.
> Oh a dialogue I'll sing you as true as me life.
> Between a coal owner and a poor pitman's wife
> As she was a-walking along the highway
> She met a coal owner and to him did say

Derry down, down, down Derry down.

'Whip the eggs till they're light yellow,' he say.

MRS BRYANT. Who say?

BEATIE. Ronnie.

> Good morning Lord Firedamp the good woman
> said
> I'll do you no harm sir so don't be afraid
> If you'd been where I'd been for most of my life
> You wouldn't turn pale at a poor pitman's wife
> Singing down, down, down Derry down.

MRS BRYANT. What song's that?

BEATIE. A coalmining song.

MRS BRYANT. I tell you what I reckon's a good song, that 'I'll wait for you in the heavens blue'. I reckon that's a lovely song I do. Jimmy Samson he sing that.

BEATIE. It's like twenty other songs, it don't mean anything and it's sloshy and sickly.

MRS BRYANT. Yes, I reckon that's a good song that.

BEATIE (*suddenly*). Listen Mother, let me see if I can explain something to you. Ronnie always say that's the point of knowing people. 'It's no good having friends who scratch each other's back,' he say. 'The excitement in knowing people is to hand on what you know and to learn what you don't know. Learn from me,' he say, 'I don't know much but learn what I know.' So let me try and explain to you what he explain to me.

MRS BRYANT (*on hearing a bus*). There go the half-past-eleven bus to Diss – blust that's early. (*Puts spuds in saucepan on oven and goes to collect runner beans, which she prepares.*)

BEATIE. Mother, I'm *talking* to you. Blust woman it's not often we get together and really talk, it's nearly always me listening to you telling who's dead. Just listen a second.

MRS BRYANT. Well go on gal, but you always take so long to say it.

BEATIE. What are the words of that song?

MRS BRYANT. I don't know all the words.

BEATIE. I'll tell you. (*Recites them.*)

> I'll wait for you in the heavens blue
> As my arms are waiting now.
> Please come to me and I'll be true
> My love shall not turn sour.
> I hunger, I hunger, I cannot wait longer,
> My love shall not turn sour.

There! Now what do that mean?

MRS BRYANT (*surprised*). Well, don't you know what that mean?

BEATIE. I mean what do they do to you? How do the words affect you? Are you moved? Do you find them beautiful?

MRS BRYANT. Them's as good words as any.

BEATIE. But do they make you feel better?

MRS BRYANT. Blust gal! That ent meant to be a laxative!

BEATIE. I must be mad to talk with you.

MRS BRYANT. Besides it's the tune I like. Words never mean anything.

BEATIE. All right, the tune then! What does *that* do to you? Make your belly go gooey, your heart throb, make your head spin with passion? Yes, passion, Mother, know what it is? Because you won't find passion in that third-rate song, no you won't!

MRS BRYANT. Well all right gal, so it's third-rate you say. Can you say why? What make that third-rate and them frilly bits of opera and concert first-rate? 'Sides, did I write that song? Beatie Bryant, you do go up and down in your spirits, and I don't know what's gotten into you gal, no I don't.

BEATIE. I don't know either, Mother. I'm worried about

Ronnie I suppose. I have that same row with him. I
ask him exactly the same questions – what make. a
pop song third-rate. And he answer and I don't know
what he talk about. Something about registers,
something about commercial world blunting our
responses. 'Give yourself time woman,' he say.
'Time! You can't learn how to live overnight. *I* don't
even know,' he say, 'and half the world don't know
but we got to try. Try,' he says, ''cos we're still
suffering from the shock of two world wars and we
don't know it. Talk,' he say, 'and look and listen and
think and ask questions.' But Jesus! I don't know
what questions to ask or *how* to talk. And he gets so
riled – and yet sometimes so nice. 'It's all going up in
flames,' he say, 'but I'm going to make bloody sure I
save someone from the fire.'

MRS BRYANT. Well I'm sure *I* don't know what he's on
about. Turn to your baking gal look and get you
done, Father'll be home for his lunch in an hour.

> *A faint sound of an ambulance is heard.* MRS
> BRYANT *looks up but says nothing.* BEATIE *turns to
> whipping the eggs again and* MRS BRYANT *to cleaning
> up the runner beans. Out of this pause* MRS BRYANT
> *begins to sing 'I'll wait for you in the heavens blue',
> but on the second line she hums the tune incorrectly.*

BEATIE (*laughs*). No, no, hell Mother, it don't go like
that. It's –

> BEATIE *corrects her and in helping her mother she ends
> by singing the song, with some enthusiasm, to the end.*

MRS BRYANT. Thank God you come home sometimes
gal – you do bring a little life with you anyway.

BEATIE. Mother, I ent never heard you express a feeling
like that.

MRS BRYANT (*she is embarrassed*). The world don't want

no feelings gal. (*Footsteps are heard.*) Is that your father home already?

> MR BRYANT *appears at the back door and lays a bicycle against the wall. He is a small shrivelled man wearing denims, a peaked cap, boots, and gaiters. He appears to be in some pain.*

BEATIE. Hello poppy Bryant.

MR BRYANT. Hello Beatie. You're here then.

MRS BRYANT. What are you home so early for?

MR BRYANT. The ole guts ache again. (*Sits in armchair and grimaces.*)

MRS BRYANT. Well, what is it?

MR BRYANT. Blust woman, I don't know what 'tis n'more'n you, do I?

MRS BRYANT. Go to the doctor man I keep telling you.

BEATIE. What is it father Bryant?

MRS BRYANT. He got guts ache.

BEATIE. But what's it from?

MR BRYANT. I've just said I don't know.

MRS BRYANT. Get you to a doctor man, don't be so soft. You don't want to be kept from work do you?

MR BRYANT. That I don't, no I don't. Hell, I just see ole Stan Mann picked up an' thaas upset me enough.

MRS BRYANT. Picked up you say?

MR BRYANT. Well, didn't you hear the ambulance?

MRS BRYANT. There! I hear it but I didn't say narthin'. Was that for Stan Mann then?

MR BRYANT. I was cycling along wi' Jack Stones and we see this here figure on the side o' the road there an' I say, thaas a rum shape in the road Jack, and he say, blust, that's ole Stan Mann from Heybrid, an' 'twere. 'Course soon ever he see what 'twere, he rushed off for 'n ambulance and I waited alongside Stan.

BEATIE. But he just left here.

MRS BRYANT. I see it comin'. He come in here an' I

shoved him off home. Get you to bed and take some rum an' a drop o' hot milk, I tell him.

BEATIE. Is he gonna die?

MR BRYANT. Wouldn't surprise me that it wouldn't. Blust, he look done in.

MRS BRYANT. Poor ole fellah. Shame though ent it?

MR BRYANT. When d'you arrive Beatie?

MRS BRYANT. She come on the half-past-ten bus. I looked for her on the nine-thirty bus and she weren't on that, so I thought to myself I bet she come on the half-past-ten. She did.

MR BRYANT. Yearp.

MRS BRYANT. You gonna stay away all day?

MR BRYANT. No I aren't. I gotta go back 'cos one of the ole sows is piggin'. 'Spect she'll be hevin' them in a couple of hours. (*To* BEATIE.) Got a sow had a litter o' twenty-two. (*Picks up paper to read.*)

BEATIE. Twenty-two? Oh Pop, can I come see this afternoon?

MR BRYANT. Yearp.

MRS BRYANT. Thought you was hevin' a bath.

BEATIE. Oh yes, I forgot. I'll come tomorrow then.

MR BRYANT. They'll be there. What you doin' gal?

MRS BRYANT. She's baking a sponge, now leave her be.

MR BRYANT. Oh, you learnt something in London then.

BEATIE. Ronnie taught me.

MR BRYANT. Well where *is* Ronnie then?

MRS BRYANT. He's comin' on Saturday a week an' the family's goin' to be here to greet him.

MR BRYANT. All on 'em?

MRS BRYANT *and* BEATIE. All on 'em!

MR BRYANT. Well that'll be a rum gatherin' then.

MRS BRYANT. And we've to be on our best behaviour.

MR BRYANT. No cussin' and swearin'?

MRS BRYANT *and* BEATIE. No.

MR BRYANT. Blust, I shan't talk then.

A young man, MR HEALEY, *appears round the garden – he is the farmer's son, and manager of the estate* BRYANT *works for.*

MRS BRYANT (*seeing him first*). Oh, Mr Healey, yes. Jack! It's Mr Healey.

MR BRYANT *rises and goes to the door.* HEALEY *speaks in a firm, not unkind, but business-is-business voice. There is that apologetic threat even in his politeness.*

MR HEALEY. You were taken ill.

MR BRYANT. It's all right, sir, only guts ache, won't be long goin'. The pigs is all seen to, just waiting for the ole sow to start.

MR HEALEY. What time you expecting it?

MR BRYANT. Oh, she 'ont come afore two this afternoon, no she 'ont be much afore that.

MR HEALEY. You're sure you're well, Jack? I've been thinking that it's too much for you carting those pails round the yard.

MR BRYANT. No, that ent too heavy, sir, 'course 'tent. You don't wanna worry, I'll be along after lunch. Just an ole guts ache that's all – seein' the doctor tonight – eat too fast probably.

MR HEALEY. If you're sure you're all right, then I'll put young Daniels off. You can manage without him now we've fixed the new pump in.

MR BRYANT. I can manage, sir – 'course I can.

MR HEALEY (*moving off outside*). All right then, Jack, I'll be with you around two o'clock. I want to take the old one out of number three and stick her with the others in seventeen. The little ones won't need her, will they? Then we'll have them sorted out tomorrow.

MR BRYANT. That's right, sir, they *can* go on their own now, they can. I'll see to it tomorrow.

MR HEALEY. Right then, Jack. Oh – you hear Stan
Mann died?

MR BRYANT. He died already? But I saw him off in the
ambulance no more'n half-hour ago.

MR HEALEY. Died on the way to hospital. Jack Stones
told me. Lived in Heybrid, didn't he?

MR BRYANT. Alongside my daughter.

MR HEALEY (*calling*). Well, good morning, Mrs Bryant.

MRS BRYANT (*calling*). Good morning, Mr Healey.

> *The two men nod to each other,* MR HEALEY *goes off.*
> MR BRYANT *lingers a second.*

MRS BRYANT (*to* BEATIE). That was Mr Healey, the new
young manager.

BEATIE. I know it Mother.

MR BRYANT (*returning slowly*). He's dead then.

MRS BRYANT. Who? Not Stan Mann!

MR BRYANT. Young Healey just tell me.

MRS BRYANT. Well I go t'hell. An' he were just here
look, just here alongside o' me not more'n hour past.

MR BRYANT. Rum ent it?

BEATIE (*weakly*). Oh hell, I hate dying.

MRS BRYANT. He were a good ole bor though. Yes he
was. A good ole stick. There!

BEATIE. Used to ride me round on his horse, always full
o' life an' jokes. 'Tell your boy he wanna hurry up
and marry you,' he say to me, 'or I'll hev you meself
on a plate.'

MRS BRYANT. He were a one for smut though.

BEATIE. I was talkin' with him last night. Only last night
he was tellin' me how he caught me pinchin' some
gooseberries off his patch an' how he gimme a whole
apron full and I went into one o' his fields near by an'
ate the lot. 'Blust,' he say, 'you had the ole guts
ache,' an' he laugh, sat there laughin' away to hisself.

MRS BRYANT. I can remember that. Hell, Jenny'll miss him – used always to pop in an' out o' theirs.

BEATIE. Seem like the whole world gone suddenly dead don' it?

MR BRYANT. Rum ent it?

Silence.

MRS BRYANT. *He's* a nice man Mr Healey is, yes he is, a good sort, I like him.

BEATIE. Don't know about being nice. Sounds to me like he were threatening to sack Father.

MR BRYANT. That's what I say see, get a rise and they start cutting down the men or the overtime.

MRS BRYANT. The Union magazine's come.

MR BRYANT. I don't want that ole thing.

BEATIE. Why can't you do something to stop the sackings?

MR BRYANT. You can't, you can't – that's what I say, you can't. Sharp as a pig's scream they are – you just *can't* do nothin'.

BEATIE. Mother, where's the bakin' tin?

MR BRYANT. When we gonna eat that?

BEATIE. You ent! It's for Jenny Beales.

MR BRYANT. You aren't making that for Jenny are you?

BEATIE. I promised her.

MR BRYANT. Not with my electricity you aren't.

BEATIE. But I promised, Poppy.

MR BRYANT. That's no matters. I aren't spendin' money on electricity bills so's you can make every Tom, Dick 'n' Harry a sponge cake, that I aren't.

MRS BRYANT. Well, don't be so soft man, it won't take more'n half-hour's bakin'.

MR BRYANT. I don't care what it'll take I say. I aren't lettin' her. Jenny wants cakes, she can make 'em herself. So put that away Beatie and use it for something else.

MRS BRYANT. You wanna watch what you're sayin' of 'cos I live here too.

MR BRYANT. I know all about that but I pay the electricity bill and I says she isn't bakin'.

BEATIE. But Poppy, one cake.

MR BRYANT. No I say.

BEATIE. Well, Mummy, do something – how can he be so mean.

MRS BRYANT. Blust me if you ent the meanest ole sod that walks this earth. Your own daughter and you won't let her use your oven. You bloody ole hyper-crite.

MR BRYANT. You pay the bills and then you call names.

MRS BRYANT. What I ever seen in you God only knows. Yes! an' he never warn me. Bloody ole hypercrite!

MR BRYANT. You pay the bills and then you call names I say.

MRS BRYANT. On four pounds ten a week? You want me to keep you *and* pay bills? Four pound ten he give me. God knows what he do wi' the rest. I don't know how much he've got. I don't, no I don't. Bloody ole hypercrite.

MR BRYANT. Let's hev grub and not so much o' the lip woman.

> BEATIE *begins to put the things away. She is on the verge of the tears she will soon let fall.*

MRS BRYANT. That's how he talk to me – when he do talk. 'Cos you know he don't ever talk more'n he hev to, and when he do say something it's either 'how much this cost' or 'lend us couple o' bob'. He've got the money but sooner than break into that he borrow off me. Bloody old miser. (*To* BEATIE.) What you wanna cry for gal? 'Tent worth it. Blust, you don't wanna let an ole hypercrite like him upset you, no

you don't. I'll get my back on you my manny, see if I
don't. You won't get away with no tricks on me.

BEATIE *has gone into the other room and returned
with a small packet.*

BEATIE (*throwing parcel in father's lap*). Present for you.
MRS BRYANT. I'd give him presents that I would! I'd
walk out and disown him! Beatie, now stop you a-
cryin' gal – blust, he ent worth cryin' for, that he ent.
Stop it I say and we'll have lunch. Or you lost your
appetite gal?

BEATIE *sniffs a few tears back, pauses, and –*

BEATIE. No – no, that I ent. Hell, I can eat all right!

Curtain.

SCENE TWO

Lunch has been eaten. MR BRYANT *is sitting at the table
rolling himself a cigarette.* MRS BRYANT *is collecting the
dishes and taking them to a sink to wash up.* BEATIE *is
taking things off the table and putting them into the larder –
jars of sauce, plates of sliced bread and cakes, butter, sugar,
condiments, and bowl of tinned fruit.*

MRS BRYANT (*to* BEATIE). Ask him what he want for his
tea.
MR BRYANT. She don't ever ask me before, what she
wanna ask me now for?
MRS BRYANT. Tell him it's his stomach I'm thinking
about – I don't want him complaining to me about
the food I cook.
MR BRYANT. Tell her it's no matters to me – I ent got no
pain now besides.
BEATIE. Mother, is that water ready for my bath?

MRS BRYANT. Where you hevin' it?

BEATIE. In the kitchen of course.

MRS BRYANT. Blust gal, you can't bath in this kitchen during the day, what if someone call at the door?

BEATIE. Put up the curtain then, I shan't be no more'n ten minutes.

MR BRYANT. 'Sides, who wants to see her in her dickey suit.

BEATIE. I know men as 'ould pay to see me in my dickey suit. (*Posing her plump outline.*) Don't you think I got a nice dickey suit?

> MR BRYANT *makes a dive and pinches her bottom.*

Ow! Stoppit Bryants, stoppit!

> *He persists.*

Daddy, stop it now!

MRS BRYANT. Tell him he can go as soon as he like, I want your bath over and done with.

BEATIE. Oh Mother, stop this nonsense do. If you want to tell him something tell him – not me.

MRS BRYANT. *I* don't want to speak to him, hell if I do.

BEATIE. Father, get the bath in for me please. Mother, where's them curtains.

> MR BRYANT *goes off to fetch a long tin bath – wide at one end, narrow at the other – while* MRS BRYANT *leaves washing-up to fish out some curtains which she hangs from one wall to another concealing thus a corner of the kitchen. Anything that is in the way is removed.* BEATIE *meanwhile brings out a change of underwear, her dressing-gown, the new frock, some soap, powder, and towel. These she lays within easy reach of the curtain.*

I'm gonna wear my new dress and go across the fields to see Frankie and Pearl.

MRS BRYANT. Frankie won't be there, what you on about? He'll be gettin' the harvest in.

BEATIE. You makin' anything for the harvest festival?

MR BRYANT (*entering with bath, places it behind curtain*). Your mother don't ever do anything for the harvest festival – don't you know that by now.

BEATIE. Get you to work father Bryant, I'm gonna plunge in water and I'll make a splash.

MRS BRYANT. Tell him we've got kippers for tea and if he don' want none let him say now.

BEATIE. She says it's kippers for tea.

MR BRYANT. Tell her I'll eat kippers. (*Goes off, collecting bike on the way.*)

BEATIE. He says he'll eat kippers. Right now, Mother, you get cold water an' I'll pour the hot.

> *Each now picks up a bucket.* MRS BRYANT *goes off out to collect the cold water and* BEATIE *plunges bucket into boiler to retrieve hot water. The bath is prepared with much childlike glee.* BEATIE *loves her creature comforts and does with unabashed, almost animal, enthusiasm that which she enjoys. When the bath is prepared,* BEATIE *slips behind the curtain to undress and enter.*

MRS BRYANT. You hear about Jimmy Skelton? They say he've bin arrested for accosting some man in the village.

BEATIE. Jimmy Skelton what own the pub?

MRS BRYANT. That's him. I know all about Jimmy Skelton though. He were a young boy when I were a young girl. I always partner him at whist drives. He's been to law before you know. Yes! An' he won the day too! Won the day he did. I don't take notice though, him and me gets on all right. What do Ronnie's mother do with her time?

BEATIE. She've got a sick husband to look after.

MRS BRYANT. She an educated woman?

BEATIE. Educated? No. She's a foreigner. Nor ent
  Ronnie educated neither. He's an intellectual, failed
  all his exams. They read and things.

MRS BRYANT. Oh, they don't do nothing then?

BEATIE. Do nothing? I'll tell you what Ronnie do, he
  work till all hours in a hot ole kitchen. An' he teach
  kids in a club to act and jive and such. And he don't
  stop at weekends either 'cos then there's political
  meetings and such and I get breathless trying to keep
  up wi' him. OOOhh, Mother it's hot . . .

MRS BRYANT. I'll get you some cold then.

BEATIE. No – ooh – it's lovely. The water's so soft
  Mother.

MRS BRYANT. Yearp.

BEATIE. It's so soft and smooth. I'm in.

MRS BRYANT. Don't you stay in too long gal. There go
  the twenty-minutes-past-one bus.

BEATIE. Oh Mother, me bath cubes. I forgot me bath
  cubes. In the little case by me pick-up.

> MRS BRYANT *finds bath cubes and hands them to*
> BEATIE.

MRS BRYANT (*continuing her work*). I shall never forget
  when I furse heard on it. I was in the village and I
  was talking to Reggie Fowler. I say to him, there've
  bin a lot o' talk about Jimmy ent there? Disgustin', I
  say. Still, there's somebody wanna make some easy
  money, you'd expect that in a village wouldn't you?
  Yes, I say to him, a lot of talk. An' he stood there, an'
  he were a-lookin' at me an' a-lookin' as I were a-
  talkin' and then he say, missus, he say, I were one o'
  the victims! Well, you could've hit me over the head
  wi' a hammer. I was one o' the victims, he say.

BEATIE. Mother, these bath cubes smell beautiful. I
  could stay here all day.

MRS BRYANT. Still, Jimmy's a good fellow with it all –
do anything for you. I partner him at whist drives; he
bin had up scores o' times though.

BEATIE. Mother, what we gonna make Ronnie when he
come?

MRS BRYANT. Well, what do he like?

BEATIE. He like trifle and he like steak and kidney pie.

MRS BRYANT. We'll make that then. So long as he don't
complain o' the guts ache. Frankie hev it too you
know.

BEATIE. Know why? You all eat too much. The
Londoners think we live a healthy life but they don't
know we stuff ourselves silly till our guts ache.

MRS BRYANT. But you know what's wrong wi' Jimmy
Beales? It's indigestion. He eat too fast.

BEATIE. What the hell's indigestion doin' a'tween his
shoulder-blades?

MRS BRYANT. 'Cos some people get it so bad it go right
through their stomach to the back.

BEATIE. You don't get indigestion in the back, Mother,
what you on about?

MRS BRYANT. Don't you tell me gal, I hed it!

BEATIE. Owee! The soap's in me eyes – Mother, towel,
the towel, quickly the towel!

> MRS BRYANT *hands in towel to* BEATIE. *The washing-up is probably done by now, so* MRS BRYANT *sits in a chair, legs apart and arms folded, thinking what else to say.*

MRS BRYANT. You heard that Ma Buckley hev been
taken to Mental Hospital in Norwich? Poor ole dear.
If there's one thing I can't abide that's mental cases.
They frighten me – they do. Can't face 'em. I'd
sooner follow a man to a churchyard than the mental
hospital. That's a terrible thing to see a person lose
their reason – that 'tis. Well, I tell you what, down

where I used to live, down the other side of the Hall,
years ago we moved in next to an old woman. I only
had Jenny and Frank then – an' this woman she were
the sweetest of people. We used to talk and do
errands for each other – Oh she was a sweet ole dear.
And then one afternoon I was going out to get my
washin' in and I saw her. She was standin' in a tub o'
water up to her neck. She was! Up to her neck. An'
her eyes had that glazed, wonderin' look and she
stared straight at me she did. Straight at me. Well, do
you know what? I was struck *dumb*. I was *struck*
dumb wi' shock. What wi' her bein' so nice all this
while, the sudden comin' on her like that in the tub
fair upset me. It did! And people tell me afterwards
that she's bin goin' in an' out o'hospital for years.
Blust, that scare me. That scare me so much she
nearly took me round the bend wi' her.

> BEATIE *appears from behind the curtain in her
> dressing-gown, a towel round her head.*

BEATIE. There! I'm gonna hev a bath every day when
I'm married.

> BEATIE *starts rubbing her hair with towel and fiddles
> with radio. She finds a programme playing Mendel-
> ssohn's Fourth Symphony, the slow movement, and
> stands before the mirror, listening and rubbing.*

(*Looking at her reflection.*) Isn't your nose a funny
thing, and your ears. And your arms and your legs,
aren't they funny things – sticking out of a lump.
MRS BRYANT (*switching off radio*). Turn that squit off!
BEATIE (*turning on her mother violently*). *Mother!* I could
kill you when you do that. No wonder I don't know
anything about anything. I never heard nothing but
dance music because you always turned off the
classics. I never knowed anything about the news

because you always switched off after the headlines. I
never read any good books 'cos there was never any
in the house.

MRS BRYANT. What's gotten into you now gal?

BEATIE. God in heaven Mother, you live in the country
but you got no – no – no majesty. You spend your
time among green fields, you grow flowers and you
breathe fresh air and you got no majesty. Your
mind's cluttered up with nothing and you shut out
the world. What kind of a life did you give me?

MRS BRYANT. Blust gal, I weren't no teacher.

BEATIE. But you hindered. You didn't open one door
for me. Even his mother cared more for me than
what you did. Beatie, she say, Beatie, why don't you
take up evening classes and learn something other
than waitressing. Yes, she say, you won't ever regret
learnin' things. But did you care what job I took up
or whether I learned things? You didn't even think it
was necessary.

MRS BRYANT. I fed you. I clothed you. I took you out to
the sea. What more d'you want. We're only country
folk you know. We ent got no big things here you
know.

BEATIE. Squit! Squit! It makes no difference country or
town. *All* the town girls I ever worked with were just
like me. It makes no difference country or town –
that's squit. Do you know when I used to work at the
holiday camp and I sat down with the other girls to
write a letter we used to sit and discuss what we
wrote about. An' we all agreed, all on us, that we
started: 'Just a few lines to let you know', and then
we get on to the weather and then we get stuck so we
write about each other and after a page an' half of big
scrawl end up: 'Hoping this finds you as well as it
leaves me.' There! We couldn't say any more.
Thousands of things happening at this holiday camp

and we couldn't find words for them. All of us the same. Hundreds of girls and one day we're gonna be mothers, and you *still* talk to me of Jimmy Skelton and the ole woman in the tub. Do you know I've heard that story a dozen times. A dozen times. Can't you hear yourself Mother? Jesus, how can I bring Ronnie to this house.

MRS BRYANT. Blust gal, if Ronnie don't like us then he –

BEATIE. Oh, he'll like you all right. He like people. He'd've loved ole Stan Mann. Ole Stan Mann would've understood everything Ronnie talk about. Blust! That man liked livin'. Besides, Ronnie say it's too late for the old 'uns to learn. But he says it's up to us young 'uns. And them of us that know hev got to teach them of us as don't know.

MRS BRYANT. I bet he hev a hard time trying to change you gal!

BEATIE. He's *not* trying to change me Mother. You can't change people, he say, you can only give them some love and hope they'll take it. And he's tryin' to teach me and I'm tryin' to understand – do you see that Mother?

MRS BRYANT. I don't see what that's got to do with music though.

BEATIE. Oh my God! (*Suddenly.*) I'll show you. (*Goes off to front room to collect pick-up and a record.*) Now sit you down gal and I'll show you. Don't start ironing or reading or nothing, just sit there and be prepared to learn something. (*Appears with pick-up and switches on.*) You aren't too old, just you sit and listen. That's the trouble you see, we ent ever prepared to learn anything, we close our minds the minute anything unfamiliar appear. *I* could never listen to music. I used to like some on it but then I'd lose patience, I'd go to bed in the middle of a symphony, or my mind would wander 'cos the music didn't mean anything

to me so I'd go to bed or start talking. 'Sit back
woman,' he'd say, 'listen to it. Let it happen to you
and you'll grow as big as the music itself.'

MRS BRYANT. Blust he talk like a book.

BEATIE. An' sometimes he talk as though you didn't
know where the moon or the stars was. (BEATIE *puts
on record of Bizet's* L'Arlésienne *Suite.*) Now listen.
This is a simple piece of music, it's not highbrow, but
it's full of living. And that's what he say socialism is.
'Christ,' he say. 'Socialism isn't talking all the time,
it's living, it's singing, it's dancing, it's being interested in what go on around you, it's being concerned
about people and the world.' Listen Mother. (*She
becomes breathless and excited.*) Listen to it. It's simple
isn't it? Can you call that squit?

MRS BRYANT. I don't say it's all squit.

BEATIE. You don't have to frown because it's alive.

MRS BRYANT. No, not all on it's squit.

BEATIE. See the way the other tune comes in? Hear it?
Two simple tunes, one after the other.

MRS BRYANT. I aren't saying it's all squit.

BEATIE. And now listen, listen, it goes together, the two
tunes together, they knit, they're perfect. Don't it
make you want to dance? (*She begins to dance a
mixture of a cossack dance and a sailor's hornpipe.*)

*The music becomes fast and her spirits are young and
high.*

Listen to that Mother. Is it difficult? Is it squit? It's
light. It make me feel light and confident and happy.
God, Mother, we could all be so much more happy
and alive. Wheeeee . . .

BEATIE *claps her hands and dances on and her mother
smiles and claps her hands and –*

The curtain falls.

ACT THREE

Two weeks have passed. It is Saturday, the day Ronnie is to arrive. One of the walls of the kitchen is now pushed aside and the front room is revealed. It is low-ceilinged, and has dark brown wooden beams. The furniture is not typical country-farmhouse type. There may be one or two windsor-type straight-back chairs, but for the rest it is cheap utility stuff. Two armchairs, a table, a small bamboo table, wooden chairs, a small sofa, and a swivel bookcase. There are a lot of flowers around – in pots on the window ledge and in vases on the bamboo table and swivel case.

It is three in the afternoon, the weather is cloudy – it has been raining and is likely to start again. On the table is a spread of food (none of this will be eaten). There are cakes and biscuits on plates and glass stands. Bread and butter, butter in a dish, tomatoes, cheese, jars of pickled onions, sausage rolls, dishes of tinned fruit – it is a spread! Round the table are eight chairs. BEATIE's paintings are hanging on the wall. The room is empty because BEATIE is upstairs changing and MRS BRYANT is in the kitchen. BEATIE – until she descends – conducts all her conversation from upstairs.

BEATIE. Mother! What you on at now?

MRS BRYANT (*from kitchen*). I'm just puttin' these glass cherries on the trifle.

BEATIE. Well come on look, he'll be here at four thirty.

MRS BRYANT (*from kitchen*). Don't you fret gal, it's another hour 'n' half yet, the postman hevn't gone by. (*Enters with an enormous bowl of trifle.*) There! He like trifle you say?

BEATIE. He love it.

MRS BRYANT. Well he need to 'cos there's plenty on it.

(*To herself, surveying the table.*) Yes, there is, there's plenty on it. (*It starts to rain.*) Blust, listen to that weather.

BEATIE. Rainin' again!

MRS BRYANT (*looking out of window*). Raining? It's rainin' fit to drowned you. (*Sound of bus.*) There go the three-o'clock.

BEATIE. Mother get you changed, come on, I want us ready in time.

MRS BRYANT. Blust you'd think it were the bloody Prince of Egypt comin'. (*Goes upstairs.*)

> *The stage is empty again for a few seconds. People are heard taking off their macs and exclaiming at the weather from the kitchen. Enter* FRANK *and* PEARL BRYANT. *He is pleasant and dressed in a blue pin-striped suit, is ruddy-faced and blond-haired. An odd sort of shyness makes him treat everything as a joke. His wife is a pretty brunette, young, and ordinarily dressed in plain, flowered frock.*

FRANK (*calling*). Well, where are you all? Come on – I'm hungry.

PEARL. Shut you up bor, you only just had lunch.

FRANK. Well I'm hungry again. (*Calling.*) Well, where is this article we come to see?

BEATIE. He ent arrived.

FRANK. Well, he want to hurry, 'cos I'm hungry.

BEATIE. You're always hungry.

FRANK. What do you say he is – a strong socialist?

BEATIE. Yes.

FRANK. And a Jew boy?

BEATIE. Yes.

FRANK (*to himself*). Well, that's a queer mixture then.

PEARL (*calling*). I hope he don't talk politics all the time.

FRANK. Have you had a letter from him yet?

PEARL. Stop it Frank, you know she hevn't heard.

FRANK. Well that's a rum boy friend what don't write. (*Looks at paintings, pauses before one of them and growls.*)

PEARL. Watch out or it'll bite you back.

> BEATIE *comes down from upstairs. She is dressed in her new frock and looks happy, healthy, and radiant.*

FRANK. Hail there, sister! I was then contemplating your masterpiece.

BEATIE. Well don't contemplate too long 'cos you aren't hevin' it.

FRANK. Blust! I'd set my ole heart on it.

PEARL. That's a nice frock Beatie.

FRANK. Where's the rest of our mighty clan?

BEATIE. Jenny and Jimmy should be here soon and Susie and Stan mightn't come.

FRANK. What's wrong wi' them?

BEATIE. Don't talk to me about it 'cos I hed enough! Susie won't talk to Mother.

PEARL. That make nearly eighteen months she hevn't spoke.

BEATIE. Why ever did *you* and Mother fall out Pearl?

FRANK. 'Cos Mother's so bloody stubborn that's why.

PEARL. Because one day she said she wanted to change her Labour Tote man, that's why, and she asked me to do it for her. So I said all right, but it'll take a couple of weeks; and then she get riled because she said I didn't want to change it for her. And then I ask her why didn't she change him herself and she say because she was too ill to go all the way to see John Clayton to tell him, and then she say to me, why, don't you think I'm ill? And I say – I know this were tactless o' me – but I say, no Mother, you don't look ill to me. And she didn't speak to me since. I only hope she don't snub me this afternoon.

BEATIE. Well, she tell me a different story.

FRANK. Mother's always quarrelling.

PEARL. Well I reckon there ent much else she *can* do stuck in this ole house on her own all day. And father Bryant he don't say too much when he's home you know.

FRANK. Well blust, she hevn't spoke to her own mother for three years, not since Granny Dykes took Jenny in when she had that illegitimate gal Daphne.

BEATIE. Hell! What a bloody family!

FRANK. A mighty clan I say.

JIMMY *and* JENNY BEALES *now enter.*

JENNY. Hello Frankie, hello Pearl, hello Beatie.

FRANK. And more of the mighty clan.

JENNY. Mighty clan you say? Mighty bloody daft you mean. Well, where is he?

FRANK. The mysterious stranger has not yet come – we await.

JENNY. Well, I aren't waitin' long 'cos I'm hungry.

PEARL. That's all this family of Bryants ever do is think o' their guts.

FRANK (*to* JIMMY). Have you formed your association yit?

JENNY. What association is this?

FRANK. What! Hevn't he told you?

JIMMY. Shut you up Frank Bryant or you'll get me hung.

FRANK. Oh, a mighty association – a mighty one! I'll tell ye. One day you see we was all sittin' round in the pub – Jimmy, me, Starkie, Johnny Oats, and Bonky Dawson – we'd hed a few drinks and Jimmy was feelin' – well, he was feelin' – you know what, the itch! He hed the itch! He started complaining about ham, ham, ham all the time. So then Bonky Dawson say, blust, he say, there must be women about who feel the same. And Starkie he say, well 'course they are, only how do you tell? And then we was all quiet a while thinkin' on it when suddenly Jimmy says, we ought to start an association of them as need a bit now and then and we all ought to wear a badge he say, and when you see a woman wearin' a badge you know she need a bit too.

JIMMY. Now that's enough Frank or I'll hit you over the skull.

FRANK. Now, not content wi' just that, ole Jimmy then say, and we ought to have a password to indicate how bad off you are. So listen what he suggest. He suggest you go up to any one o' these women what's wearin' a badge and you say, how many lumps of sugar do you take in your tea? And if she say 'two' then you know she ent too badly off, but she's willin'. But if she say 'four' then you know she's in a bad a state as what you are, see?

Long pause.

JENNY. He'd hev a fit if she said she took sixteen lumps though wouldn't he?

Pause.

PEARL. Where's mother Bryant?

BEATIE. Uptairs changin'.

PEARL. Where's father Bryant?

BEATIE. Tendin' the pigs.

FRANK. You're lucky to hev my presence you know.

BEATIE. Oh?

FRANK. A little more sun and I'd've bin gettin' in the harvest.

PEARL. Well, what did you think of that storm last night? All that thunder 'n' lightnin' and it didn't stop once.

BEATIE. Ronnie love it you know. He sit and watch it for bloody hours.

FRANK. He's a queer article then.

JENNY. He do sound a rum 'un don't he?

BEATIE. Well you'll soon see.

JIMMY. Hev he got any sisters?

BEATIE. One married and she live not far from here.

PEARL. She live in the country? A town girl? Whatever for?

BEATIE. Her husband make furniture by hand.

PEARL. Can't he do that in London?

BEATIE. Ronnie say they think London's an inhuman place.

JIMMY. So 'tis, so 'tis.

BEATIE. Here come father Bryant.

> MR BRYANT *enters. He is in denims and raincoat, tired, and stooped slightly.*

FRANK. And this be the male head of the mighty Bryant clan!

MR BRYANT. Blust, you're all here soon then.

BEATIE. Get you changed quick Father – he'll be along any minute look.

MR BRYANT. Shut you up gal, I'll go when I'm ready, I don't want you pushin' me.

> MRS BRYANT *comes from upstairs. She looks neat and also wears a flowered frock.*

FRANK. And this be the female head o' the mighty Bryant clan!

MRS BRYANT. Come on Bryant, get you changed – we're all ready look.

MR BRYANT. Blust, there go the other one. Who is he this boy, that's what I wanna know.

MRS BRYANT. He's upset! I can see it! I can tell it in his voice. Come on Bryants, what's the matters.

MR BRYANT. There ent much up wi' me, what you on

about woman. (*Makes to go.*) Now leave me be, you want me changed look.

MRS BRYANT. If there ent much up wi' you, I'll marry some other.

FRANK. Healey bin at you Pop?

BEATIE. The pigs dyin'?

MRS BRYANT. It's something serious or he wouldn't be so happy lookin'.

MR BRYANT. I bin put on casual labour.

JENNY. Well isn't that a sod now.

MRS BRYANT. Your guts I suppose.

MR BRYANT. I tell him it's no odds, that there's no pain. That don't matters Jack, he says, I aren't hevin' you break up completely on me. You go on casual, he say, and if you gets better you can come on to the pigs again.

MRS BRYANT. That's half pay then?

BEATIE. Can't you get another job?

FRANK. He've bin wi' them for eighteen years.

BEATIE. But you must be able to do something else – what about cowman again?

MR BRYANT. Bill Waddington do that see. He've bin at it this last six 'n' half years.

JENNY. It's no good upsettin' yourself Beatie. It happen all the time gal.

JIMMY. Well, we told her when she was at ours didn't we.

MRS BRYANT (*to* MR BRYANT). All right, get you on up, there ent nothin' we can do. We'll worry on it later. We always manage. It's gettin' late look.

MR BRYANT. Can he swim? 'Cos he bloody need to. It's rainin' fit to drowned you. (*Goes off upstairs.*)

MRS BRYANT. Well, shall we have a little cup o' tea while we're waitin'? I'll go put the kettle on. (*Goes to kitchen.*)

Everyone sits around now. JENNY *takes out some*

knitting and JIMMY *picks up a paper to read. There is
a silence. It is not an awkward silence, just a
conversationless room.*

PEARL (*to* JENNY). Who's lookin' after your Daphne?

JENNY. Ole mother Mann next door.

PEARL. Poor ole dear. How's she feelin' now?

JENNY. She took it bad. (*Nodding at* JIMMY.) Him too.
He think he were to blame.

PEARL. Blust that weren't his fault. Don't be so daft
Jimmy Beales. Don't you go fretting yourself or you'll
make us all feel queer look. You done nothin' wrong
bor – he weren't far off dying 'sides.

FRANK. They weren't even married were they?

JENNY. No, they never were – she started lookin' after
him when he had that first stroke and she just stayed.

JIMMY. Lost her job 'cos of it too.

FRANK. Well, yes, she would, wouldn't she – she was a
State Registered Nurse or something weren't she?
(*To* BEATIE.) Soon ever the authorities got to hear o'
that they told her to pack up livin' wi' him or quit her
job, see?

JENNY. Bloody daft I reckon. What difference it make
whether she married him or not.

PEARL. I reckon you miss him Jenny?

JENNY. Hell yes – that I do. He were a good ole bor –
always joking and buying the gal sweets. Well, do
you know I cry when I heard it? I did. Blust, that fair
shook me – that it did, there!

JIMMY. Who's lookin' after *your* kid then, Pearl?

PEARL. Father.

    Pause.

JIMMY (*to* FRANK). Who do you think'll win today?

FRANK. Well Norwich won't.

JIMMY. No.

Pause. MRS BRYANT *enters and sits down.*

MRS BRYANT. Well the kettle's on.

PEARL (*to* BEATIE). Hev his sister got any children?

BEATIE. Two boys.

JIMMY. She wanna get on top one night then they'll hev girls.

JENNY. Oh shut you up Jimmy Beales.

MRS BRYANT. Hed another little win last night.

JENNY. When was this?

MRS BRYANT. The fireman's whist drive. Won seven 'n' six in the knockout.

JENNY. Yearp.

FRANK (*reading the paper*). I see that boy what assaulted the ole woman in London got six years.

MRS BRYANT. Blust! He need to! I'd've given him six years and a bit more. Bloody ole hooligans. Do you give me a chance to pass sentence and I'd soon clear the streets of crime, that I would. Yes, that I would.

BEATIE (*springing into activity*). All right Mother – we'll give you a chance. (*Grabs* JIMMY's *hat and umbrella. Places hat on mother's head and umbrella in her arms.*) There you are, you're a judge. Now sum up and pass judgement.

MRS BRYANT. I'd put him in prison for life.

FRANK. You gotta sum up though. Blust, you just can't stick a man in prison and say nothing.

MRS BRYANT. Goodbye, I'd say.

BEATIE. Come on Mother, speak up. Anybody can say 'go to prison', but *you* want to be a judge. Well, you show a judge's understanding. Talk! Come on Mother, talk!

Everyone leans forward eagerly to hear mother talk. She looks startled and speechless.

MRS BRYANT. Well I – I – yes I – well I – Oh, don't be so soft.

FRANK. The mighty head is silent.

BEATIE. Well yes, she would be wouldn't she.

MRS BRYANT. What do you mean, I would be? You don't expect me to know what they say in courts do you? I aren't no judge.

BEATIE. Then why do you sit and pass judgement on people? If someone do something wrong you don't stop and think why. No discussin', no questions, just (*Snap of fingers.*) – off with his head. I mean look at Father getting less money. I don't see the family sittin' together and discussin' it. It's a problem! But which of you said it concerns you?

MRS BRYANT. Nor don't it concern them. I aren't hevin' people mix in my matters.

BEATIE. But they aren't just people – they're your family for hell's sake!

MRS BRYANT. No matters, I aren't hevin' it!

BEATIE. But Mother I –

MRS BRYANT. Now shut you up Beatie Bryant and leave it alone. I shall talk when I hev to and I never shall do, so there!

BEATIE. You're so stubborn.

MRS BRYANT. So you keep saying.

> MR BRYANT *enters, he is clean and dressed in blue pin-striped suit.*

MR BRYANT. You brewed up yit?

MRS BRYANT (*jumping up and going to kitchen*). Oh hell, yes – I forgot the tea look.

MR BRYANT. Well, now we're all waitin' on him.

JENNY. Don't look as if Susie's comin'.

BEATIE. Stubborn cow!

> *Silence.*

JENNY. Hev you seen Susie's television set yit?

BEATIE. I seen it.

FRANK. Did you know also that when they fist hed it
  they took it up to bed wi' them and lay in bed wi' a
  dish of chocolate biscuits?

PEARL. But now they don't bother – they say they've
  had it a year now and all the old programmes they
  saw in the beginning they're seein' again.

MRS BRYANT (*entering with tea*). Brew's up!

BEATIE. Oh, for Christ's sake let's stop gossiping.

PEARL. I aren't gossiping. I'm making an intelligent
  observation about the state of television, now then.

MR BRYANT. What's up wi' you now?

BEATIE. You weren't doin' nothin' o' the sort – you was
  gossiping.

PEARL. Well that's a heap sight better'n quotin' all the
  time.

BEATIE. I don't quote all the time, I just tell you what
  Ronnie say.

FRANK. Take it easy gal – he's comin' soon – don't need
  to go all jumpin' an' frantic.

BEATIE. Listen! Let me set you a problem.

JIMMY. Here we go.

BEATIE. While we're waitin' for him I'll set you a moral
  problem. You know what a moral problem is? It's a
  problem about right and wrong. I'll get you buggers
  thinking if it's the last thing I do. Now listen. There
  are four huts –

FRANK. What?

BEATIE. Huts. You know – them little things you live in.
  Now there are two huts on one side of a stream and
  two huts on the other side. On one side live a girl in
  one hut and a wise man in the other. On the other
  side live Tom in one hut and Archie in the other.
  Also there's a ferryman what run a boat across the
  river. Now – listen, concentrate – the girl loves
  Archie but Archie don't love the girl. And Tom love
  the girl but the girl don't go much on Tom.

JIMMY. Poor bugger.

BEATIE. One day the girl hears that Archie – who don't love her, remember – is going to America, so she decides to try once more to persuade him to take her with him. So listen what she do. She go to the ferryman and ask him to take her across. The ferryman say, I will, but you must take off all your clothes.

MRS BRYANT. Well, whatever do he wanna ask that for?

BEATIE. It don't matters why – he do! Now the girl doesn't know what to do so she ask the wise man for advice, and he say, you must do what you think best.

FRANK. Well that weren't much advice was it!

BEATIE. No matters – he give it. So the girl thinks about it and being so in love she decides to strip.

PEARL. Oh I say!

MR BRYANT. Well, this is a rum ole story ent it?

BEATIE. Shut up Father and listen. Now, er – where was I?

MR BRYANT. She was strippin'.

BEATIE. Oh yes! So, the girl strips and the ferryman takes her over – he don't touch her or nothing – just takes her over and she rushes to Archie's hut to implore him to take her with him and to declare her love again. Now Archie promises to take her with him and so she sleeps with him the night. But when she wake up in the morning he've gone. She's left alone. So she go across to Tom and explain her plight and ask for help. But soon ever he knowed what she've done, he chuck her out see? So there she is. Poor little gal. Left alone with no clothes and no friends and no hope of staying alive. Now – this is the question, think about it, don't answer quick – who is the person most responsible for her plight?

JIMMY. Well, can't she get back?

BEATIE. No, she can't do anything. She's finished. She've hed it! Now, who's to blame?

There is a general air of thought for a moment and BEATIE *looks triumphant and pleased with herself.*

MRS BRYANT. Be you a-drinkin' on your tea look. Don't you worry about no naked gals. The gal won't get cold but the tea will.

PEARL. Well I say the girl's most responsible.

BEATIE. Why?

PEARL. Well, she made the choice didn't she?

FRANK. Yes, but the old ferryman made her take off her clothes.

PEARL. But she didn't hev to.

FRANK. Blust woman, she were in love!

BEATIE. Good ole Frank.

JENNY. Hell if I know.

BEATIE. Jimmy?

JIMMY. Don't ask me gal – I follow decisions, I aren't makin' none.

BEATIE. Father?

MR BRYANT. I don't know what you're on about.

BEATIE. Mother?

MRS BRYANT. Drink you your tea gal – never you mind what I think.

This is what they're waiting for.

PEARL. Well – what do Ronnie say?

BEATIE. He say the gal is responsible only for makin' the decision to strip off and go across and that she do that because she's in love. After that she's the victim of two phoney men – one who don't love her but take advantage of her and one who say he love her but don't love her enough to help her, and that the man who say he love her but don't do nothin' to help her is most responsible because he were the last one she could turn to.

JENNY. He've got it all worked out then!

BEATIE (*jumping on a chair thrusting her fist into the air like Ronnie, and glorying in what is the beginning of a hysteric outburst of his quotes*). 'No one do that bad that you can't forgive them.'

PEARL. He's sure of himself then?

BEATIE. 'We can't be sure of everything but certain basic things we must be sure about or we'll die.'

FRANK. He think everyone is gonna listen then?

BEATIE. 'People *must* listen. It's no good talking to the converted. *Everyone* must argue and think or they will stagnate and rot and the rot will spread.'

JENNY. Hark at that then.

BEATIE (*her strange excitement growing; she has a quote for everything*). 'If wanting the best things in life means being a snob then glory hallelujah I'm a snob. But I'm not a snob Beatie, I just believe in human dignity and tolerance and cooperation and equality and –'

JIMMY (*jumping up in terror*). He's a communist!

BEATIE. 'I'm a socialist!'

There is a knock on the front door.

(*Jumping down joyously as though her excited quotes have been leading to this one moment.*) He's here, he's here! (*But at the door it is the* POSTMAN, *from whom she takes a letter and a parcel.*) Oh, the silly fool, the fool. Trust him to write a letter on the day he's coming. Parcel for you Mother.

PEARL. Oh, that'll be your dress from the club.

MRS BRYANT. What dress is this then? I didn't ask for no dress from the club.

PEARL. Yes you did, you did ask me, didn't she ask me Frank? Why, we were looking through the book together Mother.

MRS BRYANT. No matters what we was doin' together I
  aren't hevin' it.
PEARL. But Mother you distinctly –
MRS BRYANT. I aren't hevin' it so there now!

> BEATIE *has read the letter – the contents stun her. She*
> *cannot move. She stares around speechlessly at*
> *everyone.*

Well, what's the matter wi' you gal? Let's have a
read. (*Takes letter and reads contents in a dead flat but*
loud voice – as though it were a proclamation.) 'My dear
Beatie. It wouldn't really work would it? My ideas
about handing on a new kind of life are quite useless
and romantic if I'm really honest. If I were a healthy
human being it might have been all right but most of
us intellectuals are pretty sick and neurotic – as you
have often observed – and we couldn't build a world
even if we were given the reins of government – not
yet any-rate. I don't blame you for being stubborn, I
don't blame you for ignoring every suggestion I ever
made – I only blame myself for encouraging you to
believe we could make a go of it and now two weeks
of your not being here has given me the cowardly
chance to think about it and decide and I –'
BEATIE (*snatching letter*). Shut up!
MRS BRYANT. Oh – so we know now do we?
MR BRYANT. What's this then – ent he comin'?
MRS BRYANT. Yes, we know now.
MR BRYANT. Ent he comin' I ask?
BEATIE. *No he ent comin'.*

> *An awful silence ensues. Everyone looks uncomfort-*
> *able.*

JENNY (*softly*). Well blust gal, didn't you know this was
  going to happen?

> BEATIE *shakes her head.*

MRS BRYANT. So *we're* stubborn are we?

JENNY. Shut you up Mother, the girl's upset.

MRS BRYANT. Well I can see that, I can see that, he ent coming, I can see that, and we're here like bloody fools, I can see that.

PEARL. Well did you quarrel all that much Beatie?

BEATIE (*as if discovering this for the first time*). He always wanted me to help him but I never could. Once he tried to teach me to type but soon ever I made a mistake I'd give up. I'd give up every time! I couldn't bear making mistakes. I don't know why, but I couldn't bear making mistakes.

MRS BRYANT. Oh – so we're hearin' the other side o' the story now are we?

BEATIE. He used to suggest I start to copy real objects on to my paintings instead of only abstracts and I never took heed.

MRS BRYANT. Oh, so you never took heed.

JENNY. Shut you up I say.

BEATIE. He gimme a book sometimes and I never bothered to read it.

FRANK (*not maliciously*). What about all this discussion we heard of?

BEATIE. I *never* discussed things. He used to beg me to discuss things but I never saw the point on it.

PEARL. And he got riled because o' that?

BEATIE (*trying to understand*). I didn't have any patience.

MRS BRYANT. Now it's coming out.

BEATIE. I couldn't help him – I never knew patience. Once he looked at me with terrified eyes and said, 'We've been together for three years but you don't know who I am or what I'm trying to say – and you don't care do you?'

MRS BRYANT. And there she was tellin' me.

BEATIE. I never knew what he wanted – I didn't think it mattered.

MR BRYANT. And there she was gettin' us to solve the moral problem and now we know she didn't even do it herself. That's a rum 'un, ent it?

MRS BRYANT. The apple don't fall far from the tree – that it don't.

BEATIE (*wearily*). So you're proud on it? You sit there smug and you're proud that a daughter of yours wasn't able to help her boy friend? Look at you. All of you. You can't say anything. You can't even help your own flesh and blood. Your daughter's bin ditched. It's your problem as well isn't it? I'm part of your family aren't I? Well, help me then! Give me words of comfort! Talk to me – for God's sake, someone talk to me. (*She cries at last.*)

MR BRYANT. Well, what do we do now?

MRS BRYANT. We sit down and we eat that's what we do now.

JENNY. Don't be soft Mother, we can't leave the girl crying like that.

MRS BRYANT. Well, blust, 'tent my fault she's cryin'. I did what I could – I prepared all this food, I'd've treated him as my own son if he'd come but he hevn't! We got a whole family gathering specially to greet him, all on us look, but he hevn't come. So what am I supposed to do?

BEATIE. My God, Mother, I hate you – the only thing I ever wanted and I weren't able to keep him, I didn't know how. I hate you, I hate . . .

> MRS BRYANT *slaps* BEATIE*'s face. Everyone is a little shocked at this harsh treatment.*

MRS BRYANT. There! I hed enough!

MR BRYANT. Well what d'you wanna do that for?

MRS BRYANT. I hed enough. All this time she've bin

home she've bin tellin' me I didn't do this and I didn't do that and I hevn't understood half what she've said and I've hed enough. She talk about bein' part o' the family but she've never lived at home since she've left school look. Then she go away from here and fill her head wi' high-class squit and then it turn out she don't understand any on it herself. It turn out she do just the same things she say I do. (*Into* BEATIE's *face.*) Well, am I right gal? I'm right ent I? When you tell me I was stubborn, what you mean was that *he* told you *you* was stubborn – eh? When you tell me I don't understand you mean *you* don't understand isn't it? When you tell me I don't make no effort you mean *you* don't make no effort. Well, what you blaming me for? Blaming me all the time! I haven't bin responsible for you since you left home – you bin on your own. She think I like it, she do! Thinks I like it being cooped up in this house all day. Well I'm telling you my gal – I don't! There! And if I had a chance to be away working somewhere the whole lot on you's could go to hell – the lot on you's. All right so I am a bloody fool – all right! So I know it! A whole two weeks I've bin told it. Well, so then I can't help you my gal, no that I can't, and you get used to that once and for all.

BEATIE. No you can't Mother, I know you can't.

MRS BRYANT. I suppose doin' all those things for him weren't enough. I suppose he weren't satisfied wi' goodness only.

BEATIE. Oh, what's the use.

MRS BRYANT. Well, don't you sit there an' sigh gal like you was Lady Nevershit. I ask you something. Answer me. You do the talking then. Go on – you say you know something we don't so *you* do the talking. Talk – go on, talk gal.

BEATIE (*despairingly*). I can't Mother, you're right – the

apple don't fall far from the tree do it? You're right,
I'm like you. Stubborn, empty, wi' no tools for livin'.
I got no roots in nothing. I come from a family o'
farm labourers yet I ent got no roots – just like town
people – just a mass o' nothin'.

FRANK. Roots, gal? What do you mean, roots?

BEATIE (*impatiently*). Roots, roots, roots! Christ,
Frankie, you're in the fields all day, you should know
about growing things. Roots! The things you come
from, the things that feed you. The things that make
you proud of yourself – roots!

MR BRYANT. You got a family ent you?

BEATIE. I am not talking about family roots – I mean –
the – I mean – Look! Ever since it begun the world's
bin growin' hasn't it? Things hev happened, things
have bin discovered, people have bin thinking and
improving and inventing but what do we know about
it all?

JIMMY. What is she on about?

BEATIE (*various interjections*). What do you mean, what
am I on about? I'm talking! Listen to me! I'm tellin'
you that the world's bin growing for two thousand
years and we hevn't noticed it. I'm telling you that
we don't know what we are or where we come from.
I'm telling you something's cut us off from the
beginning. I'm telling you we've got no roots. Blimey
Joe! We've all got large allotments, we all grow things
around us so we should know about roots. You know
how to keep your flowers alive don't you Mother?
Jimmy – you know how to keep the roots of your
veges strong and healthy. It's not only the corn that
need strong roots, you know, it's us too. But what've
we got? Go on, tell me, what've we got? We don't
know where we push up from and we don't bother
neither.

PEARL. Well, I aren't grumbling.

BEATIE. You say you aren't – oh yes, you say so, but look at you. What've you done since you come in? Hev you said anythin'? I mean really said or done anything to show you're alive? Alive! Blust, what do it mean? Do you know what it mean? Any of you? Shall I tell you what Susie said when I went and saw her? She say she don't care if that ole atom bomb drop and she die – that's what she say. And you know why she say it? I'll tell you why, because if she had to care she'd have to do something about it and she find *that* too much effort. Yes she do. She can't be bothered – she's too bored with it all. That's what we all are – we're all too bored.

MRS BRYANT. Blust woman – bored you say, bored? You say Susie's bored, with a radio and television an' that? I go t'hell if she's bored!

BEATIE. Oh yes, we turn on a radio or a TV set maybe, or we go to the pictures – if them's love stories or gangsters – but isn't that the easiest way out? Anything so long as we don't have to make an effort. Well, am I right? You know I'm right. Education ent only books and music – it's asking questions, all the time. There are millions of us, all over the country, and no one, not one of us, is asking questions, we're all taking the easiest way out. Everyone I ever worked with took the easiest way out. We don't fight for anything, we're so mentally lazy we might as well be dead. Blust, we are dead! And you know what Ronnie say sometimes? He say it serves us right! That's what he say – it's our own bloody fault!

JIMMY. So that's us summed up then – so we know where *we* are then!

MRS BRYANT. Well if he don't reckon we count nor nothin', then it's as well he didn't come. There! It's as well he didn't come.

BEATIE. Oh, *he* thinks we count all right – living in

mystic communion with nature. Living in mystic bloody communion with nature (*indeed*). But us count? Count Mother? I wonder. Do we? Do you think we really count. You don' wanna take any notice of what them ole papers say about the workers bein' all-important these days – that's all squit! 'Cos we aren't. Do you think when the really talented people in the country get to work they get to work for us? Hell if they do! Do you think they don't know we 'ont make the effort? The writers don't write thinkin' we can understand, nor the painters don't paint expecting us to be interested – that they don't, nor don't the composers give out music thinking we can appreciate it. 'Blust,' they say, 'the masses is too stupid for us to come down to them. Blust,' they say, 'if they don't make no effort why should we bother?' So you know who come along? The slop singers and the pop writers and the film makers and women's magazines and the Sunday papers and the picture-strip love stories – that's who come along, and you don't have to make no effort for them, it come easy. 'We know where the money lie,' they say, 'hell we do! The workers've got it so let's give them what they want. If they want slop songs and film idols we'll give 'em that then. If they want words of one syllable, we'll give 'em that then. If they want the third-rate, *blust!* We'll give 'em *that* then. Anything's good enough for them 'cos they don't ask for no more!' The whole stinkin' commercial world insults us and we don't care a damn. Well, Ronnie's right – it's our own bloody fault. We want the third-rate – we got it! We got it! We got it! We . . .

Suddenly BEATIE *stops as if listening to herself. She pauses, turns with an ecstatic smile on her face –*

D'you hear that? D'you hear it? Did you listen to me?

I'm talking. Jenny, Frankie, Mother – I'm not quoting no more.

MRS BRYANT (*getting up to sit at table*). Oh hell, I hed enough of her – let her talk a while she'll soon get fed up.

> *The others join her at the table and proceed to eat and murmur.*

BEATIE. Listen to me someone. (*As though a vision were revealed to her.*) God in heaven, *Ronnie!* It does work, it's happening to me, I can feel it's happening, I'm beginning, on my own two feet – I'm beginning . . .

> *The murmur of the family sitting down to eat grows as* BEATIE's *last cry is heard. Whatever she will do they will continue to live as before. As* BEATIE *stands alone, articulate at last –*

> *The curtain falls.*

'I'LL WAIT FOR YOU IN THE HEAVENS BLUE'

I'm Talking About Jerusalem

For Della and Ralph

I'm Talking About Jerusalem was first presented at the Belgrade Theatre, Coventry, on 28 March 1960, with the following cast:

RONNIE KAHN	George Tensotti
ADA SIMMONDS	Cherry Morris
SARAH KAHN	Lala Lloyd
DAVE SIMMONDS	Alan Howard
1ST REMOVAL MAN	Kenton Moore
2ND REMOVAL MAN	Robin Parkinson
LIBBY DOBSON	Patrick O'Connell
COLONEL DEWHURST	Paul Kermack
SAMMY	Keith Crane
DANNY SIMMONDS	Peter Palmer
ESTHER KAHN	Ann Robson
CISSIE KAHN	Rosemary Leach
POSTMAN	Rex Doyle

Directed by John Dexter

Act One, Scene One: September 1946
          Scene Two: July 1947

Act Two, Scene One: Autumn 1953
          Scene Two: Autumn 1956
          Scene Three: Autumn 1959

ACT ONE

SCENE ONE

September 1946.

Norfolk. A house in the middle of fields. We see the large kitchen of the house, the garden, and the end part of an old barn.

DAVE and ADA SIMMONDS are just moving in. Boxes and cases are strewn around. DAVE and two REMOVAL MEN are manoeuvring a large wardrobe, 1930 type, from a lorry off stage. ADA is unpacking one of the cases. SARAH KAHN, her mother, is buttering some bread on a table, and from a portable radio comes a stirring part of Beethoven's Ninth Symphony. RONNIE KAHN, ADA's brother, is standing on a box conducting both the music and the movement of people back and forth. DAVE – unlike ADA and RONNIE – speaks with a slight cockney accent.

RONNIE. Gently now. Don't rush it. You're winning.

DAVE. Instead of standing there and giving orders why don't you give a bloody hand?

RONNIE. You don't need any more hands. I'm organizing you, I'm inspiring you.

DAVE. Jesus Christ it's heavy, it's heavy. Drop it a minute.

RONNIE. Lower it gently – mind the edges, it's a work of art.

DAVE. I'll work of art you. And turn that radio off – I can cope with Beethoven, but not both of you.

RONNIE (*turns off radio*). What are you grumbling for? I've been shlepping things to and fro up till now, haven't I? Only as it's the last piece I thought I'd exercise my talents as a foreman. Don't I make a good foreman? (*Calling.*) Hey, Mother, don't I make a good foreman?

SARAH (*coming from the kitchen*). What've you lost?

RONNIE. Listen to her! What've you lost! She's just like her daughter, she can't hear a thing straight. Watch this. Hey, Ada! The sea's not far away you know.

ADA. You can't have any because I haven't put the kettle on yet.

RONNIE. Lunatic family.

DAVE. Come on. We'll never get done. Ready?

They bend to lift the wardrobe. SARAH *returns to kitchen.*

RONNIE. Heave – slowly – don't strain – heave.

1ST REMOVAL MAN. Where's it going?

DAVE. Through the kitchen and upstairs.

RONNIE. You won't get through the kitchen, go round the back.

DAVE. We'll manage.

RONNIE *goes on ahead and pushes* ADA, *the box and* SARAH *and table out of their path.*

RONNIE. Make way, make way – the army is marching on its stomach. (DAVE *and the two men are bent forward in effort.*) You see, I can't help, there's not enough room for four to get round that door.

They stop at other end of the kitchen and lower the wardrobe.

DAVE. We have to get round here and along the passage.

2ND REMOVAL MAN. Never. You can't bend wardrobes.

1ST REMOVAL MAN. Could saw it in half.

RONNIE (*pretending to be offended*). Good God man! An original twentieth-century piece and you want to saw it in half? Ahhhhhhhhh. (*Weeps upon it.*)

IST REMOVAL MAN. You still at school?

RONNIE. So?

IST REMOVAL MAN. Talk a lot don't you.

RONNIE. What's that got to do with school?

IST REMOVAL MAN. Should've thought they'd taught you manners.

SARAH (*coming into battle*). Don't you think he's got manners then?

2ND REMOVAL MAN. But he talks so don't he?

ADA (*joining battle*). Sooner he talked than he remained silent.

RONNIE. My lunatic family comes to my rescue.

IST REMOVAL MAN. I'd've clipped him round the ear if he'd've called me lunatic.

DAVE. We'll have to take it back and use the front entrance.

RONNIE. What's the good of me being a foreman if you don't listen to me.

> RONNIE *again pushes back table and box which women had returned.*

Make way, make way. The retreat! (*Opens radio again and conducts them and symphony out of kitchen.*)

SARAH. Everything he makes into a joke.

> *The men raise the wardrobe and struggle back, this time going round the back of the house.* RONNIE *pauses and surveys the scene.*

RONNIE. Nineteen forty-six! The war is really over isn't it, eh, Mother? Aren't you proud that your children are the first to pick up the ruins?

SARAH. I'm proud, yes! (*Pushes radio lid closed.*)

RONNIE. Of course proud! We just put a Labour Party in power didn't we? It's right they should be the pioneers – good! E-ver-y-bo-dy is building. Out go the slums, whist! And the National Health Service comes in. The millennium's come and you're still grumbling. What's the matter, you don't like strawberries and cream?

SARAH (*looking around*). Strawberries and cream?

RONNIE. All right, so it's shmultz herring and plum pudding for the meanwhile. But it's a great saga you're witnessing. The wandering Jews strike again! None of the easy life for them, none of the comforts of electricity –

SARAH. They're madmen!

RONNIE. They don't need roads, give them a muddy lane –

SARAH. Tell me Ada, how are you going to get to the village? Not even a road here there isn't. Just fields – a house in the middle of nowhere.

ADA. Ronnie, go and get some water for tea.

RONNIE. And none of the joys of running water for these brave people, a well! A biblical well. I can see you Ada, like Miriam at the well and Dave will come like Moses and drive away the strangers and draw water for you and you shall love him and marry him, and you shall bear him a son and he will be called Adam and the son shall grow strong and the land of Israel shall grow mighty around him –

SARAH. Yes, here!

SARAH *moves to throw something on a dustheap out of hearing.*

ADA. It was Zipporah and Moses anyway.

RONNIE. Zipporah. What a beautiful name. I've always wanted to write the Bible. Ada, haven't you ever felt you've wanted to sit down and write something that's already written? God, how many times I've felt like composing the 'Autumn Journal'.

SARAH *returns in time to hear this.*

ADA. What?

RONNIE. You know – Louis MacNeice –

> Sleep, my past and all my sins,
> In distant snow or dried roses
> Under the moon for night's cocoon will open
> When day begins.

ADA. I know what you mean.

SARAH (*surprised*). It's wonderful, Ronnie.

RONNIE. Isn't it beautiful Mother? It's a poetry I can talk, I don't have to recite it. (*As if telling her something.*)

> Sleep to the noises of running water
> Tomorrow to be crossed, however deep;
> This is no river of the dead or Lethe,
> Tonight we sleep
> On the banks of the Rubicon – the die is cast;
> There will be time to audit
> The accounts later, there will be sunlight later
> And the equation will come out at last.

My God, I want to write it again and again.

SARAH. But Ronnie, you've never read me that one before. Now that one, *that* one you try and get published.

At this, ADA *and* RONNIE *break into uncontrollable laughter.* SARAH *cannot understand why.*

So what's funny?

RONNIE. Oh, Mother I love you, love you. (*He cuddles her.*)

SARAH (*pushing him away because he tends to smother her*). All right so you love me, love me, but what's funny?

RONNIE (*picking up pail and going to get water*). My

mother encourages me – get it published she says! (*Goes off laughing.*)

SARAH. Is he gone mad or something?

ADA. Oh, Mummy, you are funny – he was quoting a poem by a famous poet.

SARAH. How did I get such clever children?

RONNIE (*off*). Hey, Ada! How do I get the water out of this well?

ADA (*shouting*). Lift up the lid and hook the bucket on and just let it down.

RONNIE (*after a second*). Hey Ada! There's no water in this well.

ADA (*shouting*). Of course there is, you idiot.

RONNIE. But I can't see it.

ADA. It's a long way down.

RONNIE. You can die of thirst before you get to the bottom.

SARAH (*sighing*). Ada, Ada. You're both mad.

ADA. Next time you come down, we'll have lots of improvements.

SARAH. I don't understand it, I just don't see why you have to come out here. Is London so bad? Millions of people live there!

ADA. Thank you.

SARAH. All of a sudden they pick up and go away.

ADA (*calling*). Dave, where's the paraffin?

DAVE (*off*). I put it in the corner.

ADA. I see it. (*Picks up paraffin and proceeds to fill and light Primus stove.*)

SARAH. A Primus stove! What's the point? All this heavy work. No roads, no electricity, no running water, no proper lavatory. It's the Middle Ages. Tell me why you want to go back to the Middle Ages?

ADA. We'll get a calor gas stove in time.

SARAH. Progress!

ADA. Mummy, please, ple-ease help us. It's not easy this

move, for any of us. Doesn't it occur to you that we desperately need your blessing, please –

SARAH. I'm here aren't I? Silly girl. But how can I bless – ? I brought up two nice children, and I want to see them round me – that's wrong? But all right, so you want to go away, so you want to build a life of your own, but here? Why here? Explain it to me, maybe I'll be happier. Why here?

RONNIE (*off, shouting*). Hey, Dave – how you managing?

DAVE (*off*). We're managing. Just a few more stairs.

RONNIE. That's right boys – heave, heave!

DAVE. I'll heave this bloody thing on top of your head if you don't shut up. Go away and make some tea.

RONNIE (*entering*). The men want tea. Feed the workers. Hey Addie – you know what I discovered by the well? You can shout! It's marvellous. You can shout and no one can hear you.

ADA (*triumphantly*). Of course!

SARAH (*derisively*). Of course.

RONNIE. Of course – listen. (*Goes into garden and stands on a tea chest and shouts.*) Down with capitalism! Long live the workers' revolution! You see? *And long live Ronnie Kahn too!* (*Waits for a reply.*) No one argues with you. No one says anything. Freedom! You can jump about. (*Jumps off chest.*) You can spin in the air. (*Jumps and spins with arms akimbo.*) You can do somersaults . . . (*He rolls on the grass shouting 'wheeeee'.*) You can bang the earth. (*He thumps the ground with his fists with utter joy.*) My God – it's wonderful – you can go mad all on your own and no one'll say anything. (*Sits up wide-eyed.*)

SARAH. He's not my son. I'll swear he's not my son.

RONNIE (*crawling on all fours up to the kitchen door.*) Of course I'm not your son. My real mother was a gipsy and lived in a caravan, and one day she came to your door and instead of buying flowers from her you

bought me. And everyone believed us. They used to
look at you, and then at me and say no – no, it's true,
he doesn't look like you does he?

SARAH. Make the tea.

RONNIE (*springing up*). Where's the kettle?

ADA. In one of the boxes.

RONNIE. It's like camping.

SARAH. Camping!

ADA. Finished the bread Mummy?

SARAH. I've finished the bread. What about the soup?

ADA. Soup?

RONNIE. She made a chicken soup last night and put it
in bottles. She puts everything in bottles. (*Looks in*
SARAH's *bag.*)

SARAH. And a meat pie too I made.

ADA. Oh Mummy, you shouldn't have.

SARAH. I shouldn't have, I shouldn't have! Everything I
shouldn't have. Did *you* think about what you were
going to eat when you came here?

ADA. I brought bread and tomatoes and fruit and
cheese.

RONNIE. Cheese!

SARAH. As if I didn't know what you'd bring!

RONNIE. She always offers me cheese when I'm hungry.

ADA. You're both mad.

SARAH. *We're* mad! My children and they still don't
know how to organize their lives.

RONNIE (*holding up jar*). Bottled Chicken Soup. It looks
like – er – hum – yes, well, I hope it tastes different.

ADA. We've only one Primus so you'll have to wait until
the water's boiled. Get out a table-cloth Ronnie.

RONNIE. A table-cloth? What, here? Now?

ADA. This place may be a shambles but I don't intend
living as though it's one.

DAVE *and the* REMOVAL MEN *have returned by this*

time and RONNIE *throws out a cloth assisted by*
SARAH.

1ST REMOVAL MAN. Got a problem living here haven't
you?

2ND REMOVAL MAN. Ain't very modern is it, Jim?

RONNIE. Got the wardrobe in place?

2ND REMOVAL MAN. We got it through the door.

DAVE. You can help me manoeuvre it later, Ronnie.

1ST REMOVAL MAN. What made you move here, mate?
Not being nosey or anything, but you can't say it's
everybody's choice of a new home.

DAVE. It's a long story.

2ND REMOVAL MAN. Couldn't you find a better place?
More convenience? I mean it's not very sanitary, is it?

DAVE. Not easy to find the right place with little cash.
Saw the job advertised, a cheap house for sale near
by – grabbed it!

SARAH. Hard! Everything has to be hard for them.

1ST REMOVAL MAN. Still, they're young, missus, ain't
they? Gotta admit it's fresh out here.

2ND REMOVAL MAN. Too bleedin' fresh if you ask me.
Unnatural!

RONNIE. Come on, Dave. Give them an answer. It's a
golden opportunity this. The world has asked you
why you've come here. There stands the world. (*To*
REMOVAL MEN.) and here stand you two. You're on
trial comrade.

ADA. Don't arse around Ronnie, the men want their tea.

RONNIE. But I'm serious, girl. I want to know too.
You've always been my heroes, now you've changed
course. You've left communism behind – what now?

1ST REMOVAL MAN. Communist, are you?

2ND REMOVAL MAN. That's a dirty word, ain't it?

1ST REMOVAL MAN. Not during the war it wasn't.

RONNIE. The world is waiting, Dave.

DAVE. I'm not going to make speeches, Ronnie.

SARAH. Is a reason a speech?

DAVE. You can't talk about reasons, Sarah, just like that. A decision grows, slowly – you discover it.

RONNIE. But where did this one start?

ADA. Ceylon –

DAVE. When I was stationed out there. I was with Air Sea Rescue, boat building.

1ST REMOVAL MAN. We was in India. That's where Ted and me met. Decided on this game out there.

DAVE. I was in India for a bit. Where were you?

2ND REMOVAL MAN. Bombay.

DAVE. Karachi me. That's where I met Libby Dobson, Ada – remember? I always wrote to you about Libby Dobson? Me and him were going to do everything together when we got back to Civvy Street. Like you two. But *that* was a ship in the night.

ADA. He made a great impression on you, though.

DAVE. Taught me a lot. When we get straight we'll have him down here – shouldn't be difficult to trace him. He always wanted to do something like this with me. This'll please him this move, old Libby Dobson'd get a kick out of coming here.

1ST REMOVAL MAN. What was Ceylon like?

DAVE. Beautiful island. Being a carpenter I used to watch the local carpenters at work. They used to make their own tools and sometimes they'd show me. They'd sit out on the beach fashioning the boats or outside their houses planing and chiselling away at their timber, and they let me sit with them once they knew I was also building boats. And you know, one day, as I watched, I made a discovery – the kind of discovery you discover two or three times in a lifetime. I discovered an old truth: that a man is made to work and that when he works he's giving away something of himself, something very precious –

2ND REMOVAL MAN. We didn't see anything precious about living in mud huts and working in disease.

DAVE. No, no. You miss the point – I'm talking about the *way* they worked, not the conditions. I know about disease, I know about the mud huts, but what I was trying to say –

ADA. It's no good trying to explain. We're here and let's –

SARAH (*angrily*). Ada stop it! Stop it! Impatience! What's the matter with you all of a sudden. Don't explain! Nothing she wants to explain. No more talking. Just a cold, English you-go-your-way-and-I'll-go-mine! Why?

ADA. Because language isn't any use! Because we talk about one thing and you hear another that's why.

RONNIE. Come on, Dave, you haven't said enough. The world doesn't believe you –

ADA. The world!

RONNIE. Explain more.

ADA. Explain what? We've moved house, what's there to explain? What's so exceptional?

SARAH (*posing the real question*). What's wrong with socialism that you have to run to an ivory tower?

DAVE. Nothing's wrong with socialism Sarah, only we want to live it – not talk about it.

SARAH. Live it? Here?

ADA. Oh the city is paradise I suppose!

SARAH. The city is human beings. What's socialism without human beings tell me?

DAVE. I know the city Sarah. Believe me sweetheart! Since being demobbed I've worked in a factory turning out doors and window frames and I've seen men hating themselves while they were doing it. Morning after morning they've come in with a cold hatred in their eyes, brutalized! All their humanity gone. These you call men? All their life they're going to drain their energy into something that will give them nothing in return. Why do you think these two (*The* REMOVAL MEN.) decided to set up on their own? Eh? I'll tell you –

SARAH. But this isn't a socialist society yet –

ADA. What the hell difference do you think that'll make? All anyone talks about is taking over capitalist society, but no one talks about really changing it.

2ND REMOVAL MAN. And you're going to change it?

1ST REMOVAL MAN. On your own, cock?

DAVE. No of course we can't change it. But you see that barn out there? I'll work as a chippy on the Colonel's farm here for a year and then in a year's time that barn'll be my workshop. There I shall work and here, ten yards from me, where I can see and hear them, will be my family. And they will share in my work and I shall share in their lives. I don't want to be married to strangers. I've seen the city make strangers of husbands and wives but not me, not me and my wife.

SARAH. Words, words.

ADA. *Not* words. At last something more than just words.

Pause. Their defiance sinks in.

RONNIE (*to the* REMOVAL MEN). So now *you* (*To* ADA *and* DAVE.) and now the *world* knows. And the world – will watch you.

1ST REMOVAL MAN. Come on China. It's time to set off. These socialists can't even make us a cup of tea.

At which point the whole KAHN *family swing into action with regrets and apologies and thrust sandwiches and fruit into the arms of the startled lorry drivers.*

2ND REMOVAL MAN. Oi, oi! Whoa! Merry Christmas!

IST REMOVAL MAN. Think of us poor city sods won't you? Good luck!

> The REMOVAL MEN *go off to the lorry. We hear the lorry start, it revs and slowly moves off in gear. The family stands and watches, and waves and calls* 'Goodbye', *listening till the sound dies away. Silence.*

> *Each feels that with the going of the lorry has gone the last of the old life.*

> *It is getting dark.*

RONNIE. Well – you're here. You've come. Welcome to the Shambles.

> DAVE *moves to* ADA *and kisses her.* RONNIE *watches.* SARAH *sits unhappily in a chair away from them all.*

DAVE. We've got a house.
ADA. We've got a house.
DAVE. Tired darling?
ADA. A bit.
DAVE. It's not *such* a mess.
ADA. I know.
DAVE. It looks it but it's not such a mess.
ADA. I know, angel.
DAVE. Are you in control?
ADA. I'm in control.
DAVE. I love you very much.
ADA. I love you very much.
RONNIE (*moving to* SARAH). And I love you too sweetheart. (*His arm round her.*) Look at my sister – (*With mock passion.*) isn't she beautiful?
SARAH. I don't understand what went wrong. I don't understand how she can be like that.
ADA (*breaking away from* DAVE). I'm not like anything Mummy, only like your daughter. (*Kisses* SARAH.) You can come and visit us. Look – (*Waving arms*

around with mock majesty.) a country house. Aren't you pleased your daughter's got a country house? We can entertain in grand style! Everyone can come for a holiday – we'll have the maiden aunts down! Aunty Cissie and Aunt Esther can come and pull up weeds for us.

RONNIE. They're really very bourgeois these idealists you know.

SARAH. So far away.

ADA. Only a hundred miles.

SARAH. A hundred miles! You can say it easily. And what if Harry gets worse? It doesn't stop at one stroke, your father's never been very strong.

DAVE. I'm going to unpack some of the things upstairs.

ADA. Light the Tilley lamp for me darling before you go up. Supper won't be long. (DAVE *does so.*)

RONNIE. I'm going to look over the district. I bet there are hidden treasures and secret hideouts.

SARAH. Take your raincoat. (RONNIE *does so.*)

DAVE. I suppose *I'll* have to take a candle up with me.

ADA. Come on Mummy. Let's get some supper ready.

SARAH. Do you have to work any more Dave? Can't you rest a little?

DAVE. I'll prepare some beds and take out some of the clothes and hang them. We'll get straight bit by bit. No sense in rushing it. They're good things these lamps. There! It's alight. (*A soft glow covers part of the kitchen.*)

ADA. A lovely light.

SARAH. It took someone all this time to discover electricity – he shouldn't have bothered!

DAVE *smiles, shakes his head and goes off upstairs. The women busy themselves. They tidy the general mess and then lay plates and knives and forks on the table.* ADA*'s movements are slow and calm.* SARAH *is* *volatile and urgent, though somehow she manages to speak slowly and with deliberation – softly. The atmosphere sinks in. Then –*

And Dave doesn't like me – you know that?

ADA doesn't reply. Silence. They continue moving around.

I don't know why it should be that he doesn't like me. I don't think I've ever done anything to hurt him. (*Pause.*) Perhaps that's why he's taking you away, because he doesn't like me. Who knows!

Still ADA does not reply – instead she very softly starts humming.

He's changed you. Dave's changed a lot from the old days, Ada. (*Pause.*) Or perhaps he hasn't, perhaps it's me. Who knows. I know he fought in Spain, he's really a wonderful boy but – Ach! children! You bring them up, you teach them this you teach them that, you do what you think is right and still it's no good. They grow up and they grow away and you're left with – with – ! Where do their madnesses come from? Who knows. *I* don't know why Dave doesn't like me.

Still no word from ADA. She hums perhaps a little louder.

What you humming for? Humming! All of a sudden she does this humming when I talk to her. A new madness. Stop it Ada. Stop it! Silly girl.

An elderly gentleman appears. He is COLONEL DEWHURST, the farmer for whom DAVE will be working. He comes from the path and knocks on the kitchen door just as SARAH finishes.

COLONEL (*as door is opened to him*). Mrs Simmonds? I'm Colonel Dewhurst.

ADA. Oh hello, come in please, we're still unpacking so forgive –

COLONEL. But I understand, ma'am, I just thought –

ADA. This is my mother, Mother, Colonel Dewhurst, Dave's employer.

COLONEL (*shaking hands*). How do you do, ma'am. You must be very tired. Come a long way today, haven't you?

ADA (*calling*). Dave! Dave! Colonel Dewhurst.

DAVE. I'm coming down, a second.

ADA. Do sit down please.

COLONEL. I was telling your mother you've come a long way today.

ADA. Yes, we have.

COLONEL. It must seem strange.

SARAH. It seems very strange.

ADA. My mother thinks we're mad Colonel.

COLONEL. To come to the country? A fine life, a fine life.

SARAH. With no sanitation or electricity?

COLONEL. Thousands of places like that, thousands! But it's a large house, fresh air –

SARAH. There are parks in London.

COLONEL. *I* wouldn't change now.

SARAH. Maybe you've got some amenities my children haven't?

COLONEL. But they're young, aren't they? It's good they start off with a struggle, makes them appreciate life –

SARAH (*to* ADA). We brought you up with riches I suppose?

DAVE (*appearing and shaking hands*). Hello Colonel Dewhurst.

COLONEL. I thought I'd drop over and see you were arriving safely.

DAVE. That's very good of you.

COLONEL. It won't take you long to get used to it. It's a bracing life in the country.

DAVE. We're not rushing things. I think we'll manage.

COLONEL. Of course you will, yes, I'm sure. When do you think you'll be able to start – er – you know, when can I expect –

DAVE. Well I hoped you wouldn't mind giving us a few days to settle in and get our bearings.

COLONEL. Yes, well, there's no need to come in tomorrow, I think that'll be all right, yes, that'll be all right. But my foreman is waiting to start some fencing – want to get a few more sows in. He's been waiting a long time for a carpenter. No, no need to come in tomorrow – early start the next day'll do, do perfectly.

DAVE. Thanks.

COLONEL. Yes, well, thought I'd pop over and see you were arriving safely. Come at a good time – we've had some rain but it's gone. Doesn't do to have too much rain.

ADA (*not really knowing the reply*). No it doesn't does it?

COLONEL. Talking of rain, Simmonds, I'd advise you to buy yourself a tank to catch the soft water. Good stuff, that. Save you work, too. Not so much to pull up from the well. Buy one with a tap – easier. Don't drink it, though. Use it for washing and things.

DAVE. Thank you for telling us.

COLONEL. I'll see you right. (*Walks out into the garden. DAVE and ADA follow to doorway.*) You'll learn lots of things as you go along. (*Looks around.*) Good garden here. Grow your own veges. Apple tree there. Prune it a bit. Sturdy barn too, couple hundred years old. Use it for chickens, build a run inside it. You could do that, couldn't you? Build yourself a chicken run?

DAVE. I expect so. A little bit of intelligence can build you anything.

COLONEL (*suddenly become the employer*). Eight o'clock on Wednesday morning, then, Simmonds. Good night to you both. (*Goes off.*)

    DAVE *and* ADA *stand a second and look at each other.*

SARAH. That's the man you're working for?

ADA (*to* DAVE). He didn't give you much time to settle in did he?

DAVE. No, he didn't did he?

SARAH. You won't have time to scratch yourself, I'm telling you.

ADA. Well perhaps he needs you.

DAVE (*certain*). I'm sure he does. (*Not so certain.*) But I reckon he could have given us a couple of days to settle in.

ADA. Yes he could have.

DAVE. We're still rushing –

ADA. Seems like it.

    They are disappointed. SARAH *watches them sadly.*

SARAH. Oh my children, children! Straight away they want to walk into paradise. Perhaps it's a good thing you should start work so soon, you'll settle in the house gradually and working will get you into a stride, a routine. Always have a routine.

ADA (*brightening at this*). Perhaps Mum is right darling. Perhaps it's better to get stuck in straight away.

DAVE. No moping you mean?

ADA. I mean have no time to think we've done the wrong thing.

DAVE. *You* don't think we've done the wrong thing do you darling?

ADA. No – I do not.

DAVE. I do love you. (*Kisses her briefly.*)

ADA. Come on, let's get this food over with. Where's
Ronnie?

SARAH. Looking for hidden treasure.

DAVE. He's what?

SARAH. He's gone out exploring – in the mountains
there. (*Waves vaguely.*)

ADA. There aren't any mountains in Norfolk Mother.

SARAH. I'm very surprised.

DAVE. What's that fire there?

> *They all look at a red glow coming from behind the
> barn.* DAVE *and* ADA *rush off to one side of the barn.*

I hope the bloody fool hasn't been up to any of his
tricks.

> SARAH *stands looking in the direction they've gone.
> After a few seconds* RONNIE *strolls in from the other
> side of the barn. He walks in a kind of daze, clutching
> a branch, gazing into space.*

RONNIE. You can build fires under the night sky.

SARAH. What've you been up to you mad boy?

RONNIE. There's bracken in every hedge and you can
make fires with them.

SARAH. Have you set the barn on fire?

RONNIE. It's beautiful.

SARAH. For God's sake stop playing the fool and answer
me.

RONNIE (*looking around him*). It's all very beautiful.

> ADA *and* DAVE *appear.*

ADA. Ronnie, you are a nitwit, you could have set the
whole place alight.

RONNIE. Oh no. I know about these things.

SARAH. What did he do? I can't get any sense out of
him.

DAVE. It's all right – he made a camp fire, don't panic, nothing's burning. Let's eat.

> *They settle down to eat except* RONNIE, *who for the moment leans against a box, still enraptured.*

SARAH. He's so mad. I get so angry sometimes. Look at him, in a daze. Take your raincoat off and sit down and eat.

> RONNIE *sits down at the table but doesn't take off his raincoat.*

ADA. What are you sitting down in your raincoat for?

RONNIE. Somehow I feel, I feel – I . . . (*Unable to explain.*)

ADA. Yes, yes, but why are you eating with your raincoat on?

SARAH. Another madness! Every so often he gets a madness into his head and you can't shake him out of it. I get so annoyed. Ronnie, take your raincoat off!

DAVE. What are you getting upset for, both of you. The boy wants to eat in his raincoat let him eat in his raincoat.

ADA. He's not normal!

DAVE. All right so he's not normal, why should you worry.

ADA. I do worry. I'm not going to sit at the table with him while he's wearing a raincoat. Ronnie take your raincoat off! (RONNIE *continues eating.*)

SARAH. I don't know what makes him like this. Ronnie take your raincoat off!

ADA. He's so bloody stubborn. *Ronnie!*

DAVE. You and your mother, you're both the same. Why don't you leave the boy alone. What harm is he doing in a raincoat.

ADA. Because it annoys me that's why! (*To* DAVE.)

Don't side with him Dave because if you side with him he knows he can get away with it.

SARAH rises at this point and goes to a corner of the room where she finds an umbrella.

DAVE. Now look at us! Here we are quarrelling among ourselves just because your brother is sitting down at the table wearing a macintosh. Have you ever heard such lunacy? What's your mother up to?

SARAH sits at the table and opens the umbrella over her and proceeds to eat. Everyone looks at her in amazement. Suddenly RONNIE bursts out laughing, jumps up from the chair, kisses her, and takes off his raincoat. DAVE sees what has happened and laughs also. There is great merriment.

DAVE. Well if you Kahns aren't the most lunatic family I know.

They all begin to eat. SARAH twists the umbrella once on her shoulders, sticks her hand out to see if the 'rain' has finished, and then folds up the umbrella and eats.

SARAH. Don't I know my children.
DAVE. You're all so much alike, that's why.

They eat on in silence for a moment until suddenly SARAH gets up from the table and moves quickly out from the kitchen to the garden where she takes a handkerchief from her apron. She weeps a little. RONNIE rises and goes to the door.

RONNIE. Sarah?
SARAH. It's all right, I'm all right, leave me, go back inside and finish eating.

RONNIE returns.

RONNIE. Tears again.

ADA. I guessed this might happen. Perhaps she shouldn't have come.

DAVE. Can you blame her darling? Ronnie, sit down and let's finish this food.

RONNIE. I'm not really hungry. (*Half annoyed.*) She always makes it seem like the end of the world when she cries.

SARAH (*from the garden*). You know, it reminds me of Hungary, where I was born –

ADA. There, she's better again.

SARAH. There used to be high mountains and a river and a waterfall; my brother Hymie once fell into the river and I saved him. He nearly drowned. The mountains had snow on them.

RONNIE (*calling to her*). But there aren't any mountains or waterfalls here Mother.

SARAH (*after a pause, petulantly*). It still reminds me of Hungary.

ADA. Everything reminds her of Hungary. We were listening to Beethoven the other night and she swore black and blue it was based on a Hungarian folk song.

RONNIE. I'll wash up.

DAVE. Come on, let's finish unpacking.

> RONNIE *takes what remains of the water in the kettle and pours it into a basin, shakes some soap powder into it and begins to wash up.* ADA *and* DAVE *stand by one of the boxes, take out the contents one by one, unwrap them and lay them aside.* SARAH *enters, takes a dishcloth and begins to wipe up what* RONNIE *washes. As they do this* SARAH *begins to sing a soft and melodic Yiddish folk song. She can't remember past the first line.* RONNIE *picks up and reminds her. They sing together.* RONNIE *indicates to* ADA *to join in, she does so and in turn brings in* DAVE. *The new*

life has started and some of the old has come with them, and –

The curtain falls.

SCENE TWO

July 1947.

Everything is more in order now. Twelve months have passed and with them their first winter.

A signpost saying 'Y.H.A.', with an arrow, leans against a wall, waiting to be knocked into the ground.

The stage is empty. DAVE *appears singing 'Linden Lea' and carrying a roll of linoleum, which he lays down by the back door. He has just returned from work. At the door he pauses and looks out, surveying the countryside. From a room upstairs,* ADA *calls out.*

ADA. Dave?

DAVE. Yes sweetheart.

ADA. My God, what time is it?

DAVE. About five fifteen. Is Libby here?

ADA. No, he'll be back soon. I'm just finishing this letter.

DAVE. It's all right, don't rush.

ADA. Dave – when did we arrive here?

DAVE. Roughly twelve months ago.

> DAVE *stays by door and begins to unbutton his tall boots. After some seconds* ADA *appears. She is pregnant. She greets* DAVE *with a kiss and then he nods his head towards the view. They both gaze at it a while and inhale deeply.*

ADA. The corn is yellow now.

DAVE. Colours for each season. The children will love it.

ADA. We'll teach the children to look at things won't we Dave? I shall make it into a sort of game for them. Teach them to take notice. (*With mock pomp.*) Don't let the world pass you by, I shall tell them – (*Breathing deeply.*) breathe, I shall say breathe deeply and fill your lungs and open your eyes. For the sun, I shall say, open your eyes for that laaaarge sun.

DAVE. Not long ago that field was brown. What does Libby say to it all, now he's had a chance to look around? We didn't get much of a chance to talk last night because he arrived so late.

ADA. A very strange fish your friend Libby Dobson. He doesn't quite fit the picture you painted of him does he?

DAVE. No he doesn't does he? What's he been up to all day?

ADA. I packed him up some sandwiches and he went out for a day's walking. God knows where. He stood out here and he looked around and he said 'It's all sky isn't it?' and then he stalked off with a 'see you'.

DAVE. He looked very sad and worn old Libby – never thought he'd end up a – what does he call himself?

ADA. A business consultant.

DAVE. He was a bloody fine mechanic in the RAF.

ADA. You're disappointed aren't you darling?

DAVE. Yes I am – daft, but I am. You know there's always one person you want to show your life to – show what you've done – and I've thought Libby Dobson was the bloke – should've thought he'd've understood. Blimey! the man had a hand in shaping my ideas – people! Well that's people I suppose.

ADA. Maybe he'll be better after a day's walk. Get me some water look or he'll come and nothing'll be ready and then he will be riled.

DAVE. Riled! You're a real Norfolk girl already. (*Holding her.*) Let's pretend he's not here and let's go to bed and just lie there.

ADA. Let's get this one over first.

DAVE. We'll leave a note for old Dobson and he can get his own supper.

ADA. Darling the water.

DAVE. He's a big boy – he can look to himself.

ADA. Besides *I'm* – we're – hungry.

DAVE. Water.

> *He goes off singing 'Linden Lea' and* ADA *goes in to lay a salad.* DAVE *begins to talk to her from the back of the house.*

Darling we must start making new plans.

ADA. I'm making a salad for supper.

DAVE. What?

ADA. Salad!

DAVE. Plans!

ADA. What?

DAVE. Plans!

ADA. No, salad!

> DAVE *appears at window to kitchen.*

DAVE. Let's get together – what are *you* talking about?

ADA. I said I'm making a salad for supper.

DAVE. Oh. And I said we must start making new plans. We'll start again. (*Returns to well.*)

ADA (*waits, then calls*). What plans?

DAVE (*off*). I want to build a chicken hut –

ADA. Lovely –

DAVE. And then I want to start laying a concrete floor in the barn so that I can build a proper workshop.

ADA. Have you ever laid a concrete floor before?

DAVE. I hadn't ever made a piece of furniture before had I? You learn. You think about it and you learn.

How many more buckets of water do you want for Christ's sake?

ADA. Just fill the copper.

DAVE. But I filled it this morning.

ADA. And I used it this morning.

> DAVE *enters, puffed out, carrying a bucket of water.*

Here, put the spare one in the jug.

> ADA *draws a jug from under the sink.*

DAVE. And that's another thing. I've got to take a pipe from the sink to the well and run it into a drain outside.

ADA. A plumber too.

DAVE. And then we must start thinking about buying a soft-water tank, that'll save arms at the well.

ADA. Darling, I need storage space. The one cupboard you built there isn't enough.

DAVE. In time my darling, all in good time. We've made our garden grow haven't we? We've made our garden grow and we've stopped our roof from leaking. I've boarded the old stables up and laid by timber ready to work. The rooms are painted white and nearly all the windows have curtains, and in three months' time I reckon I can start on my own. Look, only the hedges are wild. All in good time my darling.

ADA. And Mummy asks us what we do with our time. They're mad.

DAVE. Think we'll stick it out?

ADA. What the hell kind of question is that –

DAVE. Relax Ada – you've gone all tense – you'll give birth to a poker.

ADA. Dave, and that's another thing. I'm worried about the baby. I've been reading that –

DAVE. Whatever you've been reading forget it! Look at you, you're so healthy. Your belly is high and the baby is probably so big that he's bored with it all. (*Puts his ear to her stomach and has a conversation with the baby.*) Listen, he's talking.

ADA. You're mad darling.

DAVE. I tell you he's talking. Yes. Yes, I can hear you – sounds like a dozen drains emptying – what's that? You don't want to come out? But you've got to come out, I don't care how comfortable it is you'll get cramp. No I'm not going to send a bloody taxi for you – you'll walk. Now you listen to me, you come out when you're told or I'll plug you in there for life – you hear me?

ADA. Dave, for God's sake, don't be crude.

DAVE (*snuggling up to her*). Yes, let's be crude.

ADA. In the middle of fields?

DAVE. Right in the middle of fields, one night, at full moon.

> *At this moment* LIBBY DOBSON *appears. He's stocky, about thirty years old, and looks as though he wants to be a fisherman and can only be one on holidays.*

DOBSON. Quite a hideout you've got here, haven't you?

DAVE (*hopefully*). What do you think of it now you've seen it Libby?

DOBSON. You're going to turn it into a youth hostel?

DAVE. Got to make some spare cash somehow mate.

DOBSON. These places really do cater for the hale and bloody hearty, don't they? There – (*Puts two bottles on the table.*) wine for the table and the whisky's for me. I'm going up to change. (*Goes off.*)

DAVE. Well, I wonder what sort of evening this is going to be?

ADA (*picking up a bucket of waste from under sink and throwing it outside back door*). It'll be all right Dave. People aren't ever as you remember them – you'll just have to get to know each other again.

Outside ADA *notices the rolls of linoleum. Puts down bucket and undoes them.*

What's this darling?

DAVE. Some old lino the Colonel threw away. We can use that in the hallway.

ADA. Threw away?

DAVE. Well I saw it lying around in the shed. It's been there for months.

ADA. Did you ask him?

DAVE. But it's been lying around for ages.

ADA. Dave I'm not very moral about taking odd things from employers but I'd hate to have him –

DAVE. It's all right sweetheart I tell you.

ADA. You say it's all right but –

DAVE. Ada, the supper. Libby's hungry and so am I. I want to wash. (*Pours himself water into the bowl and strips to the waist to wash, as* ADA *proceeds to lay the table.*)

ADA. Shall I bring out the wine glasses?

DAVE. Bring out the wine glasses.

ADA. Darling don't be cross.

DAVE. But you go on so.

ADA. I don't want things to go wrong.

DAVE. Well a lot will go wrong – so? Are you going to get upset each time?

ADA. Will you light the lamp when you've finished please?

DAVE. I mean a lot *is* going to go wrong isn't it?

ADA. This is different, I –

DOBSON *returns at this point and sits down, waiting for the next move. Remember, he has already caught them embracing.* DAVE *and* ADA *glance at each other,* DAVE *shrugs his shoulders.* ADA *proceeds to lay out a clean shirt for* DAVE, *he is drying himself. The rest of this scene happens while* ADA *prepares a salad. They never get round to eating it.*

Don't forget the lamp when you've done please Dave.

DOBSON. Tilley lamps – the lot. You two have really taken your backward march seriously, eh? Dead serious – cor!

DAVE. Libby – what is it mate, come on, out with it – what's nettled you?

DOBSON. Oh no, Simmonds, please. No old chums and their war memories – I'm on holiday. I'll help you chop your wood – I'll even dance round the maypole with you – but no heart-searching, I'm a tired man.

Throughout an awkward silence the lamp is lit. During this next scene DOBSON *drinks his whisky, becoming more and more tipsy; just now he stares at the sky.*

DOBSON. The countryside smells like a cow with diarrhoea.

ADA. Perhaps your nose is still full of smoke and petrol fumes.

DOBSON. Jesus! I could've recognized that remark a mile off. If I hadn't known, it would have told me your whole story. Our horrible industrial civilization. We hate the large, inhuman cities. Eh? Back to nature, boys.

An embarrassed silence.

ADA (*to* DAVE). I had a letter from Ronnie today.

DAVE. What does your mad brother say?

ADA. You remember his girl friend Jacqueline? The one he told us knew it all? Well he's come to the dramatic conclusion that people who are similar aren't much good to each other so he's going to marry a prostitute!

DOBSON. Oh God! I bet your mother's in the Salvation Army.

ADA *and* DAVE *laugh uproariously at this.*

ADA. Can you imagine Sarah in the Salvation Army? 'Comrades, Jesus Christ was the first communist to be born among us.'

DOBSON. Now the picture is complete. Two ex-communists! There's nothing more pathetic than the laughter of people who have lost their pet faith.

The laughter is dead. That was a bomb.

DAVE. What the hell *is* the matter with you Libby? Within a few minutes you've called us idealists as if you were swearing at us, and then you express disgust because you think we've lost our faiths.

ADA. Let's have some of your wine shall we?

DOBSON. Yes, let's.

DAVE. You're being offensive Libby.

DOBSON (*wearily*). Oh, come off it! I'm a cynic. You can recognize a cynic, can't you? You should be using me, sharpening your ideas on me. The more sceptical I become the higher your ideals should soar, shouldn't they? Eh? Well, soar then – soar! Be heroic! There's nothing wrong with idealism, only when it's soft and flabby. The smell of petrol in my nose! So what! You can't change the world because it smells of petrol.

ADA. Who's talking about changing the world?

DOBSON. Then go home. Be good children and go home, because you'll never make the beautiful, rustic estate.

ADA. My God darling – it's come to something when we're sneered at for wanting beautiful things.

DOBSON. Because it's a lie. Outdated! Because it's not new!

DAVE. New! New! Everything has to be new! Contemporary! You could walk around on your hands all day – that's new – but it wouldn't be achieving much would it?

DOBSON. That's better – you're bristling, you're bristling. Soon you'll be able to devour me. That's what a cynic's for, Davey mate, to be devoured, gobbled up.

DAVE (*to* ADA). I don't understand it darling. Everyone accuses us of something or other – rustics, escapists, soft-headed. (*To* DOBSON.) You think there aren't problems here?

ADA. There isn't a servant to draw our water, you know.

DAVE. Or a gardener to grow our vegetables.

ADA. Do you think I'm going to have a nanny to see to my child?

DAVE. Or that there's a private income somewhere?

ADA. In London you waste your time solving the wrong problems.

DAVE. Leaving early to catch the bus! Is that living?

ADA. But God forbid we should ever imagine that we're changing that world by living here.

DOBSON. Then there's not much point in doing this sort of thing, is there?

DAVE. Not even on an individual level?

DOBSON. What do you mean, 'an individual level'?

DAVE. For God's sake stop asking us what we mean by perfectly simple phrases.

DOBSON. That's just it! They are simple phrases. Simple, inane and irresponsible! Individual level! Have you ever taken your ideas to their logical conclusion? Well, have you? Hasn't a worker in a factory ever looked at you as though you were mad – a little potty, you know? Would you have the world do without cars, planes, electricity, houses, roads? Because *that's* the logical conclusion. If no man

should be tied to turning out screws all his life, then
that's what it means. No screws – no transport! No
labourers – no roads! No banks or offices – no
commercial market! No humdrum jobs, then no
anything! There you are, solve it! Go on. Think
about it. Reorganize the world so's everyone's doing
a job he enjoys, so everyone's 'expressing' himself.
Go on. Universal happiness? Get it!

DAVE. Now who's being wet? Happiness? (*Mimicking.*)
What do you mean by happiness? It's the *doing*, the
doing! Do you think we care that the city was large or
smelt of petrol? It was the boredom man – the sheer
boredom. Nine to five! Mass production! Remember? It numbed us, made us soggy and soft. There!
That's being soggy and soft! Happiness! My God,
you cynics are the soggiest.

DOBSON. Nicely, nicely, Davey. Look, only my head
and arms are left.

ADA. You sound as though you really believe in
Jerusalem.

DOBSON. Shrewd girl. Of course I believe in Jerusalem,
only *I* personally can't measure up to it.

ADA. Because your type always tries to win with words
that's why – but you never *do* anything, you're never
at peace long enough.

DOBSON (*the harshness gone*). The idyll was really
broken, wasn't it? I could see it in your faces. Dave's
old blood brother has sold his soul. But what do you
really know about me, that you think you can say
that?

DAVE. We hadn't much of a chance had we comrade?
You weren't exactly inviting were you?

DOBSON. I've tried it, Dave – listen to me and go home
– I've tried it and failed. Socialism? I didn't sell out
that easily. You've gone back to William Morris, but
I went back to old Robert Owen. Five thousand

pounds my old man left me, and I blushed when I heard it. But I still hung on. It's not mine, I decided – the profits of exploitation, I said. Right! Give it back! So I worked out a plan. I found four other young men who were bright mechanics like myself and who were wasting their talents earning ten pounds a week in other men's garages, and I said 'Here's a thousand pounds for each of you – no strings, no loans, it's yours! Now let's open our own garage and exploit no one but ourselves. There's only one provision,' I said, 'only one: as soon as there is an excess profit of another thousand pounds, we find someone else to inherit it and we expand that way!' See the plan! A chain of garages owned and run by the workers themselves, the real thing, and I will build it myself. Can you imagine what a bloody fool they must have thought me? Can you guess the hell of a time they had planning to buy me out? Democracy, mate? I spit it! Benevolent dictatorship for me. You want Jerusalem? Order it with an iron hand – no questions, no speeches for and against – bang! It's there! You don't understand it? You don't want it? Tough luck, comrade – your children will! (*To* ADA.) No peace? You're right, Mrs Simmonds. I'm dirtied up. Listen to me, Dave, and go home before you're dirtied up.

ADA. You've nearly finished that whisky Libby.

DOBSON. Is that all you can say? I've just related a modern tragedy and you're warning me against alcohol. She's a real woman this Ada of yours. A woman dirties you up as well, you know. She and the world – they change you, they bruise you, they dirty you up – between them, you'll see.

DAVE. And you call the idealist soft and flabby do you?

ADA. Let's drop it Dave – I think Libby's had enough.

DOBSON. Oh no, you mean you've had enough. The little woman senses danger – marvellous instinct for self-preservation. I suppose you two consider you are happily married for ever and ever and ever. (*Pause.*) I was married once. God knows how it happened – just after demob. I used to watch her as the weeks and months went by; I used to sit and watch fascinated and horrified as – as she changed. This was before the old man died and we both went out to work. After supper we'd wash up and she'd sit by the fire and fall asleep. Just fall asleep – like that. She might glance at a newspaper or do a bit of knitting, but nothing else – nothing that might remind me she was alive. And her face would go red in front of the fire and she'd droop around and be slovenly. And I just watched her. She chewed food all the time, you know. Don't believe me? I watched her! Chewing all the time. Even in bed, before she went to sleep – an apple or a piece of gateau – as though terrified she wasn't getting enough into her for that day. And she became so gross, so undelicate, so unfeeling about everything. All the grace she had was going, and instead there was flesh growing all around her. I used to sit and watch it grow. How does one ever know, for Christ's sake, that a woman carries the seeds of such disintegration? Then I tried what your brother wants to do – take a simple girl, a girl from an office, lively, uncluttered. Wife number two! Just about the time I inherited my five thousand pounds. A real socialist enterprise and a simple wife. Ironic, really. There was I putting a vision into practice, and there was she watching me in case I looked at other women – making me feel lecherous and guilty. She's the kind that dirties you up. There was I sharing out my wealth and there was she – always wanting to possess things, terrified of being on her own. She marries a man in order to have something to attach to herself, a possession! The man provides a home – bang! She's got another possession. *Her* furniture, *her* saucepans, *her* kitchen – bang! bang! bang! And then she has a baby – bang again! All possessions! And this is the way she grows. She grows and she grows and she grows and she takes from a man all the things she once loved him for – so that no one else can have them. Because you see, the more she grows, ah! the more she needs to protect herself. Clever? Bloody clever! I think I hate women because they have no vision. Remember that, Davey – they haven't really got vision – only a sense of self-preservation, and you will get smaller and smaller and she will grow and grow and you will be able to explain nothing because everything else will be a foreign language to her. You know? Those innocent I-don't-know-what-you're-talking-about eyes?

DAVE. Make an early night Libby, yes?

> DOBSON *rises, suddenly, furious at being told to go to bed. But his own terrible honesty defies him. He shrinks, looks at them for a sort of forgiveness, and then shrugging his shoulders turns and goes, taking maybe something to chew from the table.*

ADA. Do you realize he was talking about what I might become darling?

DAVE. Are you worried?

ADA. Do we really appear like that to you men?

DAVE. You *are* worried aren't you?

ADA. I suddenly feel unclean.

DAVE. A cynic works that way darling. Perhaps he's right when he says we should use him, sharpen ourself on him. I don't know what to say – the man's certainly been bruised hasn't he? Does that make him more reliable or less – I never know.

ADA. The futile pursuit of an ideal. Suddenly it all makes me sick. Like eating too many good things.

DAVE. Right! Then enough now. We're not going to be dragged into this discussion again. We are not going to go around apologizing for the way we live. Listen to people and we'll go mad. Enough now!

Someone is coming from the lane. A torchlight appears. A voice calls. It is COLONEL DEWHURST.

COLONEL. Is anyone at home? Hello there. Simmonds.

ADA. It's Dewhurst. At this hour! (*Opens door to him.*) In here Colonel. Come in.

COLONEL. Good evening.

DAVE. Good evening Colonel Dewhurst. Have a seat. Would you like some wine?

COLONEL. This is not a social visit, Simmonds.

DAVE. That sounds very ominous.

ADA. Do have wine Colonel – it's very good.

COLONEL. Please, Mrs Simmonds. You're making it very difficult for me.

DAVE. Difficult?

COLONEL. I've treated you well, Simmonds, haven't I?

DAVE (*not knowing how it's coming*). Ye-es.

COLONEL. That's right, I have. Helped you when you started. Gave you advice.

DAVE. I'm very grateful Colonel but –

COLONEL. Well, you don't show it!

DAVE. I'm sorry but I don't know what you're talking about.

COLONEL. The lino, the lino! That's what I'm talking about and you know that's what I'm talking about. Look, Simmonds, you're an intelligent man – you're not the usual sort who works for me, and I didn't expect you to lie. Still, I didn't expect you to steal from me, but you did. Now don't waste time, just tell me and we'll see what we can do: did you or didn't you take two rolls of lino from the shed near the workshop?

DAVE. Those rolls you threw away and said were no use?

ADA. Dave –

DAVE. Darling – let *me*. No Colonel, I did not.

COLONEL. But I don't understand why you're lying. In fact I don't understand you at all, Simmonds. What did you come to the country for? It's a different way of life here, y'know. They're a slow people, the country people – slow, but sound. I know where I am with them, and they know their place with me. But with you I could never –

DAVE. Never get the right sort of master-servant relationship?

COLONEL. Yes, if you like. But you didn't like, did you? You spoke to me as if I were a – a –

DAVE. An equal.

COLONEL. I don't like it, Simmonds. I'm not a slave driver, but I believe each person has his place.

DAVE. You're decent like, but it's a favour like?

COLONEL. Are you talking to me about decency, Simmonds?

DAVE. You didn't come all the way up that lane just to find out whether I stole two rolls of lino did you Colonel?

ADA. For God's sake Dave –

DAVE. Now Ada!

COLONEL. Yes I did come all the way up that lane, and I'm damn well furious that I had to. Listen Simmonds, I've got to sack you, because by now all my other men know you took the rolls, and they know I know, and if I don't sack you they'll all think they can get away with pilfering. But thinking you were a decent chap, I thought I'd come here and just tell you what a fool you'd been, and discuss what we could do about it. Now I find you're a petty liar and

I'm furious, and I don't care what you do. Good night.

DAVE. But you haven't even any proof – I mean –

COLONEL. You must be insane. And what's outside your back door? (*Silence.*) Well, what is it?

DAVE (*weakly*). You said you didn't want it.

COLONEL. Of course I didn't. Junk! Two and sixpence worth of junk – but that isn't the point.

ADA. What is the point Colonel?

COLONEL. You don't really know the point, do you? We 'ask', Simmonds: in my sort of society we ask. That's all. It's twenty-four hours' notice I'm giving, but there is no need to turn up tomorrow. (*He leaves.*)

ADA. You bring the habits of factory life with you? What got into you?

DAVE. Oh God. What a bloody fool I am.

ADA. But I don't understand. Didn't you *know* the lino was outside and that he might see it?

DAVE. I took a chance that it might be dark –

ADA. Oh my God!

DAVE (*surprised*). I feel so ashamed.

ADA. It was so humiliating – if only you'd admitted it –

DAVE. To be caught for something so petty –

ADA. To be doubly caught for lying as well.

DAVE. Jesus! I feel so ashamed.

> *For some seconds* DAVE *sits, thoroughly crushed.* ADA *is appalled and uncertain what to do.*

ADA. Well we're not going back to London because of this ridiculous blunder. You're so bloody soft some times.

DAVE. Ada I'm sorry.

ADA. You'll have to start your workshop earlier that's all.

DAVE. But we can't afford it.

ADA. Well we'll *have* to afford it. I'm *not* giving up.

We'll eat less, we'll buy less, we'll do something but I'm not going away from all this. Thank God the house is still ours anyway. By Christ, Dave – your ideals have got some pretty big leaks in places haven't they?

> DAVE *is deeply hurt by this and* ADA *realizes she has struck deeply. Perhaps this is the first time she has ever hurt him so deeply. They wander round the room in silence now, clearing up the table.*

DAVE. Could you *really* see me leaving?

> *More silence – the battle dies in silence and the wounds heal quietly. The meal is being finally set.*

ADA. I can help mix cement for the workshop floor you know – I've developed big muscles from drawing water up the well.

DAVE (*looks at her gratefully*). Oh God I feel such a fool.

> *Then after a second* DAVE *lays his hands on* ADA's *shoulders, takes her to a chair, sits her gently on it, places a stool under her feet, takes an olive branch from out of the pot and, first offering it to her, lays it on her lap. Then he looks around and finds a large red towel which he shrouds on her head and shoulders. Then he steps back and kneels in homage. There he remains for a moment till gently he laughs and gradually* ADA *laughs too. And on their laughter –*

> *The curtain falls.*

ACT TWO

SCENE ONE

Late autumn afternoon, 1953. Six years have passed.

The front wall of the barn has been raised, revealing a furniture-maker's workshop.

DAVE *is just stepping out of the barn carrying, triumphantly, a chair that he and* SAMMY *have just made.* SAMMY *is* DAVE's *apprentice.* DAVE *is singing (pom-pom) 'Land of Hope and Glory' while* SAMMY *is on his knees applauding and bowing at the spectacle. As* DAVE *majestically lays chair on the 'horse'* SAMMY *speaks. It is fine craftsmanship.*

SAMMY. Looks as though it's sitting down don't it!

DAVE. When a chair does that, it works. (*Pause.*) But there's something wrong with this one.

SAMMY. Shall us have it apart?

DAVE. No, no. Leave it a while. Pour us out another cuppa. We'll look at it. (*Walks round the chair.*) The legs are too tall.

SAMMY. Hell! Have 'em any shorter and you'll be sitting on the floor.

DAVE. True, true. (*Thinks.*) A wrinkle! A little wrinkle! Old Dave's learnt a lot in six years. Give 'em a slight curf with the saw at the shoulder *in between* the joints. Won't need much. Now then, let's have a little clear-up shall we? Get the glue on!

SAMMY. When's he coming to see his chair?

DAVE. Who, Selby? Shortly, shortly.

SAMMY. I don't go much on him you know. He run a seed-sorting factory. Selby's seeds! Old compost!

And they reckon he don't pay his men too well neither.

DAVE. Bit fly eh?

SAMMY. Yearp, fly. And he started as a farm labourer hisself look.

DAVE. Well we've agreed on a good price for the chair anyway.

SAMMY. And you mind you stick to it too. I'll sharpen your chisels. (*Does so.*)

DAVE. The boy say anything to you when you took him to school this morning?

SAMMY. He jabbers a lot don't he?

DAVE. He's like all the Kahns. A funny kid. Comes home with the strangest stories. He's a smasher. Misses his mummy though.

SAMMY. What time train is Ada catchin' from London?

DAVE. Left about twelve this morning I think.

SAMMY. You heard from her? She say how her father was?

DAVE. Not well at all, not well at all poor Harry. This is his second stroke and it seems to have knocked him quite hard. (*He is looking at the chair now.*) I don't think I will. I'll leave the seat as it is. Once you start taking off a piece here and there it makes it worse. It's not all that out of proportion. What say you bor?

SAMMY. Well listen to you then! What say you bor! A proper Norfolk article you're talking like.

DAVE. You taking the mickey out of me? (*Throws a handful of shavings over* SAMMY's *head.*) Are you? (*Another.*) Are you? Are you? Eh?

> SAMMY *throws back shavings, at which* DAVE *cries* 'War!' *and picks up a stick. A fencing duel takes place till* SAMMY *falls defeated.*

SAMMY. Hey pack it in ole son. Mister what's-his-

name'll be here soon to have a look at this here
squatting chair of his.

DAVE. Look at this mess you've made. Sweep it up at
once. Untidy ole bugger.

> SAMMY *gathers shavings on his hands and knees with
> brush and pan. He wants to say something to* DAVE,
> *and is uncertain how to start.*

SAMMY. Dave, it'll be a while before Ada comes won't
it?

DAVE. Yes.

SAMMY. I want a little word with you then.

DAVE. Go on son. I'm listening, but I must get this
ready for glueing.

SAMMY. I want to leave soon.

DAVE. That was a very short word. Leave?

SAMMY. I aren't satisfied Dave.

DAVE. Satisfied?

SAMMY. Well I don't seem to be getting anywhere then.

DAVE. But you're learnin' something boy, you're learnin' to do something with your hands.

SAMMY. But nothing a factory can't do just as well as
what we do.

DAVE (*shocked*). Have you ever seen inside a factory?
You want to stand by a machine all day? By a planer
or a sander or a saw bench?

SAMMY. They change around all the time.

DAVE. Excitement! You change machines! Big difference! All your life Sammy, think of it, all your life.

SAMMY. But you get more money for it.

DAVE. That I do not have an answer to. (*Pause.*)
Sammy, remember that chair? Remember what you
said about it? It looks as though it's sitting down you
said. That's poetry boy, poetry! No not poetry, what
am I talking about. Er – it's – it's – O Jesus how do
you start explaining this thing. Look Sammy, look at

this rack you made for your chisels. Not an ordinary rack, not just bits of wood nailed together, but a special one with dove-tail joints here and a mortise and tenon joint there, and look what you put on the side, remember you wanted to decorate it, so you used my carving tools and you worked out a design. For no reason at all you worked out a design on an ordinary chisel rack. But there was a reason really wasn't there? You enjoyed using those tools and making up that design. I can remember watching you – a whole afternoon you spent on it and you used up three pieces of oak before you were satisfied. Twenty-seven and six you owe me.

SAMMY. Hell, that were only messing around.

DAVE. *Not* messing around. Creating! For the sheer enjoyment of it just creating. And what about the fun we had putting up this workshop?

SAMMY. It's not that I don't enjoy myself Dave.

DAVE. But that's not all cocker. It's not only the fun or the work – it's the place. Look at it, the place where we work. The sun reaches us, we get black in the summer. And any time we're fed up we pack up and go swimming. Don't you realize what that means? There's no one climbing on our backs. Free agents Sammy boy, we enjoy our work, we like ourselves.

SAMMY. You think I don't know these things, hell Dave. But I've seen the boys in the village, I know them, they don't care about things and I see them hang around all their lives, with twopence halfpenny between them an' half a dozen dependents. But I want to get on – don't you think I ought to get on?

DAVE. A bait! A trap! Don't take any notice of that clap-trap for God's sake boy. For every hundred that are lured only one makes it. One, only one. Factories? Offices? When you're in those mate you're there for good. Can't you see that? (*No answer.*) No, you can't

can you? Of course you can't. Jesus, I must be mad to
imagine I could fight everyone. Sammy, I'm sorry
mate – I just –

> *At this moment* ADA *appears. She looks pale and*
> *weary.*

Ada! Sweetheart! (*He doesn't know who to talk to first.*)
SAMMY. I'm away home to my tea now Dave. See you
tomorrow. How are you Ada? (*Retires quickly.*)
DAVE. Sammy, think again boy, we'll talk some more
tomorrow, we'll talk tomorrow, you hear?
ADA. What's been happening?
DAVE. He wants to leave. Work in a factory. Ada, how
ill you look. (*Goes to embrace her, she takes his kiss but*
does not respond.)
ADA. I met Selby in the village.
DAVE. And?
ADA. He wants to cancel the order for the chair.
DAVE. Cancel it? But it's made.
ADA. The price is too high he says.
DAVE. High? But we agreed – the bastard. That's the
third person's done this on me. Blast them, all of
them. Twentieth-centuy, short-sighted, insolent,
philistine-type bastards! And the world depends
upon them, you know that Ada? Oh sweetheart, what
an awful welcome.

> *Again he moves towards her but she moves away to sit*
> *on a stool.*

What is it Ada? Why don't you let me touch you all
of a sudden, so long and – O my God, it's Harry,
idiot I am, I didn't ask, he's not . . .
ADA. No, he's not dead.
DAVE. Then how is he?
ADA. He was raving when I got there.
DAVE. Raving? Old Harry?

ADA. The second stroke affected his brain. He was in a padded cell.

DAVE. O God, Ada –

DAVE *stetches to her but she continues to refuse his comfort.*

ADA. He didn't recognize me at first. He was lying on his back. You know how large his eyes are. They couldn't focus on anything. He kept shouting in Yiddish, calling for his mother and his sister Cissie. Mummy told me he was talking about Russia. It seems when they first brought him into the ward he threw everything about – that's why a cell. He looked so frightened and mad, as if he were frightened of his own madness.

DAVE. But what brought it on? I mean don't the doctors know?

ADA. A clot of blood. It's reached the brain. And then he recognized me and he looked at me and I said 'Hello Daddy – it's Ada' and he started screaming in Yiddish. 'Dir hasst mir, dir hasst mir, dir host mirch alle mul gerhasst!' You hate me and you've always hated me. (*She breaks down uncontrollably.*) Oh darling I haven't stopped crying and I don't understand it, I don't understand it because it's not true, it's never been true.

DAVE *holds her tightly as she cries, and smothers her with kisses.*

DAVE. Hush darling, gently, gently. It was a sick man screaming, a sick man, hush – O good God.

They stand a while. Then ADA *pulls away and starts mechanically unpacking her case.*

ADA. He smiled and kissed me a lot before I left, it was

an uncanny feeling, but you know Dave (*Surprised at the thought.*) I feel like a murderer.

DAVE. *Ada!* You gone mad? A murderer? Stop this nonsense. You think you were responsible for his illness?

ADA (*calmly*). No, I don't think I was responsible for his illness and neither did I hate him. But perhaps I didn't tell him I loved him. Useless bloody things words are. Ronnie and his bridges? 'Words are bridges,' he wrote, 'to get from one place to another.' Wait till he's older and he learns about silences – they span worlds.

DAVE. No one made any rules about it. Sometimes you use bridges. Sometimes you're silent.

ADA. What bridges? Bridges! Do you think I know what words go to make *me*? Do you think I know why I behave the way I behave? Everybody says I'm cold and hard, people want you to cry and gush over them. (*Pause.*) During the war, when you were overseas, I used to spend nights at home with Sarah and the family. There was never a great deal of money coming in and Mummy sometimes got my shopping and did my ironing. Sometimes she used to sit up late with me while I wrote to you in Ceylon, and she used to chatter away and then – fall asleep. She'd sit, in the chair, straight up, and fall asleep. And every time she did that and I looked at her face it was so sweet, so indescribably sweet – that I'd cry. There! Each time she fell asleep I'd cry. But yet I find it difficult to talk to her! So there! Explain it! Use words and explain that to me.

DAVE. What's going to happen to Sarah, Ada? Do you reckon we ought to think about returning?

ADA (*turning to him, slowly and deliberately*). Dave, listen to me. My mother is a strong woman. She was born to survive every battle that faces her. She doesn't

need me. You say I'm like her? You're right. I'm also
strong, I shall survive every battle that faces me too,
and this place means survival for me. We – are –
staying – put!

> DAVE *takes her hands and kisses them, then her lips.*
> *A child's voice calls:* 'Mummy, Ada, Mummy, Ada,
> Mummy, Ada!'

DAVE. It's the boy. Watch how pleased he'll be, he kept
asking when you were coming. I bet you a dollar the
first thing he'll want you to do is play your game with
him.

ADA. Danny?

DANNY (*off, assuming a gruff voice*). I'm Daniel the lion
killer.

ADA. You're who?

DANNY. I've come to slay your lions for you.

ADA. How much do you charge?

DAVE (*taking out his pipe*). Mothers!

DANNY. I charge sixpence a lion.

ADA. The last time I saw you you were so small, I don't
know whether I could trust you to slay my lions.

DANNY. I'm as tall as an elephant.

ADA. I can't possibly believe that. Come out and show
yourself Daniel the lion killer.

DANNY. I shan't show myself until you play the game
with me.

ADA. Oh! And what is the game today Daniel?

DANNY. It is called 'Look I'm alive!'

> DAVE *does a there-I-told-you-so-look.*

ADA. Oh that one. All right. Are you ready?

DANNY. Yes. Now you do it with me.

> *Now* ADA *faces us and goes through the same actions
> as we must assume* DANNY *does. She starts crouched*

down, with her face hidden in her arm – as in the womb.

ADA. Are you crouched down?
DANNY (*in his own voice*). Yes Mummy.

DAVE *pulls a face at her so she draws him into the game too.*

ADA. Do you mind if my friend here plays Mr Life? (DAVE *tries to run away.*) *Dave!*
DANNY. No, hurry up, I'm getting cramp.

What happens from now must have the touch of magic and of clowning. The day has gone and now the light fades slowly into evening.

DAVE (*bowing first to* ADA, *then to* DANNY). I am – (*Pause – to* ADA.) what's it?
ADA. You're Mr Life.
DAVE. Oh yes, Mr Life. I am Mr Life. I have spent all day making furniture and now I am going to make a human being. You are clay and I am going to make you into a human being. I am going to breathe the fire of life into you. Hissssss, Hissssss, Hissssss.

As DAVE *breathes the fire* ADA *unfolds and rises very slowly – this is what* DANNY *is doing unseen – her eyes are closed.*

Now you have life and you can breathe.

ADA *breathes deeply.*

Now I will give you sight.

He snaps his fingers at DANNY *then at* ADA. ADA *opens her eyes. There is wonder and joy at what is revealed.*

Now I will give you movement.

> DAVE *beckons to* DANNY *then to* ADA. ADA *raises and lowers her arms twice, moving her head from left to right at the same time, full of curiosity and excitement at what she is doing.*

Now I will give you speech. (*He draws something unseen from his mouth and throws it to* DANNY, *then he kisses his finger and places the kiss on* ADA's *lips.*) Tell me, what does it feel like to be a human being?

DANNY (*in his gruff voice*). It's a little strange. But I'm getting used to it. It's very exciting.

> ADA *relaxes and becomes herself and involved in the questioning.*

ADA. Now that you have eyes and tongue to see and talk and limbs to move – move, and tell me what you see.

DANNY (*in his own voice*). Hedges!

ADA. No no Daniel. That's a name, that's not what you see.

DANNY (*in his own voice from now on*). I see thin pieces of wood. Going all over the place. With bumps on them, and thin slips of green like paper, and some funny soft stuff on them.

ADA. *Now* you can use names.

DANNY. They're hedges with leaves and berries.

ADA. Any colours?

DANNY. The hedges are brown, the leaves are green and the berries are red and black.

ADA (*becoming excited*). What else can you see, O Daniel?

DANNY. A blue sky with white cloud.

ADA. More?

DANNY. Birds with long necks.

ADA. More?

DANNY. Green fields with brown bumps.

ADA. More?

DANNY. A red brick house and that's where I live.

ADA. Now you are a real human being Daniel who can look and think and talk and you can come out and slay the lions.

> *We hear* DANNY *run right across the back of the stage (past barn and hedges) crying: 'I'm coming I'm coming I'm coming!' and* ADA *crouches down with her arms outstretched to receive him as the night and –*
>
> *The curtain falls.* *

SCENE TWO

It is warm autumn. Three years have passed. 1956. The wall in front of the barn is lowered. No one works there now.

Two women are seated in the garden. CISSIE *and* ESTHER KAHN, *maiden aunts of* ADA. *The first is a trade unionist, the other owns a market stall.* CISSIE *is shelling peas.* ESTHER *is peeling potatoes.*

There is a lovely light in the sky and two deck chairs near the back door.

ESTHER. A guest house they call it.

CISSIE. Esther, stop grumbling – peel!

ESTHER. Three hundred ditches we had to jump over before we even reached the house – and they advertise in newspapers. For peace and quiet and a modest holiday – the Shambles. A very inviting name. Mind you, for a dirty weekend, this place – you know what I mean?

CISSIE (*not* really *minding*). Why must you be so bloody crude Esther?

ESTHER. All these years she's been my sister and she doesn't know me yet?

---

* The boy could perhaps rush on to the stage as the lights fade. Director's decision.

CISSIE. What time does Dave come back for lunch?

ESTHER. One o'clock.

CISSIE. Ada'll come back from shopping with him, I suppose.

ESTHER. They better be on time else that dinner'll be burnt.

CISSIE. What?

ESTHER. Don't say 'what', say 'ah?' Fine bloody holiday this. Only two mad maiden aunts like us would do this. Do you realize that we haven't stopped working since we've been here? Look at that job we did yesterday. Pulling up weeds. Agricultural workers!

CISSIE. Stop grumbling. You know you're enjoying yourself.

ESTHER. You think they make all their other guests work like this? No wonder they get so few. Cissie – I think we should tell them.

CISSIE. What?

ESTHER. Don't say 'what', say 'ah?' We should tell them that people when they go on holiday they don't like digging gardens and feeding chickens.

CISSIE. Don't be daft woman. It's only us. We spoil her. Both her and Ronnie we spoilt.

ESTHER. A guest house they call it. Not even a bleedin' flush lavatory. Just three hundred ditches.

CISSIE. Hush Esther.

ESTHER. What's the matter for Gawd's sake? You frightened someone'll hear me? (*Shouting.*) *Cissie, have you stopped peaing yet?*

CISSIE. So help me you're mad.

ESTHER. I'm keeping in training. Though I must say this ain't the most inspiring place for selling underwear. I mean what do their guests do here? The only sights to see are sixty clucking hens waiting to be slaughtered – poor sods – and a two-hundred-year-old barn. A historical monument!

CISSIE. That used to be Dave's workshop.

ESTHER. What did he leave it for?

CISSIE. Ada was telling me that one day about six months ago, he built a beautiful dressing-table for someone and he had a lorry come to collect it, and the driver took no care on the bumpy lane so that by the time they reached the main road they'd knocked all the corners off it. A two-hundred-pound job it was, all his own design, ruined! So he found a new workshop in the village.

ESTHER. And he still can't earn money. Poor sod. He works hard that one – and what for? For peanuts that's what for!

CISSIE. Well today may change all that.

ESTHER. You mean the loan?

CISSIE (nodding). If he's managed to persuade the bank to loan him money he can buy machinery and his work'll be easier.

ESTHER. Now that's something I don't understand. I can remember him saying when he first moved here that he wanted to make furniture with his own hands. Now he's buying machinery, he'll be like a factory only not big enough to make their turnover. So where's the ideals gone all of a sudden?

CISSIE. Esther, you're a stall-owner, you don't understand these things.

ESTHER. All right, so I'm a coarse stall-owner. I'm a silly cow. So I'm a silly cow and you're a clever trade-union organizer – you explain it to me.

CISSIE. It's all got to do with the work of another socialist furniture-maker, William Morris.

ESTHER. Jewish?

CISSIE. No, famous! He used to say 'Machines are all right to relieve dull and dreary work, but man must not become a slave to them.'

ESTHER. So?

CISSIE. So Ada says Dave says if he can buy a machine
to saw the wood, and another to plane it, that will
save him a lot of unnecessary labour and he can still
be a craftsman.

ESTHER. I'll tell you something Cissie! Our nieces and
nephews are all mad. Look at Ronnie – working in a
kitchen, and that silly arse has fallen in love with a
waitress.

CISSIE. So what's wrong with a waitress? Beatie
Bryant's a very nice girl, very active, bless her.

ESTHER. I know she's a nice girl but she doesn't know
what Ronnie's saying half the time.

CISSIE. If it comes to that neither do I. You know where
she comes from? About twenty miles from here.
Ronnie met her when he came to work in Norwich.

> CISSIE *rises and enters kitchen to put peas in pot.*
> ESTHER *follows.*

ESTHER. Another wandering Jew. Another one can't
settle himself. Hopping about all over the country
from one job to another. I'll tell you something Cissie
– it's not a joke. Ronnie worries me. He worries me
because his father was just the same. You know
Harry? Before he fell ill? The way he couldn't stick at
one job? The same thing! All over again. It worries
me.

CISSIE. Now Esther don't you ever tell him that – you
hear me?

ESTHER. Me? I wouldn't say a word! But it worries me.
And he wants to spread socialism. Everybody's busy
with socialism. 'Aunty Esther' he says 'I've finished
making speeches, I'm going to marry a simple girl
and hand it all on to her.' So I says to him 'Ronnie' I
says 'be careful. Don't hand it on to her *before* you're
married.' The meat! (*Turns to oven.*)

> At this point ADA and DAVE appear.

ADA. What's happened to Aunty Esther?

CISSIE. It's all right darling, she's just gone to look at the meat. She always rushes like that – as if the world was on fire. What's the matter Simmonds? You look all done in.

DAVE. Bank managers. How do you talk to them?

CISSIE. Like I talk to employers when I'm negotiating a strike – as though you're doing them a favour by coming at all.

ESTHER (*coming out of the kitchen*). Fifteen more minutes and we can eat.

ADA. You're bricks, the pair of you.

ESTHER. You mean we got thick skulls?

CISSIE. Stop grumbling.

ESTHER. All she can say to me is 'Esther stop grumbling'. I'm a happy woman, let me grumble. So tell us, what happened? (*Returns to chair in garden.*)

CISSIE. Wait a minute, let me get my knitting. (*Goes to kitchen.*)

ESTHER. Can't you ever sit still and do nothing?

CISSIE. No I bloody can't. The good Lord gave me hands and I like using them.

ESTHER. The good Lord gave you an arse but you don't have to be sh . . .

CISSIE. *Esther!*

ESTHER. She's so squeamish your aunt.

CISSIE (*returning and sitting on deck chair*). Right, now let's hear what happened – I'm very interested.

ADA. I must go in and lay the table, I can hear from inside.

DAVE *moves to the barn and cleans some of his tools.*

ESTHER. What's the matter with everybody? No one can sit still for five minutes. This one knits, this one must lay the table, that one mucks about with his tools –

CISSIE. He's cleaning his chisels, Esther.

ESTHER. Don't split hairs with me. It's a bleedin' conspiracy to make me feel guilty – well nuts to yers all, I'm sitting still. I'm a lady. A bleedin' civilized lady on holiday. Fan me somebody!

CISSIE. Esther, maybe the kids don't feel like joking.

ESTHER. Dave Simmonds, are you going to tell us what happened at the bank or not?

DAVE. Nothing much. He said I could have an overdraft of two hundred pounds but no loan.

ESTHER. So what you feeling unhappy for? With an overdraft you can lay down deposit on two machines and pay off over three or five years. Who buys anything outright these days anyway.

DAVE. Yeah.

CISSIE. Hey Addie – what kind of school dinners does Danny get?

ESTHER. A real grasshopper mind you've got. Can't you stick to one subject at a time?

CISSIE. Leave off Esther, can't you see the boy doesn't want to talk about it?

> ADA *comes out of the kitchen. She is rubbing her hands and face on a towel very slowly. Although she looks red-eyed from washing, she really has been crying and is covering up with a wash.*

ADA. They're not bad. A little bit dull but he gets plenty of it.

ESTHER. Have you been crying Ada?

CISSIE. Leave off Esther, I tell you.

ESTHER. For crying out loud what's been happening to you two?

> DAVE *looks up and sees that, in fact,* ADA *has been crying. He lays down his saw, approaches her and takes her in his arms. After a bewildered moment of looking at them and each other –*

CISSIE *and* ESTHER (*between them*). Ah Ada darling. My pet. Sweetheart. Don't cry love. Ah there poppit, what is it then?

> *Both aunts start fussing the couple but are unable to do anything except commiserate and get in each other's way while moving around trying to get in somewhere. They cannot reach either of the two.* DAVE *and* ADA *stand locked together and rocking, their own misery being the centre of the aunts' faintly comic and frustrated concern.*

CISSIE (*having tripped over* ESTHER'*s feet*). Get back to your deck chair, I'll handle this.

ESTHER. Cissie, carry on knitting and leave off. You always were heavy-handed with people.

CISSIE. That's how it should be. As soon as *you* start handling people you have them in tears.

ESTHER. And you treat every upset as though it was an industrial dispute.

ADA. Listen to those two. Anyone would think we were still fifteen.

DAVE. Feeling better sweetheart?

ADA. How can anyone feel depressed with those two old hens clucking round you.

ESTHER. Here, let me tell you about the time Ronnie made a supper of rice.

CISSIE. That's it, tell them about the time Ronnie made us a. supper of rice.

DAVE. Listen to them darling, don't they sound like a music-hall act?

CISSIE. Ronnie invites himself to supper and says he want to try out a special pork curry –

ESTHER. A very kosher dish he assures us –

CISSIE. We don't even like curry –

ESTHER. Never mind, we agree. What a mess! A whole pound of rice he puts into a saucepan and he starts to boil it – so you know what happens when you boil rice –

CISSIE. It swells!

ESTHER. The whole pound of rice began to swell. And what does he do when it reaches the top of the saucepan? He puts half of it in another saucepan and sets them both to boil. And do you think it was cooked?

CISSIE. Of course it wasn't! And the two saucepans got full again – so he gets two more saucepans and halves them again. For two hours before we got home he was cooking rice –

ESTHER. And by the time we arrived he had five saucepans and two frying-pans filled with rice for a supper of three people.

> *Everyone is in a paroxysm of laughter until, as they emerge out of it,* ESTHER *suddenly remembers –*

Oh yes – there's some mail for you.

DAVE. Thank God – at last!

ESTHER. At last, what?

CISSIE. We thought all you wanted was a loan.

ADA. You have to have people to buy the furniture as well you know.

CISSIE. And there's no people?

ADA. Some, but it mostly for window sashes.

ESTHER. What's so important with the letter then?

DAVE. The letter is important because three weeks ago I had an enquiry for an originally designed suite of dining-room chairs and table and I sent in an estimate and this should be a reply. If they don't want it, it means I have to carry on doing window sashes.

ESTHER. And what's Ada crying for?

DAVE. She's having a baby.

Cries of joy and surprise and 'muzzeltov' and more fussing from the aunts.

ESTHER. So what's there to cry about? Are you sure?

ADA. Of course I'm sure you silly bitch.

ESTHER. Right, then if you don't mind I'm going to say something.

DAVE. Esther, I think we're going to mind –

ESTHER. I'm still going to say it.

ADA. Aunts, please, we're really very tired.

ESTHER. For Gawd's sake! It's not as though we're strangers. We're your aunts. All your life, till we die.

DAVE. What are you going to tell us? We're mad to stay here? Everyone's told us this. Half our battle here has been against people who for a dozen different reasons have tried to tell us we're mad.

ESTHER. Never mind about madness – but you've changed. You're not the same. Once upon a time we could talk to you. You got troubles? So tell us. What's the matter – you think we're going to laugh?

DAVE. We're tired Esther, leave us alone, yes?

ESTHER. Nice life! Lovely! It's a pleasure knowing you! Open the letter.

DAVE. I *know* what's in the letter. Dear Mr Simmonds, after having carefully considered your designs and estimate we feel sorry to have to inform you – God! I'm learning to hate people!

ESTHER (*taking down washing and telling a story*). My mother loved her children. You know how I know? The way she used to cook our food. With songs. She used to hum and feed us. Sing and dress us. Coo and scold us. You could tell she loved us from the way she did things for us. You want to be a craftsman? Love us. You want to give us beautiful things? Talk to us. You think Cissie and I fight? You're wrong, silly boy. She talks to me. I used to be able to watch everything on television, but she moaned so much I can't even enjoy rubbish any more. She drives me mad with her talk.

DAVE. I talked enough! You bloody Kahns you! You all talk. Sarah, Ronnie, all of you. I talked enough! I wanted to do something. Hands I've got – you see them? I wanted to do something.

ESTHER. Hands is the only thing? I'm a worker too. Haven't I worked? From selling flags at a football match to selling foam cushions in Aylesbury market. From six in the morning till six at night. From pitch to pitch, all hours, all my life! That's not work? It doesn't entitle me to a house? Or a fridge? I shouldn't buy a washing machine? How do you *measure* achievement for Christ's sake? Flower and Dean Street was a prison with iron railings, you remember? And my one ambition was to break away from that prison. 'Buy your flags' I used to yell. 'Rattles at rattling good prices' I used to try to be funny. So I sold rattles and now I've got a house. And if I'd've been pretty I'd've had a husband and children as well and they'd've got pleasure from me. Did money change me? You remember me, tell me, have I changed? I'm still the same Esther Kahn. I got no airs. No airs me. I still say the wrong things and nobody minds me. Look at me – you don't like me or something? That's all that matters. Or no, not that, not even like or dislike – do I harm you? Do I offend you? Is there something about me that offends you?

DAVE (*simply*). You haven't got a vision Esther.

ESTHER. A prophet he is!

DAVE. No! We should turn to *you* for prophecies! With your twopenny halfpenny flags and your foam cushions? With your cheap jewels, your market lies and your jerry houses?

ADA. Dave, sweetheart – there's no point – you'll only upset yourself – and she doesn't mean –

DAVE. No, no. She can take it. Straight Jane and no nonsense she says. Let's talk back a little. I know we decided not to bother to explain but I'm fed up being on the receiving end. I'll tell them. (*To* ESTHER.) Once and for all I'll tell you – you call me a prophet and laugh do you? Well, I'll tell you. I *am* a prophet. Me. No one's ever heard of me and no one wants to buy my furniture but I'm a bleedin' prophet and don't anyone forget that. As little as you see me so big I am. Now you look at me. I picked up my spear and I've stuck it deep. Prophet Dave Simmonds, me. With a chisel. Dave Simmonds and Jesus Christ. Two yiddisha boys –

ESTHER. Hatred, Cissie. Look at our nephew-in-law, hatred in every spit.

DAVE. Well, what have you left me for God's sake? You want an angel in me? Ten years I spent here trying to carve out a satisfactory life for my wife and kids and on every side we've had opposition. From the cynics, the locals, the family. Everyone was choking with their experience of life and wanted to hand it on. Who came forward with a word of encouragement? Who said we maybe had a little guts? Who offered one tiny word of praise?

ESTHER. Praise pretty boy?

DAVE. Yes, praise! It would hurt you, any of you? There isn't enough generosity to spare a little pat on the back? You think we're cranks – recluses? Well, I'll surprise you, look – no long hair, no sandals. Just flesh and blood. Of course we need a little praise. (*Dips in his pocket for coins.*) Or maybe you want me to buy it from you! Like in the market! Here, two half-crowns for a half-minute of praise. I'll buy it! You can't afford to give it away? I'll pay for it! Five bob for a few kind words, saying we're not mad. Here y'are – take it! Take it!

CISSIE. There! You satisfied Esther? Now you've upset him, you happy?

ESTHER (*subdued*). I know, I know. I'm just a silly old cow. You want to build Jerusalem? Build it! Only maybe we wanted to share it with you. Now open the letter.

> DAVE *opens the letter, just before he has had a chance to look at it the curtain comes down so that we do not know what it says.*

SCENE THREE

Three years later. 1959.

The Simmondses are moving out. SARAH *and* RONNIE *are helping them. Everyone is that much older.*

SARAH *is sweeping up the kitchen.* ADA *is attending to a third baby, who is in a carry-cot up stage.* DAVE *is just taking a box off stage to where the removal lorry is waiting.* RONNIE *is beside a pile of books that are waiting to be packed away.*

*But at this moment they are all listening to the radio.**

ANNOUNCER. Captain Davies, Conservative 20,429. J. R. Dalton, Labour, 10,526. L. Shaftesbury, Liberal, 4,291. Conservative majority 9,903. The Liberal candidate forfeits his deposit. These latest results bring the Conservative majority up to 93 and will ensure the return to power in the House of Commons of the Conservative Party for a third time in succession since the end of the war. Mr Gaitskell

---

* Alternatively, the words given here as a radio announcement could be read out by Ronnie from a newspaper, in which case instead of switching off the radio at the end of the announcement Ronnie would crumple up the newspaper.

went to Transport House this morning to confer with other Labour leaders – he looked very tired –

RONNIE (*switching off*). Well – you've chosen the right time to return anyway. You came in with them and you go out with them – whisht. (*Continues looking through books in silence.*) I'm all washed up. I don't know why the hell you asked me to help with this morbid job.

ADA. Go home then dear boy.

DAVE (*returning with an empty tea chest*). Here's the box to put the books in.

RONNIE. I said I'm all washed up. I'm complaining. (*No response.*) No one listens to me now. Funny that, everybody loo-ves me but nobody listens to me. I can't keep a job and I can't keep a girl so everyone thinks what I say doesn't count. Like they used to say of Dad. Poor old Harry – poor old Ronnie. But you forgive me my trespasses don't you Addie? Look at my sister, she's still beautiful.

DAVE. It was good of you to help us cocker.

RONNIE. *That's* all I ever get away with – gestures. You give someone a hand and they think you're a saint. Saint Ronnie Kahn.

> *All continue with their respective jobs. The removal is in its last stages.* DAVE *is going round picking up stray tools to place in a tool box.* RONNIE *sings to himself.*

RONNIE.

> Come O my love and fare ye well,
> Come O my love and fare ye well,
> You slighted me but I wish you well.
> The winter is gone and the leaves turn green,
> The winter is gone and the leaves turn green,
> Your innocent face I wish I never had seen.

You realize you two that having come with explanations you must leave with explanations.

ADA. Is anyone going to care that much Ronnie?

RONNIE. Yes, me! Jesus, one of us has got to make a success of something. You can understand the Labour Party losing the elections again, they change their politics like a suit of clothing or something, but us – well you two, you put it into practice, God knows why you lost.

ADA. Let's forget it Ronnie.

RONNIE (*jumping up*). No, don't let's forget it. You can still change your mind. Let's unpack it all. Pay the removers and try again. There must be something –

DAVE. Don't go on Ronnie, I keep telling you.

RONNIE. But you can't just pack up –

DAVE. I said shut up!

RONNIE.

> The rope is hung and the noose hangs high
> The rope is hung and the noose hangs high
> An innocent man you have all sent to die.

SARAH. What is it, a funeral here?

DAVE. Any chance of a last cup of tea before we go Mum?

SARAH. Tea I can always make.

RONNIE. Tea she can always make.

> There ain't a lady livin' in the land
> What makes tea like my dear old mum –
> No there ain't a lady livin' in the land
> What –

What rhymes with 'mum'?

SARAH. Everything he makes into a joke.

DAVE. Did you ever hear what happened to Beatie Bryant, Ronnie?

RONNIE. No.

DAVE. The girl you wanted to change.

RONNIE. Change! Huh! You know what my father once said to me? 'You can't change people Ronnie,' he said, 'you can only give them some love and hope they'll take it.' Well, Beatie Bryant took it but nothing seemed to happen.

DAVE. Three years is a long time to go with a girl.

RONNIE. I don't regret it. Maybe something did happen. After all little Sarah, wasn't it you who was always telling us that you don't know people without something happening?

SARAH. I'm always telling you you can't change the world on your own – only no one listens to me.

RONNIE. We carry bits and pieces of each other, like shrapnel from a war. Ada's like you Sarah, strong! I'm charming, like my father, and weak. O God! Isn't it all terribly, terribly sad. (*Suddenly.*) Let's do an Israeli dance before we go – come on, let's dance. (*Starts doing a Zanny Hora on his own.*) The wandering Jews move on – bless 'em. Let there be music, let there be –

ADA. Stop clowning Ronnie, we won't be done in time.

RONNIE. Don't argue! Don't sing! Don't clown!

ADA. You don't have to do anything.

RONNIE. That's right. I don't *have* to do anything – except pack up and go home. We're none of us what you could call 'returning heroes' are we? If only we could squeeze a tiny victory out of it all. God, there must be a small victory somewhere for one of us. Maybe I was a good son eh? Before he died I used to wash Harry and shave him. It took him too long to walk so I used to carry him in my arms, like a cooing baby. Then I'd bounce him on the bed and play with him and he used to laugh, a really full laugh. Funny that, in the last months he couldn't talk but his laughter was full. Mummy even used to try to play cards with him but he couldn't hold them. Sometimes I laid *my* head in *his* arms to make him feel he could still – (*It is too painful to continue.*) No – I don't have to do anything. Only the old worthies are left biding their time, waiting for the new generation. Look at old Mother there, like a patient old tigress – she's still waiting. Nothing surprises you does it Sarah? You still think it'll come, the great millennium?

SARAH. And you don't?

RONNIE. Well, I haven't brought it about – and they (*Of* ADA *and* DAVE.) haven't brought it about, and the Monty Blatts and Cissie and Esther Kahns haven't brought it about. But then Dad said it would never happen in our lifetime – 'It'll purify itself' he used to say. The difference between capitalism and socialism he used to say was that capitalism contained the seeds of its own destruction but socialism contained the seeds of its own purification. Maybe that's the victory – maybe by coming here you've purified yourselves, like Jesus in the wilderness. Yes? No? (*No response. Places last three books in box, reading titles out like a list of the dead and softly kissing each one.*) *Mother* by Maxim Gorky. *My Son, My Son* by Howard Spring. *Madame Bovary* by Gustave Flaubert. Lovely sound that – Flaubert. Ronnie de Flaubert.

DAVE. Did you ever finish your novel?

RONNIE. No.

DAVE. You've grown older in these last years, haven't you mate?

RONNIE. Yes.

ADA. I don't think there's anything more to pack away.

RONNIE (*making it up*).
    Pull down the blind, put away the stars,
    The lovers have left their fond house for the town,
    No more leaves will be gathered again
    And the last nightingales have gone.

ADA. Come on darling – put away your books and poems and let's be having you.

RONNIE. *You're* still smiling anyway.

ADA. Well, we shall be back for the summer holidays.

DAVE. Anyone would think it's your experiment that failed, you with your long face.

RONNIE. O my God, how near the knuckle that is.

SARAH. Come and have some tea and stop depressing each other.

RONNIE. And Mother says little. Quietly packs and takes her children home with her.

SARAH. I've been lonely for long enough Ronnie. A few more years and I'll be dead. I'm committing no crimes.

RONNIE. I never know whether to say at this point (*Melodramatically.*) 'we're all lonely' or not. As soon as I say something, somehow I don't believe it. Don't you find that with things? As soon as you pronounce something it doesn't seem true?

The REMOVAL MEN *enter.*

IST REMOVAL MAN. That the lot?

DAVE. That's it. Just this last case. We're leaving the rest for the holidays.

RONNIE. The radio too?

DAVE. No, bring the radio.

2ND REMOVAL MAN. Like vicars aren't we? Brought you into the world now we're taking you out!

SARAH. It's not a funeral you know.

IST REMOVAL MAN. You mustn't mind him, missus, he's got a morbid streak.

2ND REMOVAL MAN. On account of me profession – always moving things. Makes life seem uncertain. Who'll see to your garden and weeds?

IST REMOVAL MAN. Have to weed it in their holidays won't they.

2ND REMOVAL MAN. Good socialist holiday, weeding
  gardens.

SARAH (*defensively*). And why not!

> RONNIE *and* DAVE *pick up packing-case and go off
> with the* REMOVAL MEN.

ADA. Let's make it quick Dave, because Danny and
  Jake'll be waiting up for us. (*To* SARAH.) I wonder
  how the children'll take to London?

SARAH. Are you sure Aunty Esther met them at the
  station?

ADA. Yes, we had a telegram.

> RONNIE *and* DAVE *return.*

RONNIE (*trying to be cheerful*). Righto me hearties. The
  cheerful side. Let's look at the rainbow. The silver
  lining. Because remember – in the words of that
  immortal American prophet – (*Does an Al Jolson act.*)

> When April showers may come your way
> They bring the flowers that bloom in May,
> So when it's raining have no regrets
> Because it isn't raining rain you know it's . . .

(*Gives up.*) . . . etcetera, etcetera, et bloody cetera!

DAVE. I've found a basement workshop in London and
  I'll set up shop there.

RONNIE (*sadly*). A basement! The man who started
  work singing 'Linden Lea' in the open air returns to a
  basement.

ADA (*after a silence*). The sun is setting Dave. We really
  must be moving.

DAVE (*picking up again*). Who knows, maybe people
  will buy furniture in town. They say you can sell
  them anything in London.

ADA. We've found a house – a roof over our heads.

RONNIE (*jumping on crate*). Oh bloody marvellous!

We've got sixpence, jolly jolly sixpence
Di dum dee da to last us all our life
Pom-pom to lend
And pom-pom to spend
And pom-pom to take home to our wives
Hallelujah!

ADA (*finally unnerved*). Ronnie!

DAVE (*after a second*). I can't make you out cock. Not at all I can't make you out.

RONNIE. I'm crying Dave, I'm bloody crying.

Everyone is unnerved. Everyone is feeling the reality of leaving. A long pained silence.

DAVE. So? We're all crying. But what do you want of us – miracles?

SARAH. I don't know what's happened to you all. Suddenly you're talking and then you're shouting and then you're crying. Suddenly you start hitting each other with words.

DAVE. Well, why must he put us on pedestals.

SARAH. You were the God that fought in Spain, Dave, remember?

DAVE (*to* RONNIE). Is that it? (*Pause.*) You can't really forgive me because I didn't speak heroically about Spain, can you?

RONNIE (*reflectively*). The war that was every man's war.

DAVE. A useless, useless bloody war because evil and Hitler still made it, didn't they, eh? And out went six million Jews in little puffs of smoke. Am I expected to live in the glory of the nineteen-thirties all my life?

SARAH. Sick! You're all sick or something! Who says evil ever finishes? Nothing finishes! A Rasputin comes, you oppose him; a Bismarck comes, you oppose him; a Hitler comes, you oppose him! They won't stop coming and you don't stop opposing.

Stop opposing and more will come and the garden'll get covered with weeds and that's life you mad things, you. Everything must be measured. We won the last war didn't we? You forgotten that? We put a Labour Party in power and . . .

RONNIE (*with irony*). Oh, yes, that's right! We put a Labour Party in power. Glory! Hallelujah! It wasn't such a useless war after all, was it, Mother? But what did the bleeders do, eh? They sang the Red Flag in Parliament and then started building atom bombs. Lunatics! Raving lunatics! And a whole generation of us laid down our arms and retreated into ourselves, a whole generation! But you two. I don't understand what happened to you two. I used to watch you and boast about you. Well, thank God, I thought, it works! But look at us now, now it's all of us.

SARAH. Did you expect the world to suddenly focus on them and say 'Ah, socialism is beautiful', did you, silly boy? Since when did we preach this sort of poverty?

ADA (*turning on* SARAH). We were never poor! (*Softer to* RONNIE, *putting an arm round him.*) You want reassuring, sweetheart? I'll reassure you, shall I? Remember what you said about carrying bits and pieces of each other? Well it's true . . .

RONNIE. The justifications!

ADA. Will you shut up and listen to me for Christ's sake? The kind of life we lived couldn't be a whole philosophy, could it?

RONNIE. Did it have to be?

ADA. Exactly! Did it have to be. Any more than your life with Beatie Bryant or Sarah's life with Harry. Whose life was ever a complete statement? But they're going to have to turn to us in the end, they're going to . . .

RONNIE. Are you mad? To us?

ADA. Us! Us! Because *we* do the living. We *do* the living.
   (*Pause.*)

DAVE. What do you think I am, Ronnie? You think I'm
   an artist craftsman? Nothing of that sort. A designer?
   Not even that. Designers are ten a penny. I don't
   mind, Ronnie, believe me I don't. (*But he does.*) I've
   reached the point where I can face the fact that I'm
   not a prophet. Once I had – I don't know – a – a
   moment of vision, and I yelled at your Aunty Esther
   that I was a prophet. A prophet! Poor woman, I don't
   think she understood. All I meant was I was a sort of
   spokesman. That's all. But it passed. Look, I'm a
   bright boy. There aren't many flies on me and when I
   was younger I was even brighter. I was interested and
   alive to everything – history, anthropology, philosophy, architecture. I had ideas. But not now. Not
   now, Ronnie. I don't know – it's sort of sad this what
   I'm saying, it's a sad time for both of us, Ada and me,
   sad, yet – you know – it's not all that bad. We came
   here, we worked hard, we've loved every minute of it
   and we're still young. Did you expect anything else?
   You wanted us to grow to be giants, didn't you? The
   mighty artist craftsman! Well, now the only things
   that seem to matter to me are the day-to-day
   problems of my life, my kids and my work. Face it –
   as an essential member of society I don't really count.
   I'm not saying I'm useless, but machinery and
   modern techniques have come about to make me the
   odd man out. Here I've been, comrade citizen,
   presenting my offerings, and the world's rejected
   them. I don't count, Ronnie, and if I'm not sad about
   it you mustn't be either. Maybe Sarah's right, maybe
   you can't build on your own.

RONNIE. Remember your phrase about people choking
   with their own experience?

DAVE. I remember a lot of things – come on, let's go.

RONNIE. That was your apology for defeat, was it?

DAVE (*wearily*). All right, so I'm defeated. Come on, let's go –

RONNIE (*desperately*). Then where do we look for our new vision?

DAVE (*angrily*). *Don't* moan at me about visions. Don't you know they don't work? You child you – visions don't work.

RONNIE (*desperately*). They *do* work! And even if they don't work then for God's sake let's try and behave as though they do – or else nothing will work.

DAVE. Then nothing will work.

RONNIE (*too hastily*). That's cowardice!

DAVE. *You* call me a coward? You? I know your kind, you go around the world crooning about brotherhood and yet you can't even see a sordid love affair through to the end. I know your bloody kind.

ADA. Dave! This is so silly –

DAVE. Well, I've tried haven't I? Everybody wants explanations and I've tried. Do you think I want to go?

RONNIE. It wasn't sordid, you know Dave. I know I didn't see it through to the end but it wasn't sordid. Beatie Bryant could have been a poem – I gave her words – maybe she became one. But you're right. There isn't anything I've seen through to the end – maybe that's why you two were so important to me. Isn't that curious? I say all the right things, I think all the right things, but somewhere, some bloody where I fail as a human being. Like my father – just like poor old Harry. O Christ! Look at me.

> RONNIE *sinks to his knees in utter despair.*
> *They stand and watch him a while.*
> ADA *moves to him, but* DAVE *holds her back.*
> SARAH *is about to move to him but* DAVE *stops her with* 'Sarah!'

RONNIE *is to receive no more comfort. No one can help him now but himself.*
Slowly, very slowly, he unfolds and they all watch him.
Slowly, very slowly, he rises to his feet. He knows what is wanted of him but still cannot do more than stand in a sort of daze, looking from one to another – then –

DAVE (*to* ADA). Darling, did you post those letters off?

ADA (*she understands that they must indicate that they are going on*). Yes, Dave, and the estimates went off too.

DAVE. Where did you put the drawings?

ADA (*indicating brief-case*). It's all right, they're here. All those you've decided to keep I've rolled up into one pile. The rejects I burned last night.

DAVE. Now don't forget, first thing tomorrow morning I must get in touch with the electricians and tell them to start wiring the place up. Then there's that appointment with Mrs What's-her-name for her bloody awful wardrobe.

ADA *goes over to pick up the carry-cot.*

ADA. When we've finished unpacking tonight we'll make a list of all the things we must do – just before we go to bed. (*She and* DAVE *pick up cot.*) Come on Simmonds number three, we'll soon be back again for your holidays, you can still grow up here, yes you can, or won't *you* care?

DAVE. Ronnie – lock up and stick the key in your pocket, there's a good lad. Sarah, you take your daughter's bags, God knows what she's got in them.

DAVE *picks up his brief-case and he and* ADA *go off with the carry-cot, still talking.*

ADA. Are you sure you turned the calor gas off properly?

DAVE. Positive. Now look darling – you mustn't let me

forget to phone those electricians – Hey! Did we pack my drawing boards away?

ADA. Yes, yes, Simmonds. In those first boxes, don't you remember?

DAVE. Funny, I don't remember . . .

ADA (*to* SARAH *and* RONNIE). Come on, you two, the men are waiting.

> *They have gone off by now.* RONNIE *has locked the door and* SARAH *is waiting for him. He takes one of the baskets from her and puts an arm on her shoulder.*

RONNIE. Well Sarah – your children are coming home now.

SARAH. You finished crying, you fool you?

RONNIE. Cry? We must be bloody mad to cry, Mother.

> SARAH *goes off leaving* RONNIE *to linger and glance once more around. Suddenly his eye catches a stone, which he picks up and throws high into the air. He watches, and waits till it falls. Then he cups his hands to his mouth and yells to the sky with bitterness and some venom –*

We – must – be – bloody – mad – to cry!

> *The stage is empty.*

> *Soon we hear the sound of the lorry revving up and moving off. A last silence.*

> *Then –*

> *A last slow curtain.*

HOOLYIT HOOLYIT

1. Hool-yit hool-yit baiz-a vin-ten Yetzt iss ei-er
2. Brent a licht-el er-getzt toon-kle Lesht mit tzor-en

tseit Long vet dor-en noch der-er vin-ter
aus Rize die sho-ben fon d-ie lut-ten

Zu-mer i-is no-och vi-ite Long vet dor-en
Fen-s ter ri-ist a- rau- aus Rize die sho-ben

noch de-er vin-ter Zu-mer i-is no-och vite.
fon d-ie lut-ten Fen-ster ri-ist a- raus.

COME OH MY LOVE

Old American Folk Song

Methuen Contemporary Dramatists
include

Peter Barnes (three volumes)
Sebastian Barry
Dermot Bolger
Edward Bond (six volumes)
Howard Brenton
  (two volumes)
Richard Cameron
Jim Cartwright
Caryl Churchill (two volumes)
Sarah Daniels (two volumes)
Nick Darke
David Edgar (three volumes)
Ben Elton
Dario Fo (two volumes)
Michael Frayn (three volumes)
John Godber (two volumes)
Paul Godfrey
John Guare
Peter Handke
Jonathan Harvey
Declan Hughes
Terry Johnson (two volumes)
Sarah Kane
Bernard-Marie Koltès
David Lan
Bryony Lavery
Deborah Levy
Doug Lucie

David Mamet (three volumes)
Martin McDonagh
Duncan McLean
Anthony Minghella
  (two volumes)
Tom Murphy (four volumes)
Phyllis Nagy
Anthony Nielsen
Philip Osment
Louise Page
Stewart Parker (two volumes)
Joe Penhall
Stephen Poliakoff
  (three volumes)
Christina Reid
Philip Ridley
Willy Russell
Ntozake Shange
Sam Shepard (two volumes)
Wole Soyinka (two volumes)
David Storey (three volumes)
Sue Townsend
Michel Vinaver (two volumes)
Arnold Wesker (two volumes)
Michael Wilcox
David Wood (two volumes)
Victoria Wood

Methuen World Classics
include

Jean Anouilh (two volumes)
John Arden (two volumes)
Arden & D'Arcy
Brendan Behan
Aphra Behn
Bertolt Brecht (six volumes)
Büchner
Bulgakov
Calderón
Čapek
Anton Chekhov
Noël Coward (eight volumes)
Eduardo De Filippo
Max Frisch
John Galsworthy
Gogol
Gorky
Harley Granville Barker
  (two volumes)
Henrik Ibsen (six volumes)
Lorca (three volumes)

Marivaux
Mustapha Matura
David Mercer (two volumes)
Arthur Miller (five volumes)
Molière
Musset
Peter Nichols (two volumes)
Clifford Odets
Joe Orton
A. W. Pinero
Luigi Pirandello
Terence Rattigan
  (two volumes)
W. Somerset Maugham
  (two volumes)
August Strindberg
  (three volumes)
J. M. Synge
Ramón del Valle-Inclán
Frank Wedekind
Oscar Wilde

Methuen Modern Plays
include work by

Jean Anouilh
John Arden
Margaretta D'Arcy
Peter Barnes
Sebastian Barry
Brendan Behan
Dermot Bolger
Edward Bond
Bertolt Brecht
Howard Brenton
Anthony Burgess
Simon Burke
Jim Cartwright
Caryl Churchill
Noël Coward
Lucinda Coxon
Sarah Daniels
Nick Darke
Nick Dear
Shelagh Delaney
David Edgar
David Eldridge
Dario Fo
Michael Frayn
John Godber
Paul Godfrey
David Greig
John Guare
Peter Handke
David Harrower
Jonathan Harvey
Iain Heggie
Declan Hughes
Terry Johnson
Sarah Kane
Charlotte Keatley
Barrie Keeffe
Howard Korder

Robert Lepage
Stephen Lowe
Doug Lucie
Martin McDonagh
John McGrath
Terrence McNally
David Mamet
Patrick Marber
Arthur Miller
Mtwa, Ngema & Simon
Tom Murphy
Phyllis Nagy
Peter Nichols
Joseph O'Connor
Joe Orton
Louise Page
Joe Penhall
Luigi Pirandello
Stephen Poliakoff
Franca Rame
Mark Ravenhill
Philip Ridley
Reginald Rose
David Rudkin
Willy Russell
Jean-Paul Sartre
Sam Shepard
Wole Soyinka
Shelagh Stephenson
C. P. Taylor
Theatre de Complicite
Theatre de Workshop
Sue Townsend
Judy Upton
Timberlake Wertenbaker
Roy Williams
Victoria Wood

For a complete catalogue of Methuen Drama titles
write to:

Methuen Drama
215 Vauxhall Bridge Road
London SW1V 1EJ

or you can visit our website at:

www.methuen.co.uk

CPSIA information can be obtained
at www.ICGtesting.com
Printed in the USA
LVHW041642100519
617429LV00001B/5

9 780413 758309